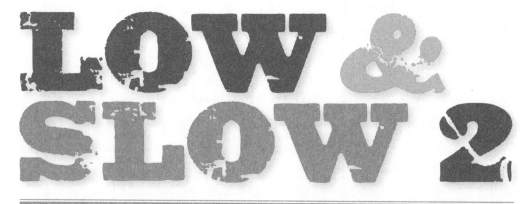

LOW & SLOW 2

THE ART OF BARBECUE, SMOKE-ROASTING, AND BASIC CURING

BY GARY WIVIOTT
AND COLLEEN RUSH

RUNNING PRESS
PHILADELPHIA · LONDON

© 2015 by Gary Wiviott and Colleen Rush
Photography © 2015 by Andrew Purcell

Published by Running Press,
A Member of the Perseus Books Group

Books published by Running Press are available at special discounts for bulk purchases in the United States by corporations, institutions, and other organizations. For more information, please contact the Special Markets Department at the Perseus Books Group, 2300 Chestnut Street, Suite 200, Philadelphia, PA 19103, or call (800) 810-4145, ext. 5000, or e-mail special.markets@perseusbooks.com.

ISBN 978-0-7624-5395-5
Library of Congress Control Number: 2015934685

E-book ISBN 978-0-7624-5606-2

9 8 7 6 5 4 3 2 1
Digit on the right indicates the number of this printing

Designed by Frances J. Soo Ping Chow
Edited by Sophia Muthuraj
Illustrations by T. L. Bonaddio
Food Stylist: Carrie Purcell
Prop Stylist: Megan Hedgpeth
Typography: Archive, Brandon, Downcome, Hawksmoor,
ITC Berkeley, and Trade Gothic Condensed

Running Press Book Publishers
2300 Chestnut Street
Philadelphia, PA 19103-4371

Visit us on the web!
www.offthemenublog.com

TABLE of CONTENTS

DEDICATION

What a wonderful journey since *Low & Slow* came out in 2009, taking me from backyard to back of the house as pitmaster of a busy BBQ restaurant in Chicago, BBQ restaurant consultant, and cofounder of the Windy City BBQ Classic. Along the way I've met incredible people, tried the patience of my lovely, and loving, bride, made friends, and developed an even greater understanding and appreciation of collaboration. Hugs to my mother and father, supportive through thick and thin. Tip of the hat to Chicago-based journalists John Kass and Mike Sula, and never-ending appreciation to my friend, the ever-patient, organized and linear Colleen Rush, rudder to my low-and-slow BBQ ship. And finally to Ellen Wiviott, my life would be so much less . . . less everything without you.
—Gary Wiviott

Many thanks to the devoted students of *Low & Slow*. You followed Gary's straight and narrow path, you embraced the unorthodox structure of the program, and you made the first book a steadfast success. We owe a debt of gratitude to you, and you shall be repaid in delicious, delicious brisket. Big thanks to Dave Weiner, Edith LeBlanc, Tonette Navarro, Alex Rodriguez, Tenney Flynn, and Doug Rush—the inner circle who offered encouragement, expertise, and sweetness. To the friends and family who enjoyed the rigorous trials of recipe testing and provided solid feedback—thank you. And, I'm coming over to your house for dinner tonight. To my favorite barbecue guy Gary: Just when I thought I was out . . . you pulled me back in. You and Ellen are family. Thanks for opening your home and food brain vault to me.
—Colleen Rush

INTRODUCTION

DEAR STUDENT,

NEARLY 25 YEARS AGO, MY WIFE, ELLEN, AND I WALKED OUT OF THE TITLE OFFICE where we signed the papers for our first house, and we drove directly to an Ace Hardware store to buy a classic Weber kettle grill. That night, we grilled steaks in our new backyard and slept on the floor of our furniture-less new home. Home ownership was meaningful for many reasons, but getting back to charcoal cooking after years of living in an apartment where grills were banned was pretty close to the top of the list. I've loved grilling since I was a kid growing up in Milwaukee, when my dad boiled chicken and pork ribs, then burned them beyond recognition on a grill and drowned everything in Open Pit barbecue sauce. I still give in to a hankering for charred chicken covered in Open Pit at least once a year. I'm a sentimental guy like that. Likewise, I look back on the last twenty-five years in awe of what I've achieved by pursuing this borderline obsessive interest in charcoal cooking.

When *Low & Slow: Master the Art of Barbecue in 5 Easy Lessons* was released in 2009, I was a backyard barbecue guy at the top of my game. After years of learning, proselytizing, and teaching the art of low-and-slow cooking, my 5 Easy Lessons program went from being a bare-bones online tutorial for Weber Smokey Mountain (WSM) cookers seen by a curious few to a 250-page handbook for beginners, cooks with bad barbecue habits, and everyone in between. And it worked. *Low & Slow* has been a steady success because no other barbecue book tackles the step-by-step, detailed process of building and maintaining a clean-burning fire in different styles of charcoal cookers.

Since the first book, I've achieved the backyard barbecue guy's ultimate dream, turning a weekend hobby into a job as a full-time pitmaster in Chicago. It's been a wild ride. And while I stand by the first book's rigid do-or-die style of teaching the basics, I will say the experience in a professional kitchen has mellowed and refined my approach to barbecue and charcoal cooking even more. I still preach following each cook to a tee at first, but if you've followed Lessons 1 through 5 in the first book, I know you've got the chops to read your cooker, the charcoal, and the meat. If your instincts kick in and tell you that your brisket needs another hour or you need to adjust a vent on your cooker to stabilize the temperature . . . then by all means, go for it. The step-by-step time and vent instructions in the cooks are designed to keep you on track and moving in the right direction, but in charcoal cookery, no two cooks are ever identical. You always have to leave wiggle room to compensate for the many variables that can and will affect a charcoal cook: the type of cooker and charcoal you're using, the vent openings that regulate the temperature, the weather, and even the marbling in the meat.

If this is the first you're hearing of Lessons 1 through 5, don't worry. In Chapters one and two, we'll go over the basics of lighting and running the most common types of charcoal cookers: the 18.5-inch and 22.5-inch Weber Smokey Mountain (WSM), the offset cooker, the 22-inch and 26-inch kettle grill, and—new to the *Low & Slow* family—the ceramic kamado-style Big Green Egg (BGE). Great barbecue is part instinct, part skill—traits you learn gradually in this series of cooks designed to coax you into charcoal cooking mastery.

The cooks in this book follow the same tenets of the original program, and I only ask two things of you: One, don't incorporate a hodge-podge of other barbecue and charcoal cooking techniques you cobbled together from nineteen different websites, books, or cooking shows. If you stray from the method, I can't guarantee the results. And two, don't overthink it. Follow my step-by-step methodology, and not only will you master cooking more herds, flocks, and schools, you will also reach a point of blissful nonchalance and ease in charcoal cookery. *"Oh, that 15-pound smoked brisket? The Norman Rockwell, perfect Thanksgiving turkey? It was nothing."*

I will also teach you new charcoal cooking methods, including smoke-roasting, lower-and-slower smoking, and basic meat curing. I'll have you flaunting your charcoal mastery with Standing Rib Roast (page 110), Smoked Corned Beef (page 102), Four-Pepper Cured Bacon (page 193), and yes, even Neapolitan-Style Pizza (page 198). With 100 recipes for poultry, beef, lamb, fish, and seafood, including rubs, brines, sauces, marinades, and side dishes to match, you've got your work cut out for you. Enjoy every minute!

Sincerely,

Gary Wiviott

1:

THE
STUFF

The essential gear you need in charcoal cooking
(plus, the stuff you don't need)

DEAR STUDENT:

LET'S START WITH A SUMMARY OF MY OPINION ABOUT MOST CHARCOAL COOK-ing gadgets: waste of money, waste of time. The more "stuff" you have, the easier it is to stray from the path of charcoal cooking enlightenment. Beyond a few basic tools, I believe in caveman simplicity with cooking gear. Good meat + good fire = good food.

Unfortunately, there is a booming industry focused on arming amateur and casual barbecue enthusiasts with totally unnecessary gizmos and accessories that, at best, are a waste of money and, at worst, can ruin your cook. For your own sake, I ask you to stick to the basics and avoid the high-tech, highly specialized barbecue tools (steam-cleaning grill brushes, marinade-infusing meat tenderizers, etc.) found in airline magazines and Hammacher Schlemmer catalogs. I also discourage using wood chips (unless you're hot smoking seafood or fish) and quick-lighting charcoal briquettes. Do not use lighter fluid or liquid smoke. Ever.

By the same token, there are a few essential items that I insist on using. The step-by-step methodology of the cooks and recipes in this book rely on using these (sometimes very specific) tools. They're not expensive or fancy, but they are important. All of the gear is outlined in this chapter, along with an introduction to the four styles of charcoal cookers. Get ready to start the fire. . . .

Sincerely,

Gary Wiviott

THE ONLY STUFF YOU NEED

THESE ARE THE essentials for following the Low & Slow program—the gear you've gotta have in order for my step-by-step method to work on your cooker.

CHIMNEY STARTER

You'll find countless varieties of this metal cylinder and other styles of charcoal starters in hardware and grill stores, but I use Weber's Rapidfire Chimney Starter as the measuring cup for charcoal for each of the cooks in this book. The 12 x 7½-inch charcoal chamber is bigger than other models.

NEWSPAPER

You'll need three full broadsheets rolled into a loose circle to light the chimney starter. Don't use glossy colored paper or any other type of treated paper; use plain newsprint only.

HARDWOOD LUMP CHARCOAL

Natural lump charcoal is burned, broken wood—plain and simple. It is not processed, it has no chemical additives, and it burns clean, producing less ash and residue than standard briquettes. You'll find brands like Royal Oak, Holland, Lazzari, Cowboy, and Nature-Glo lump charcoal in some grocery stores and most national retailers, like Home Depot, Lowe's, and Walmart.

WOOD

The most authentic barbecue makes good use of local wood, whether it's a bag of hickory wood chunks from a hardware store or a pile of seasoned pecan wood from your backyard. Use whatever wood is readily available and produces the smoke flavor you like. I don't recommend mesquite in my program, simply because it is very strong and using too much can produce harsh, bitter flavors in meat. If you use it, use it sparingly.

If you're cooking on a WSM, BGE, or kettle, you'll use clean wood chunks about the size of your fist. "Clean" means the chunks are not moldy or wet, and have no patches of bark. (Use a hand hatchet or wedge to pry bark off of the wood.) If you're cooking on an offset, you'll use splits of wood cut from logs. Splits should be approximately 1 foot long and the diameter of a baseball. If the wood is narrower, use two splits when the directions call for one split of wood.

WATER PANS

Water pans set over or near the fire help deflect heat and regulate the temperature inside a cooker. You'll fill the pans with water for low-and-slow cooks, with sand for hot smoke-roasting, and with ice for lower-and-slower cooking. If you're using a kettle or off-set, buy a stack of disposable 12½ x 6½-inch aluminum loaf pans. I use 10 x 12 x 2-inch half pans in the BGE, less for the affect it has on temperature, and more for catching messy drips that can cause flare-ups.

The 18.5-inch WSM has a built-in water pan, but I recommend swapping it out for a 15 x 12-inch Brinkman charcoal pan. There are two stock WSM water pans (depending on the year the cooker was made), and both have well-documented design flaws. They are shallow and prone to slipping and spilling. The Brinkman pan was meant to hold charcoal, but the deep, flat-bottomed, 2-gallon bowl is the perfect size and shape. The wider outer rim makes it less prone to slipping off of the flanges inside the WSM. (The stock water pan in the 22.5-inch WSM works just fine; there's no need to modify the water pan if this is the cooker you're using.)

HEAVY-DUTY WORK GLOVES

If you don't already own a pair, buy thick, high-quality leather gloves or padded welder's gloves. You'll be pouring white-hot coals into your cooker and maneuvering hot grates, among other tasks that can sizzle your hands.

LONG-HANDLED TONGS

You need a pair of long, thick metal tongs (not the lightweight cheapie ones) to move charcoal, lift hot grates, and rotate meat.

PLATE SETTER

On the BGE, the plate setter is essential for cooking low and slow; it provides a barrier between your food and the fire for indirect cooking. I recommend covering it with aluminum foil before every cook to make cleanup easier.

OVEN THERMOMETER

The lid-mounted temperature gauges on some cookers are inaccurate (particularly inexpensive offsets); this analog thermometer is your backup. Set it in the center of the cooking grate to verify grate temperatures at prescribed times in each recipe, such as when you're refilling a water pan or restocking charcoal. You don't need it if you're cooking on a BGE or WSM, but I consider it an essential on most offsets, and it's a handy tool to verify grate temperature if you're running a new cooker or suspect your cooker's thermometer is off.

WIRE GRATE BRUSH

Buy one or two inexpensive grate brushes with long, wooden handles. Always clean your grates when they are still hot, right after a cook.

INSTANT-READ THERMOMETER

ThermoWorks Super-Fast Thermapen is my weapon of choice. It registers internal temperature in about three seconds. Buy a neon-bright color which will make it easier to find when you accidentally toss it in the garbage after a long, bourbon-fueled cook.

THE EXTRAS

THESE ITEMS AREN'T essential, but they make cooking with charcoal easier. They're not expensive, and chances are you already have a few of them lying around your house.

EXTRA CHARCOAL GRATE

Set crosswise over the stock charcoal grate in a WSM or kettle grill, this grate will prevent smaller, irregular pieces of lump charcoal from falling to the bottom of the cooker so you get a longer, more efficient burn out of the charcoal (and less waste).

ROASTING RACK

The V-racks sold with most roasting pans beat any overpriced "rib rack" you'll buy, and you probably already own one that you only use once or twice a year to roast a turkey. Flip it upside down, and you've got a rib rack.

PLASTIC SQUEEZE BOTTLES

You need a few basic condiment bottles for the Tart Wash (page 15) you'll spritz on cooking meat. You don't need bottles with brushes or spray nozzles attached—these features are unnecessary, at best, and they are difficult to keep clean.

SUGARCANE KNIFE

This knife is as useful as it is intimidating. You can use it like a spatula; the small divot at the tip hooks easily onto searing-hot grates for easy lifting; and the sharpened blade can slice through bone and large cuts of meat.

PIZZA STONE

If you are using a BGE and you want to take your charcoal-cooking prowess to the next level, buy a round, ceramic 14-inch pizza stone. You can buy pizza stones direct from BGE or online from www.CeramicGrillStore .com. For step-by-step instructions and recipes for making pizzas on a charcoal cooker, see pages 198.

ELECTRIC SPICE GRINDER

Freshly ground whole spices are essential for making the best rubs and seasoning blends. I use an electric grinder—the same kind used to grind coffee beans—but a mortar and pestle or crank grinder will work just fine, too.

ESSENTIAL BARBECUE SEASONING, SPICES & HERBS

THERE'S NOTHING MORE aggravating than having $75 worth of meat ready to go on your cooker and discovering you're short on a vital ingredient for a rub or sauce. The Spice House (www.spicehouse.com) is my go-to resource for all spices. Keep these ingredients stocked.

KOSHER SALT

Diamond Crystal kosher and Morton's kosher are my all-purpose salts. These coarse, flaky salts are free of iodine and anticaking agents (additives in standard table salt), and they have a better flavor and texture. These salts have different grain structures, which means they each have different volumes and weights and should be measured accordingly. The recipes in this book were developed using Morton's kosher salt. Be sure to adjust the measurements if you are using another variety.

1 tablespoon table salt = 1½ tablespoon Morton kosher salt = 2 tablespoons Diamond Crystal kosher salt

WHOLE BLACK PEPPERCORNS

Please don't use the pulverized, dusty ground black pepper that's been sitting in your spice cabinet for three years. You'll get more flavor and crunch if you use lightly toasted peppercorns, freshly ground or cracked.

PAPRIKA

Good, high-quality paprika is the cornerstone of a great rub. I recommend having a few types on hand: sweet, half-sharp, and hot. Because of the higher turnover, I also recommend buying from a specialty spice store like The Spice House or Penzey's. Grocery store paprika sits on the shelf for too long and takes on the flavor of cardboard. It can also turn pasty in a long low-and-slow cook. Good paprika has a brighter flavor and it develops a better bark on barbecue.

GARLIC AND ONION POWDER

Along with paprika, you'll find these spice cabinet staples in many barbecue rubs and sauces. You get what you pay for in spices, so spend a few extra pennies and buy quality. Granulated options are nearly interchangeable with powdered garlic and onion, although I'd use a smidge less granulated if the recipe calls for powder. You can also make your own powders by grinding chopped, dried onion or garlic in your spice grinder.

MUSTARD

I use cheap yellow mustard as an adhesive to get rubs to stick to ribs, pork shoulder, brisket, and other meats.

VINEGAR

Cider vinegar is a major component in barbecue sauce. I use white vinegar to remove the stickiness and off odors of meats that have been vacuum-sealed.

FLAVOR AND GRIND

YOU KNOW HOW WINE CONNOISSEURS TALK ABOUT THE PROGRESSION OF FLAVORS and aromas in a sip of a fine vintage? I blend different grinds (think: fine, medium, coarse) of the same spice for a similar effect. I like the different textures, and mixing the grinds creates a progression in the intensity of a flavor. A fine grind (think: granular, like sand) packs a more pungent, immediate flavor; coarser grinds deliver more crunch and a flavor that lingers a bit longer. I started experimenting with different grinds of black pepper in barbecue rubs, and now I use the technique with a wide variety of spices to create layers of flavor in sauces and seasoning blends.

TOASTED MEXICAN CHILE BLEND (AKA HOMEMADE CHILI POWDER)

Freshly ground, dried Mexican chiles are ubiquitous in my rubs and other recipes. Whole, dried chiles are far less expensive than the preground, bottled variety and far more flavorful when they are freshly toasted and ground for recipes. This is the standard blend and ratio of Mexican chiles I use in my signature rub and other sauces and seasonings.

4 parts dried, ground guajillo or cascabels

2 parts dried, ground ancho or New Mexico red

2 parts dried, ground pasilla or ancho

1 part dried, ground morita or chipotle

1 part dried, ground pequin
or chile de arbol or cayenne

½ part dried, ground habañero (optional, for added heat)

You can also customize your own blend based on the flavor profile of the chile.

ANCHO: Dark, rich, smoky

CHIPOTLE: Smoky, subtle, long finish

GUAJILLO: Fruity, mild, workhorse (it's my go-to chile)

CAYENNE, CHILE DE ARBOL: Bright, up-front, bracing

PASILLA: Rich, lingering flavor, moderate heat

PEQUIN: Spicy, immediate heat, bee sting

HABAÑERO: Fruity, flavorful, powerful

TART WASH

Don't be fooled by its simplicity—I use this basic wash in almost every low-and-slow cook to reinforce the flavor of the rub. Use whichever rub you are applying to the meat in the wash. A spritz of wash in the last hour of a cook—when you are already opening the cooker to check the temperature of the meat—gives the meat a fresh, but diluted, coat of the rub. You can substitute with apple juice and any neutral vegetable oil. Don't use olive oil or a highly acidic juice, like lemon, orange, or grapefruit.

MAKES 1 CUP

¾ cup cranberry juice

¼ cup canola oil

2 tablespoons rub

Pour the cranberry juice, oil, and rub into a plastic squeeze bottle. Shake vigorously for about 1 minute, until the rub is dissolved and the mixture is blended like vinaigrette.

THE COOKERS

MOST OF THE COOKS can be run on the Weber Smokey Mountain (WSM), both the 18.5-inch and 22.5-inch, Big Green Egg (BGE), offset cooker and a kettle grill, both the 22-inch and 26-inch. Due to size limitations of the kettle-style grill, there are a handful of cooks I do not recommend on it because it requires a lower-and-slower temperature of very lengthy cook, Goose Breast Pastrami, Smoked Corned Beef, Smoked Brisket, Burnt Ends, and Four-Pepper-Cured Bacon.

COOK INSTRUCTIONS

In addition to the standard components of a recipe (serving size, ingredient list, cooker temperature, cook time), we have organized each cook by time (30 MINUTES BEFORE THE COOK, 2 HOURS INTO THE COOK, etc.) to help you plan, prepare, and time your meals. AT THE END OF THE COOK summaries give you a clear, up-front picture of the final stages of the cook, including internal temperature, physical signs of doneness, and resting times. After the meat preparation and charcoal setup instructions, the recipe splits into instructions for each cooker, including vent closures, meat temperature checkpoints, and charcoal restocks.

VENT CLOSURES

To maintain or modify the temperature in a charcoal cooker, you must control the airflow via vent closures. These closures are referenced in every cook to help you maintain a clean-burning fire and steady temperature in your cooker. I have outlined some vent closures in the following illustrations.

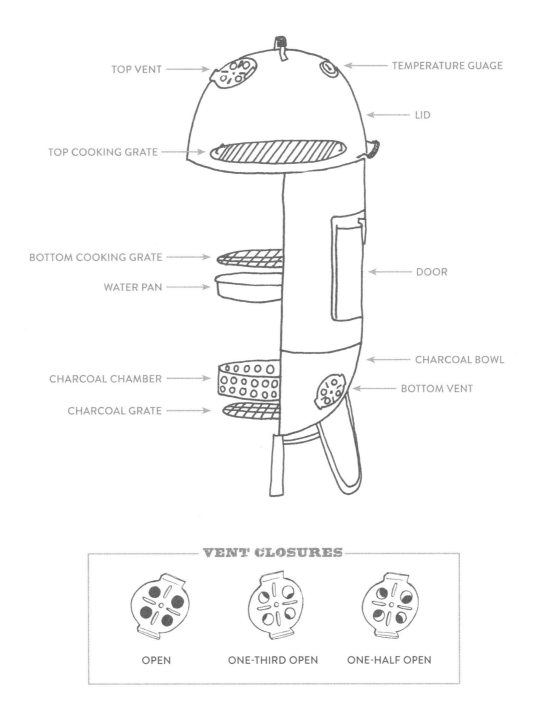

TOP VENT

TEMPERATURE GUAGE

LID

TOP COOKING GRATE

BOTTOM COOKING GRATE

WATER PAN

DOOR

CHARCOAL BOWL

CHARCOAL CHAMBER

BOTTOM VENT

CHARCOAL GRATE

VENT CLOSURES

OPEN

ONE-THIRD OPEN

ONE-HALF OPEN

BIG GREEN EGG (BGE)

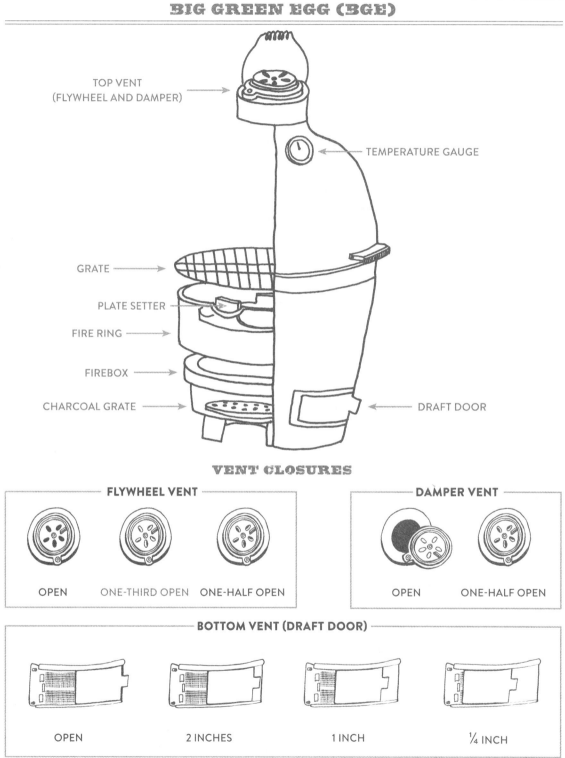

TOP VENT
(FLYWHEEL AND DAMPER)

TEMPERATURE GAUGE

GRATE

PLATE SETTER

FIRE RING

FIREBOX

CHARCOAL GRATE

DRAFT DOOR

VENT CLOSURES

FLYWHEEL VENT

OPEN   ONE-THIRD OPEN   ONE-HALF OPEN

DAMPER VENT

OPEN   ONE-HALF OPEN

BOTTOM VENT (DRAFT DOOR)

OPEN   2 INCHES   1 INCH   ¼ INCH

CLEANING A BGE

THE BIG GREEN EGG AND OTHER CERAMIC KAMADO-STYLE COOKERS HAVE ONE fatal flaw: they are *extremely* fragile. Sellers tend to tell potential buyers things like "Oh, hey, you can re-use leftover charcoal!" and "You never have to clean it!" to rationalize the hefty price. Neither statement is true. In addition to the standard cleaning and maintenance (page 22), here are the extra cleaning steps, if you own a BGE or kamado-style cooker:

- When you clean out the firebox, poke a finger into the air holes around the firebox to clear any ash clogging the holes.
- DO NOT use water to clean a BGE or other ceramic charcoal cooker. Ceramic is porous and will absorb water, which could cause the ceramic to crack when it reaches peak temperatures.
- After every 8 to 10 cooks, carefully remove all interior pieces (grate, plate setter, charcoal grate, firebox) and sweep the cooker clean with a dry brush. Sweep the interior of the lid and top vent, as well.

IMPORTANT SAFETY NOTE: BURP YOUR BGE

Because airflow is so efficiently controlled in BGE and other kamado cookers, a blast of air can cause a major backdraft or flare-up when you open the cooker. Any time your BGE is running at a high temperature (over 400°F), such as when you are making pizzas, you must slightly crack open and shut the domed lid several times to allow air slowly into the cooker before fully opening the lid.

OFFSET SMOKER

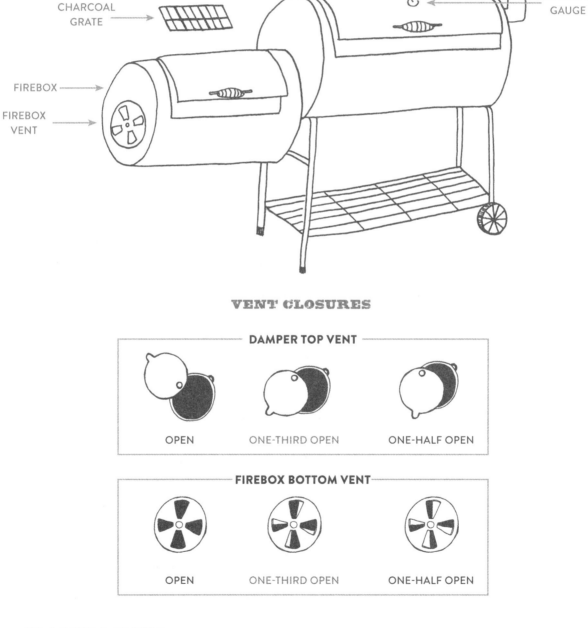

SMOKESTACK WITH TOP (DAMPER) VENT

COOKING GRATE

CHARCOAL GRATE

TEMPERATURE GAUGE

FIREBOX

FIREBOX VENT

VENT CLOSURES

DAMPER TOP VENT

OPEN

ONE-THIRD OPEN

ONE-HALF OPEN

FIREBOX BOTTOM VENT

OPEN

ONE-THIRD OPEN

ONE-HALF OPEN

KETTLE GRILL

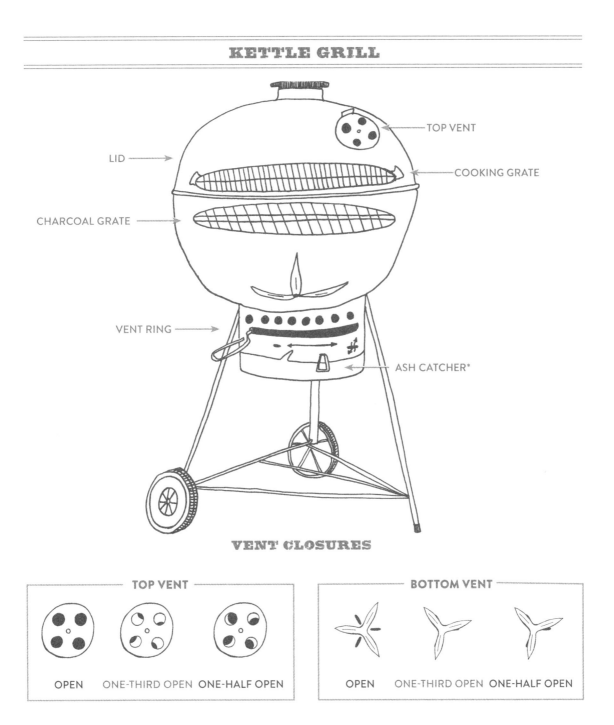

LID

TOP VENT

CHARCOAL GRATE

COOKING GRATE

VENT RING

ASH CATCHER*

VENT CLOSURES

TOP VENT		
OPEN	ONE-THIRD OPEN	ONE-HALF OPEN

BOTTOM VENT		
OPEN	ONE-THIRD OPEN	ONE-HALF OPEN

*NOTE: The ash catcher on some models of the Weber kettle grill make it difficult to see the bottom vent and accurately adjust the vent openings as prescribed in the program. The solution? Mark the lever position for vent closures on the ash catcher.

CLEANING AND MAINTENANCE FOR ALL COOKERS

A clean cooker is essential for a clean-burning fire. Follow these steps after every cook.

- Immediately after a cook, while the cooker is still hot, use your grill brush to scrub off charred bits stuck to the grate.
- Never use a chemical or soap to clean the inside of the cooker. At the end of a cook, open all vents to stoke the charcoal, but keep the lid of the cooker closed. Any remaining food or residue will burn off.
- Always discard leftover charcoal and ashes and sweep out the firebox/charcoal bowl when the coal has cooled completely.
- Store your cooker with all vents open to keep moisture and mold down.

2.

THE
SETUP

Charcoal and vent setups for low-and-slow,
hot smoke-roasting, and lower-and-slower cooks

DEAR STUDENT,

I CAN SUMMARIZE THE SECRET TO GREAT BARBECUE AND CHARCOAL COOKING in two steps: 1) build a clean-burning fire and 2) control airflow. In this chapter, you will learn how to set up your cooker for three types of cooks that run at different temperatures ranges: the low-and-slow KISS (Keep It Simple, Stupid) method (225°F to 250°F); the hot smoke–roasting method (300°F to 375°F); and the lower-and-slower method (160°F to 180°F).

This is not your typical barbecue book. It is designed to teach you all of the things your charcoal cooker can do and, more important, help you develop your instincts for cooking with charcoal. Because charcoal cooking is anything but predictable, my method factors in many of the variables that can affect a fire—the vent closures, the type of charcoal, the cooker you're using—and delivers clear instructions on how to adjust the temperature and maintain the fire for a successful cook.

Here's the catch: you've gotta follow the instructions for it to work. Obvious? Yes. But I know how tempting it is to tinker, futz, and improvise when you're playing with fire. The charcoal setups in this chapter are straightforward and strict. These techniques are not meant to be combined with barbecue tips and tricks you read online. It won't work with charcoal briquettes, gas grills, or electric pellet smokers. I've been accused of being dogmatic in my approach to barbecue, and I am guilty as charged. But my method is centered on helping you hone *your* barbecue instincts. If you follow the program, eventually the process will become second nature. You will be able to troubleshoot or modify cooks based on reading your cooker, the fire, and the meat—not a recipe.

Sincerely,

Gary Wiviott

CHARCOAL COOKING SETUPS

I OFFER THREE distinct setups for the cookers in this book, and each setup outlines charcoal and wood loads, vent closures, and water pan arrangements that allow each cooker to run in different temperature ranges. Here are the types of cooks and the temperatures at which they are designed to run:

LOW-AND-SLOW KISS (KEEP IT SIMPLE, STUPID): 225°F to 250°F
HOT SMOKE-ROASTING: 300°F to 375°F
LOWER AND SLOWER: 160°F to 180°F

LIGHTING THE CHIMNEY STARTER

I WILL NEVER UNDERSTAND WHY ANYONE USES LIGHTER FLUID WHEN THERE IS a faster, easier, and cleaner way to start a charcoal fire. Use this method and you'll have glowing-hot charcoals to start a fire in 10 minutes, minus the lingering chemical odor and flavor of lighter fluid.

1. Roll 3 full sheets of plain newspaper into separate, loosely crumpled doughnuts. Insert these paper rings in the bottom section of the charcoal chimney. Do not pack the paper into the starter. You need space and looseness between the sheets to allow air to flow around the paper, which will cause it to flare up and ignite the charcoal.

2. Set the chimney on the cooking grate or on any other fireproof surface that allows air to flow under the starter.

3. Pour lump charcoal into the chimney starter in the amount prescribed for your cooker and the type of cook.

4. Light the newspaper in two or three places. After the newspaper flares up and thick smoke pours out of the chimney, you'll hear the crackle of the charcoal starting to catch and burn. In about ten minutes, you'll start to see red-hot charcoal through the holes in the side of the chimney. If the paper smokes and smolders, but does not light the charcoal, you've packed the chimney too tight or used too much newspaper.

5. When the charcoal is fully engaged—you should see glowing, red coals, flames shooting from the top, and a gray-white ash edging the top layer of coals in about 10 minutes—gently pour the lit charcoal over the unlit charcoal and wood in your cooker.

KISS (KEEP IT SIMPLE, STUPID)

THIS IS THE classic low-and-slow setup designed to run 225°F to 250°F for long, slow cooks (think: brisket, pork shoulder, spare ribs). Once you've mastered running your cooker for five or six hours steady in this temperature range, you'll have the know-how for the other setups and vent closures.

WEBER SMOKEY MOUNTAIN (WSM)

The 18.5-inch WSM was my gateway cooker to barbecue—the cooker that turned me into a weekend warrior in the backyard, then a full-time pitmaster and barbecue life coach. In 2009, Weber introduced the massive 22.5-inch WSM. Beyond the significant increase in its cooking capacity, the most important feature of the 22.5-inch model is the additional airflow around the cooker, which means that it burns through charcoal faster and runs slightly hotter than the smaller model. The 18.5-inch WSM settles in at 240°F, but the sweet spot on a 22.5-inch WSM is closer to 265°F. It's not a huge difference, but it's worth noting. With the KISS setup, the 18.5-inch WSM will run for 5 to 6 hours and the 22.5-inch WSM will run for 6 to 7 hours with little more work checking and refilling the water pan.

YOU WILL NEED:

Natural lump charcoal

6 clean, debarked wood chunks, plus more depending on the length of the cook and desired smoke flavor

Charcoal chimney starter

3 sheets of newspaper, plus more as needed for restocking

Long metal tongs

1. Open the top and bottom vents completely.

2. Remove the center ring and the lid of the WSM. Fill the charcoal chamber halfway with unlit charcoal—about 2 chimney starters full of charcoal on the 18.5-inch model or 3 chimney starters full on the 22.5-inch model.

3. Lay 3 wood chunks on top of the unlit charcoal in the chamber.

4. Pour on another layer of unlit charcoal, filling the chamber to the top edge of the charcoal ring.

5. Prepare and light a full chimney of charcoal (See page 25 for detailed instructions).

6. When the charcoal is fully engaged in the chimney starter, carefully pour the lit charcoal in an even layer over the unlit charcoal. If pieces of charcoal spill outside of the chamber into the bowl of the cooker, use tongs to pick up and return the stray charcoal to the chamber, so it doesn't end up blocking vents.

7. Add 3 more wood chunks to the pile.

8. Reassemble the cooker with the empty water pan and grates in place in the center ring.

9. Using a slow-running garden hose or clean watering can, carefully pour water through the center of the grates to fill the water pan within 1 inch of the top edge. Avoid splashing water into or down the sides of the cooker.

10. As the lit charcoal engages the unlit charcoal, the cooker will continue to billow white smoke for another 5 to 10 minutes. When the smoke dies down to steady, lighter puffs, close the cooker and adjust the vents according to the cook instructions.

How to restock the 18.5-inch WSM

For cooks running 6 hours or longer, you'll need to add a fresh batch of charcoal to the charcoal ring. You'll be tempted to use the side door, but this door is one of the major design flaws in the 18.5-inch WSM. It's flimsy, it leaks air, and the latch isn't secure. Use this method for adding charcoal:

1. At the 5- or 6-hour mark, or when one half to three quarters of the initial batch of charcoal has burned through, prepare the chimney starter (page 25).

2. When the charcoal in the chimney is fully engaged, put on a pair of heatproof gloves. Carefully remove the center ring and lid together from the charcoal bowl and set them on an even surface. Use extra caution and move slowly to avoid sloshing the hot water in the pan.

3. Pour fresh, unlit charcoal over the burning coals, filling the chamber to the top edge.

4. Pour the freshly lit charcoal from the chimney starter into the chamber. Remember to check the bottom vents and remove any stray pieces of charcoal. Add up to 3 additional wood chunks if you want more smoke flavor.

5. After 5 to 10 minutes, when the charcoal is engaged and the clouds of white smoke stop billowing, reassemble the cooker.

How to restock the 22.5-inch WSM

The 22.5-inch WSM is a beast, with more than 725 square inches of cooking area. I can fit four full packer-cut briskets on it, which is a nice option if you're running it for a restaurant or cooking for a small army. At full capacity (3-gallon water pan, 60+ pounds of meat, 20 pounds of cooker), it can be a cumbersome piece of equipment to disassemble and restock.

Fortunately, the latch and door on the 22.5-inch model are more secure than those on the 18.5-inch model. With a long-handled trowel or shovel, you can restock the charcoal ring with unlit charcoal. Be sure the shovel end of the tool is small enough and easily clears the door to avoid bumping and spilling charcoal.

1. Unlatch the side door and assess the amount of lit charcoal in the ring.

2. If the ring is very low on lit charcoal (one quarter or less), use a long-handled trowel or shovel to refill the chamber with unlit charcoal to three-quarters full. (Don't fill the ring to the top with unlit charcoal. This will smother the fire.) If the charcoal ring is one-half full with glowing, lit charcoal, add enough unlit charcoal to bring the pile to the top edge of the charcoal ring. Be sure to spread the charcoal in an even layer across the pile. Add up to 3 more wood chunks to the fire, depending on the level of smoke flavor you desire.

3. After restocking the charcoal, remove the lid of the cooker. The influx of air helps the charcoal and wood ignite faster and burn more evenly. It also clears the initial billowing clouds of fresh charcoal smoke, which can overwhelm the flavor of the meat.

4. When the fresh charcoal is engaged and the billowing clouds of smoke have died down (5 to 10 minutes), return the lid and continue cooking.

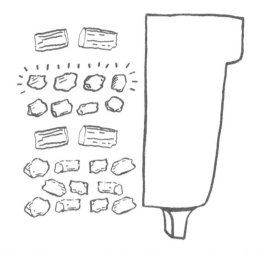

The BGE is incredibly efficient and can hold the low-and-slow temperature range on the bull's-eye for more than 12 hours if it is set up correctly. The one mistake I see people make most often: using too much lit charcoal to start the fire.

YOU WILL NEED:

Natural lump charcoal

4 clean, debarked wood chunks plus 3 to 6 more, depending on the length of the cook and desired smoke flavor

Charcoal chimney starter

3 sheets of newspaper, plus more as needed for restocking

12 x 10 x 2-inch aluminum half pan

1. Remove the cooking grate and fill the firebox with unlit charcoal to the top edge, just below the fire ring.

2. Place 2 wood chunks on top of the unlit charcoal in the firebox.

3. Open the flywheel (top) and draft (bottom) vents completely, but keep the ash/coal screen closed.

4. Prepare and light a half-full chimney starter of charcoal (see page 25 for detailed instructions).

5. When the charcoal is fully engaged, carefully pour the lit charcoal in an even layer over the unlit charcoal and wood in the firebox.

6. Add 2 more wood chunks to the pile.

7. Put on a pair of heatproof gloves and carefully insert the plate setter, legs up, over the fire ring.

8. Place the aluminum pan on the plate setter and fill it three-quarters full with water. Set the cooking grate over the plate setter.

9. When the charcoal stops billowing white smoke (about 5 minutes after pouring lit charcoal into the firebox), close the cooker and adjust the vents according to the cook instructions.

NOTE: The recommended vent closures on the BGE are a starting point for stabilizing the temperature in the cooker. You may need to make additional adjustments to the vent closures, but give the BGE at least 10 to 15 minutes to settle into a temperature before making another vent adjustment. Example: If the cooker is running hotter than 275°F, close the bottom vent in ¼-inch increments as needed.

How to restock the BGE

A full KISS setup on the BGE should burn for more than 12 hours and hold steady between 225°F and 250°F with the correct vent closures, which means you may never have to restock. If you want to add more wood on longer cooks for more smoke flavor, use clean, debarked wood "slivers" that are small enough to fit in the gaps around the plate setter. Wear a pair of heatproof gloves and remove the cooking grate, then drop the wood through the openings around the plate setter.

The only time you may ever need to restock charcoal in the BGE is during very high-heat cooks, when the cooker needs to maintain a 500°F+ temperature for more than an hour. Think: cranking out 10 to 15 Neapolitan-style pizzas (page 198). To restock, follow steps one through nine of the KISS setup (page 29), but be sure to carefully "burp" the BGE (page 19) before opening the lid.

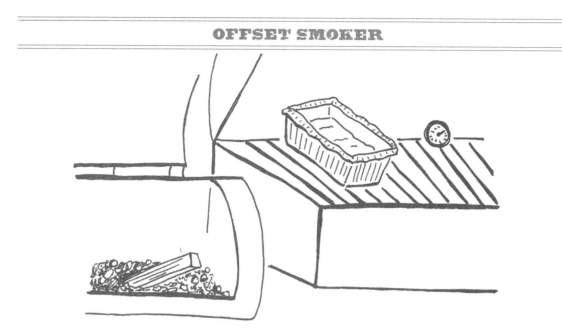

The offset smoker comes in a variety of shapes and sizes, and the charcoal setups and cook instructions in this book are based on years of trial and error on several popular brands (mainly Char-Broil and Brinkman). If I've learned anything about cooking on an offset, it is this: The cheaper the offset, the more frequently you'll have to fiddle with it to adjust the temperature during the cook. Inexpensive, lightweight offsets tend to be "leaky," which makes them run hotter. The KISS setup, vent closures, and timed checks/restocks in the cook instructions are all written with this flaw in mind, so even if you are cooking with an inexpensive, "leaky" model, the cooker should run for 45 minutes to 1 hour with little interference. Read the cooker, keep an eye on the grate temperature, and follow your instincts.

YOU WILL NEED:

Natural lump charcoal

12½ x 6½-inch aluminum loaf pan

Oven thermometer

Charcoal chimney starter

3 sheets of newspaper, plus more as needed for restocking

1 split of clean, debarked wood plus 3 to 5 more, depending on the length of the cook (for more about wood splits, see page 9)

1. Open the top (damper) and bottom (firebox) vents of the smoker.

2. Pour 2 chimneys full of unlit charcoal onto the grate inside the firebox.

3. Fill the aluminum loaf pan three-quarters full with water. Place the pan on the cooking grate, about 1 inch from the firebox vent. Set the oven thermometer in the middle of the cooking grate.

4. Prepare and light a full chimney starter of charcoal (See page 25 for detailed instructions).

5. When the charcoal is fully engaged in the chimney starter, carefully pour the lit charcoal in an even layer over the unlit charcoal in the firebox and place 1 split of wood on top of the lit charcoal in the firebox.

6. When the charcoal stops billowing white smoke and the wood begins to blacken or ignite (after about 10 minutes), close the lid on the firebox and adjust the vents according to the cook instructions.

How to restock the offset smoker

1. Open the firebox and assess the charcoal. If the grate is less than half full of ignited, glowing coals, add ½ chimney of unlit charcoal and 1 full chimney of lit charcoal. If the grate is more than half full of hot coals, add 1 full chimney of unlit charcoal.

2. Add 1 clean, debarked split of wood to the pile of lit charcoal.

3. Five to 10 minutes after restocking the charcoal, when the smoke from the new charcoal and wood stops billowing, close the firebox and continue cooking.

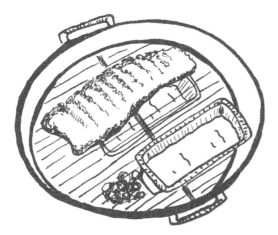

The classic 22-inch Weber kettle-style grill is one of the most popular backyard grills on the market, but it requires a bit of tinkering and frequent restocking to run most low-and-slow cooks. The additional charcoal and cooking space on the 26-inch Weber grill means less fiddling with the fire during the cook, and more distance between the food and the fire. With this charcoal and water pan setup, you should be able to run the 22-inch model for 45 minutes to 1 hour and the 26-inch model for 1 to 1½ hours with little interference.

But—and this is an important "but"—you must understand that kettles typically run 25°F to 50°F hotter than the optimum low-and-slow temperature. For most of the cooks in this book, the higher temperature means only one thing: the meat will be done faster. Do not obsess about exact low-and-slow temperature on the kettle. I've excluded the kettle from long-running

cooks of 6 hours or longer, and recipes where maintaining an exact temperature is critical, namely brisket, pastrami, and bacon. If you are intent on lowering the temperature in the kettle, fill and restock the water pan with ice throughout the cook. I do not recommend closing the top or bottom vents more than halfway because you can easily snuff the fire.

YOU WILL NEED:

Natural lump charcoal

Long metal tongs

2 clean, debarked wood chunks plus 2 or more, depending on the length of the cook and desired smoke flavor

Two 12½ x 6½-inch aluminum loaf pans

Charcoal chimney starter

3 sheets of newspaper, plus more as needed for restocking

1. Open the top and bottom vents.

2. Remove the top grate and pour ¾ chimney (for a 22-inch grill) or 1 full chimney (for a 26-inch grill) of unlit charcoal on one side of the charcoal grate, using the tongs to "bank" the charcoal in a slight slope against one side of the kettle.

3. Lay 1 wood chunk in the middle of the unlit charcoal.

4. Set 1 aluminum loaf pan (the drip pan) on the charcoal grate, opposite the banked pile of charcoal.

5. Prepare and light a three-quarters full

chimney starter of charcoal (see page 25 for detailed instructions).

6. When the charcoal is fully engaged, carefully pour the lit charcoal in an even layer over the banked pile of unlit charcoal. Use your tongs to return any lit charcoal that spills off of the pile.

7. When the charcoal stops billowing white smoke (about 5 minutes after you pour the lit charcoal into the chamber), add 1 additional wood chunk if you desire a heavier smoke flavor.

8. Fill the second aluminum loaf pan (the water pan) three-quarters full with water. Set the pan on the top grate over the fire.

9. Close the lid and adjust the vents according to the cook instructions.

How to restock the kettle grill
Follow Steps 5 to 7.

HOT SMOKE-ROASTING

WITH THE RIGHT setup and vent closures, there's a sweet spot between cooking with indirect heat (low and slow) and direct heat (grilling) on a charcoal cooker—anywhere from 300°F to 375°F. With this setup, you get the distinct flavor of wood smoke infused in lean or tender cuts of meat that cook quickly, such as Tri-Tip (page 121) or chicken wings (page 57), and heartier roasts, such as 7-bone Standing Rib Roast (page 110), and Smoke-Roasted Leg of Lamb (page 165), benefit from the sizzle of a higher heat.

WEBER SMOKEY MOUNTAIN (WSM)

1. Use the KISS method charcoal setup (page 26), but fill the water pan two-thirds full with sand (yes, sand). The "sand pan" is a heat sink that allows the cooker to maintain a steady, higher temperature.

NOTE: For some hot smoke–roast cooks, such as the Standing Rib Roast (page 110), I recommend removing the water/sand pan entirely from the WSM. For cooks like this, the meat benefits from direct heat, but the distance between the top grate and the fire is great enough to avoid flare-ups.

2. Keep the top vent open at all times and open the bottom vents according to the cook instructions to create more airflow across the coals and reach the desired temperature. The bottom vent openings will depend on the level of heat the meat can withstand, anywhere from 300°F to 375°F.

NOTE: For hot smoke roasts that run less than 2 hours, use half the amount of unlit charcoal in the fire ring to start.

BIG GREEN EGG (BGE)

1. Use the KISS method charcoal setup (page 29), including the plate setter, but do not use the disposable water pan. Cover the plate setter in foil to make cleanup easier.

2. Keep the top vent open and open the bottom vent according to the cook instructions to increase airflow across the coals and reach the desired temperature. The bottom vent opening will depend on the level of heat the meat can withstand, anywhere from 300°F to 375°F.

NOTE: For hot smoke roasts that run less than 2 hours, use half the amount of unlit charcoal in the firebox to start.

OFFSET SMOKER

1. Use the KISS method charcoal setup (page 31), but fill the water pan three-quarters full with sand and increase the amount of unlit charcoal in the firebox to 3 full chimneys to start.

2. Keep the top vent open and open the firebox vent according to the cook instructions to create more airflow across the coals and reach the desired temperature. The firebox vent opening will depend on the level of heat the meat can withstand, anywhere from 300°F to 375°F.

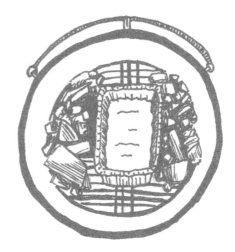

KETTLE GRILL

1. Use the same amount of unlit charcoal and wood prescribed in the KISS charcoal setup (¾ chimney for the 22-inch model, 1 chimney for the 26-inch model), but build two small piles of charcoal banked against opposite sides of the charcoal grate.

2. Lay 1 wood chunk on top of one of the piles of unlit charcoal.

3. Place an aluminum loaf pan in the middle of the charcoal grate and fill it with water.

4. When the charcoal is fully engaged in the chimney, gently pour the lit charcoal in an even layer over the banked piles of unlit charcoal. Use your tongs to return any charcoal that falls away from the pile.

5. Keep the top vent open. Open the bottom vent according to the cook instructions to create more airflow across the coals and reach the desired temperature. The bottom vent opening will depend on the level of heat the meat can withstand, anywhere from 300°F to 375°F.

LOWER AND SLOWER FIRE

THIS IS MY barbecue riff on cold smoking, which runs a bit warmer (160°F to 180°F) than true cold smoking (less than 100°F). I use this technique to infuse smoke flavor in cured meats and seafood, such as goose or duck breast pastrami (page 69), shrimp (page 148), salmon (page 140), and bacon (page 193).

The lower-and-slower fire requires a modified version of the KISS setup, using half or less than half the amount of charcoal and filling the water pan with ice to keep the temperature in the cooker low. It is difficult to reduce the temperature in a cooker once it heats up (particularly the BGE), so the key here is to start with a very small fire. You'll need to restock more frequently on longer cooks, but you'll use a minimal amount of unlit charcoal to keep the fire low.

Vent closures are also important. The closures outlined here are starting points for each cooker, but because there are so many variables that can affect the grate temperature, you must rely on your instincts and adjust the vents as needed. Be mindful that you don't close the vents too much and snuff the fire.

NOTE FOR KETTLE USERS: Sorry, folks. Running a clean-burning lower-and-slower fire is very difficult on a kettle-style grill. The risk of restricting the airflow and snuffing the fire is too high with these vent closures combined with the small amount of charcoal required to run the lower temperature. However, feel free to use the ice-in-the-water-pan trick if you find it difficult to keep the kettle temperature below 250°F on low-and-slow cooks.

YOU WILL NEED:

Natural lump charcoal

4 clean, debarked wood chunks, plus more depending on the length of the cook and desired smoke flavor

Charcoal chimney starter

3 sheets of newspaper, plus more as needed for restocking

Long metal tongs

Ice, to fill and restock water pan

1. Open all vents on the cooker.

2. Fill the WSM charcoal chamber one third full with unlit charcoal—about 1 chimney full on the 18.5-inch model and 1½ chimneys full on the 22.5-inch model.

3. Lay 2 wood chunks on top of the unlit charcoal in the chamber.

4. Prepare and light the chimney starter with half full of charcoal for the 18.5-inch model or three-quarters full of charcoal for the 22.5-inch model (see page 25 for detailed instructions).

5. When the charcoal is fully engaged in the chimney, carefully pour the lit charcoal into the charcoal chamber. Use tongs to return any stray charcoal to the chamber.

6. When the charcoal stops billowing white smoke, about 5 minutes after you pour the lit charcoal into the chamber, add 2 more wood chunks to the fire.

7. Reassemble the cooker with the empty water pan in place. Fill the water pan with ice and insert the cooking grates.

8. Close the cooker and adjust the vents at the prescribed time in the recipe, generally about 5 to 10 minutes after pouring the lit charcoal into the charcoal chamber.

9. When the temperature in the cooker has stabilized between 160°F and 180°F, set the meat on the grate, close the cooker, and continue as instructed in the recipe.

10. If the cooker dips below 160°F, assess the fire. If there is plenty of unlit charcoal but it has not engaged, slightly open the bottom vents to increase airflow. If the charcoal pile is low but burning (start checking around the 1½-hour mark), restock the cooker with ½ chimney of unlit charcoal. Replenish the ice in the water pan as needed, and drain the pan whenever it is more than half full of water.

BIG GREEN EGG (BGE)

YOU WILL NEED:

Natural lump charcoal

3 clean, debarked wood chunks plus 2 to 4 more, depending on the length of the cook and desired smoke flavor

Charcoal chimney starter

3 sheets of newspaper, plus more as needed for restocking

12 x 10 x 2-inch aluminum half pan

Ice, to fill and restock half pan

1. Remove the cooking grate and fill the firebox halfway with unlit charcoal, about 1 full chimney of charcoal.

2. Place 2 wood chunks on top of the charcoal in the firebox.

3. Prepare and light a one-third full chimney of charcoal (see page 29 for detailed instructions).

4. When the charcoal is fully engaged, gently pour the lit charcoal in an even layer over the unlit charcoal and wood in the firebox. Add 1 wood chunk to the fire.

5. Put on a pair of heatproof gloves and carefully insert the plate setter, legs up, over the fire ring.

6. Fill the aluminum half pan with ice and place it on the plate setter. Set the cooking grate over the plate setter.

7. When the charcoal stops billowing white smoke, about 5 minutes after pouring lit charcoal into the firebox, close the cooker and adjust the vents.

8. When the temperature in the cooker has stabilized between 160°F and 180°F, place the meat on the grate and close the cooker.

9. Follow the temperature checks and vent adjustments according to the cook instructions. If the cooker is running hotter than 200°F, close the bottom vent in ¼-inch increments as needed. Give the BGE 10 to 15 minutes to settle into a new temperature before making another vent adjustment.

10. Replenish the ice in the pan as needed, and drain the pan whenever it is more than half full of water.

YOU WILL NEED:

Natural lump charcoal

1 split of clean, debarked wood plus 2 to 4 more,
   depending on the length of the cook
   (for more about wood splits, see page 9)

Charcoal chimney starter

3 sheets of newspaper, plus more as needed
   for restocking

12½ x 6½-inch aluminum loaf pan

Ice, to fill and restock the loaf pan

Oven thermometer

Long metal tongs

1. Open all vents on the smoker.

2. Open the firebox and pour 1 chimney full of unlit charcoal onto the grate. Set 1 small split of wood (about half the size of a regular split) or 2 wood chunks on top of the charcoal.

3. Prepare and light a one-third full chimney of charcoal (see page 25 for detailed instructions).

4. Fill an aluminum loaf pan with ice and place it on the cooking grate, about 1 inch away from the firebox opening.

5. When the charcoal in the chimney starter is engaged, carefully pour the lit charcoal into the firebox.

6. Five minutes after adding the lit charcoal, close the firebox and close the top and firebox vents halfway.

7. When the temperature in the cooker has stabilized between 160°F and 180°F, set the meat on the far end of the grate, away from the firebox, and close the cooker.

8. If the temperature in the cooker drops below 160°F, assess the fire. If there is plenty of unlit charcoal but it has not engaged, slightly open the firebox vent to increase airflow. If the charcoal pile is low but burning, restock the firebox with ½ chimney of unlit charcoal and 1 small split of wood or 2 wood chunks.

9. Replenish the ice in the water pan as needed, and drain the pan whenever it is more than half full of water.

EXTEND THE LIFE OF YOUR FIRE WITH NATURAL BRIQUETTES

Natural briquettes burn slower and more evenly than the irregular pieces of lump charcoal, and they use vegetable starch as a binder, not the funky additives found in standard quick-light briquettes. I only use natural briquettes when I want to extend a cook without having to restock the charcoal as often. But, I never use natural briquettes alone. I layer in a bed of the briquettes (like Royal Oak's Ridge Briquets or Wicked Good Weekend Warrior Briquettes) with regular lump charcoal to build a slower-burning fire. With this setup, the fast- and clean-burning lump charcoal ignites the fire and in due course engages the slow-burning briquettes.

PLEASE NOTE: I don't recommend using natural briquettes on the BGE; it's unnecessary on such an efficient cooker, and the vegetable binder can produce residue that will gunk up a ceramic cooker.

WEBER SMOKEY MOUNTAIN (WSM)

1. Fill the charcoal ring halfway with unlit natural briquettes, then top them with wood chunks and unlit lump charcoal according to the KISS setup (page 26).
2. Ignite the bed of unlit charcoal with 1 full chimney of lit charcoal.

OFFSET SMOKER

1. Pour 1 chimney full of unlit natural briquettes on the charcoal grate, then top them with 1 split of wood and 1 chimney full of unlit lump charcoal according to the KISS setup (page 31).
2. Ignite the bed of unlit charcoal with 1 full chimney of lit charcoal.

KETTLE GRILL

1. Bank 10 to 12 natural briquettes on one side of the charcoal grate, then top them with 1 wood chunk and ½ chimney of unlit lump charcoal (for a 22-inch grill) or 1 full chimney of unlit charcoal (for a 26-inch grill).
2. Ignite the bed of unlit charcoal with a ¾-full chimney of lit charcoal.

3.
TURKEY, DUCK
&
MORE POULTRY

DEAR STUDENT:

YOU'VE GOT TO LEARN TO CRAWL BEFORE YOU CAN WALK—THAT'S THE GIST OF the Low & Slow method, and it's why I like to start with a turkey that cooks in 2 to 3 hours instead of an expensive brisket that requires 12 hours of vigilance and fire maintenance. If you've already learned how to run your cooker for a steady 8 hours or longer, turkey and other poultry may seem like a step backward. I assure you, the recipes in this chapter are essential building blocks in complete charcoal cooking mastery. Even if you're a pro on your cooker, running through more basic cooks is how you hone your technique and develop your own signature flavor profile and style of cooking. In this chapter, you'll also baby step into the world of curing and smoking meat.

    With my method, the best barbecue isn't just a plate of meat—it's proof that you understand the nuances of running your cooker. In addition to low-and-slow charcoal cooks (where the optimum temperature is in the 225°F to 250°F range), this chapter also includes introductory cooks in hot smoke-roasting (300°F to 375°F) and lower-and-slower smoking (180°F to 200°F). As much as these cooks are about delicious meat, they are even more so about the art of building and controlling a clean-burning fire and maintaining different temperature ranges on your cooker.

Enjoy!

Gary Wiviott

SMOKED TURKEY

You know the perfectly burnished Normal Rockwell turkey you dream of serving guests on Thanksgiving? This is it, and you can cook it in as little as 2 hours. (This bird cooks surprisingly fast. Don't overcook it.) You only need three elements to make it happen: a backboneless turkey trussed just right, 24 hours in a fool-proof buttermilk brine, and a clean-burning, low-and-slow fire. Just remember: Do not (ever!) buy a "prebrined", "basted", or "self-basting" turkey. These birds have been injected with salt water and flavorings, and if you brine this type of turkey, it will result in very, very salty meat. My buttermilk brine ensures a juicy bird every time and removing the backbone makes the turkey cook quickly and evenly.

Please note: With a full KISS load of charcoal burning, the WSM and BGE will run steady for many hours longer than it takes to cook a turkey. You can use this time to smoke more meat or vegetables for side dishes (be sure to check and refill the water pan as needed), or open the vents and carefully remove the water pan or plate setter to increase the heat and grill or hot smoke roast other foods. If you're confident operating your cooker, you can also start the cook with half the amount of unlit charcoal to reduce the cooker's running time.

SERVES 8 TO 10

COOKER TEMPERATURE: 225°F to 250°F

COOK TIME: 1½ to 2 hours

FOR THE RECIPE:

2 gallons Basic Buttermilk Brine (page 218)

1 (12- to 14-pound) unbasted turkey

1 tablespoon canola or olive oil

1 cup Citrus-Herb Rub (page 227)

FOR THE COOK:

3 feet of kitchen twine

¼ cup red wine vinegar (optional)

AT THE END OF THE COOK: To help crisp the skin and give the turkey a burnished, mahogany color, spritz the skin with red wine vinegar and completely open the bottom vents about 10 to 15 minutes before the turkey is done. The turkey is done when the breast reads 155°F and the thigh reads 165°F. Carryover cooking will continue to increase the temperature several degrees as it rests. Let the turkey rest at least 10 to 15 minutes before slicing and serving.

24 HOURS BEFORE THE COOK

Make the Basic Buttermilk Brine and set it aside to cool. Meanwhile, prepare the turkey.

Remove the backbone: Lay the turkey breast-side down on a cutting board. Using heavy-duty kitchen or poultry shears, cut along both sides of the backbone. Start at the thigh end, cut alongside the backbone, then turn the turkey around and cut from the neck side down along the backbone. (Save the backbone for stock.) A whole turkey takes about 30 minutes of cooking time per pound of meat. Removing the backbone significantly decreases the cook time.

Disconnect the leg/thigh joint: Turn the turkey breast-side up. Grip the thigh and leg firmly, then bend the leg backward to break the connecting joint. If the joint doesn't pop, you may need to leverage it against a solid surface (like the separator wall in a double sink) when you snap the leg backward. Repeat on the other leg/thigh.

When the brine is completely cool, submerge the turkey in the liquid, cover the brining container, and refrigerate for at least 12 hours or up to 24 hours.

1 HOUR BEFORE THE COOK

Remove the turkey from the brine, rinse it under cool running water, and discard the brine. Pat the interior and exterior of the turkey dry with paper towels.

Truss the turkey: Position the brined turkey breast-side up on a cutting board with the legs facing you. Lay the center of the twine beneath the tailbone of the turkey, with the ends extending left and right. Double loop the end of each leg with twine, then raise the legs so they are pointing directly upward. Secure the legs tightly together so they are "pinching" the breast and remain upright. If the legs slip out of this position, you can loop and anchor the twine around the neck bone.

Rub the turkey, inside and out, with the canola or olive oil. Coat the skin and cavity with the Citrus-Herb Rub (page 227) and gently work it underneath the skin of the breast.

30 MINUTES BEFORE THE COOK

Start a KISS method fire according to the instructions for your

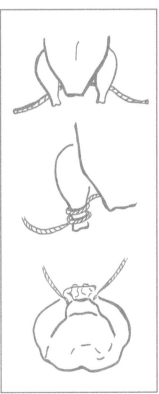

REMOVE THE BACKBONE

TRUSS THE TURKEY

cooker of choice: WSM (page 26), BGE (page 29), or offset (page 31).

If you're cooking on a kettle grill, start a hot smoke–roast fire (page 36).

WSM

◇◇

WHEN THE CHARCOAL is engaged in the fire ring and the cooker is reassembled, place the turkey breast-side up in the middle of the top grate. Close the cooker and adjust the vents.

TOP VENT:
18.5-INCH MODEL: Open.
22.5-INCH MODEL: Open.

BOTTOM VENTS:
18.5-INCH MODEL: Close two vents by one third.
22.5-INCH MODEL: Close two vents halfway.

1 HOUR INTO THE COOK

Check the cooker temperature. If the WSM is running hotter than 275°F, double-check the vent closures. Because the 22.5-inch WSM tends to run hotter, you may also need to close the third bottom vent by one half and/or the top vent by one third to lower the temperature in the cooker. Adjust one vent at a time, and allow 10 to 15 minutes for the temperature to settle in before making another adjustment.

1½ HOURS INTO THE COOK

Check the temperature of the breast and thigh with an instant-read thermometer and continue checking the turkey every 15 to 20 minutes until the breast registers 155°F. Refill the water pan if it is less than half full.

◇◇

BGE

◇◇

FIVE MINUTES AFTER adding the lit charcoal and inserting the plate setter and water pan, set the turkey breast-side up in the middle of the grate. Close the cooker and adjust the vents.

TOP VENT:

Close halfway.

BOTTOM VENT:

Open 1 inch.

30 MINUTES INTO THE COOK

Check the cooker temperature. If the BGE is running hotter than 275°F, close the bottom vent by ¼ inch. Allow 10 to 15 minutes for the temperature to settle in before making another adjustment.

1½ HOURS INTO THE COOK

Check the temperature of the breast and thigh with an instant-read thermometer and continue checking the turkey every 15 to 20 minutes until the breast registers 155°F. Refill the water pan if it is less than half full.

◇◇

OFFSET

WHEN THE CHARCOAL and wood are engaged in the firebox and no longer billowing smoke, about 5 to 10 minutes after adding the lit charcoal, place the turkey breast-side up on the opposite side of the cooking grate with the breast facing the water pan and firebox. Close the cooker and adjust the vents.

TOP VENT:
Open.

FIREBOX VENT:
Close by one third.

EVERY 30 TO 45 MINUTES IN THE COOK

Check the cooker temperature. If the offset is running hotter than 275°F, close the firebox vent halfway. You may also need to close the top (damper) vent by one third to reduce the temperature. Allow 10 to 15 minutes for the temperature to settle in between vent adjustments.

Check the charcoal level in the firebox. If half of the charcoal is burned through, restock the charcoal (see page 32). Check and refill the water pan as needed.

Rotate the turkey 180 degrees on the grate so the side facing the firebox is now turned away from the fire.

1½ HOURS INTO THE COOK

Check the temperature of the breast and thigh with an instant-read thermometer and continue checking the turkey every 15 to 20 minutes until the breast registers 155°F. Refill the water pan if it is less than half full.

KETTLE

WHEN THE CHARCOAL is engaged on the banked piles, about 5 minutes after adding the lit charcoal, place the turkey breast-side up on the grate, directly above the water pan. Close the cooker and adjust the vents.

TOP VENT:

22-INCH MODEL: Open.

26-INCH MODEL: Open.

BOTTOM VENT:

22-INCH MODEL: Close by one third.

26-INCH MODEL: Close halfway.

EVERY 20 TO 30 MINUTES IN THE COOK

Check the cooker temperature. If the kettle is running hotter than 350°F, close the top vent by one third. Allow 10 to 15 minutes for the temperature to settle in between vent adjustments.

If the temperature in the cooker drops below 300°F, assess the fire. If the charcoal in the piles is not engaging, you may need to open the vents to increase airflow. If more than half of the charcoal has burned to ash, restock the piles with ½ chimney of lit charcoal (see page 34). Refill the water pan as needed.

1 HOUR INTO THE COOK

Check the temperature of the breast and thigh with an instant-read thermometer and continue checking the turkey every 15 to 20 minutes until the breast registers 155°F. Refill the water pan if it is less than half full.

HOT SMOKE-ROASTED DUCK

When I first met Ellen, my lovely bride of 28 years (and counting), I learned that her family loved duck. To get in their good graces, I offered to cook duck for Christmas dinner, so I employed my usual obsessive method of learning: by cooking about ten ducks over a 20-day period leading up to the holiday. I became the Duck Master, and I married Ellen soon after—win-win!

Since then, I've perfected this ace-in-the-hole method of cooking duck that keeps me mostly out of trouble and in her good graces. I remove the backbone and split the duck in half, dry-cure it with a French magret-style rub for 12 hours, and hot smoke–roast the duck to get the kind of crackly, crispy skin even your most polite dinner guests will fight over.

SERVES 2 TO 4

COOKER TEMPERATURE: 300°F to 350°F

COOK TIME: 30 minutes to 1 hour

FOR THE RECIPE:

1 whole (approximately 5-pound) duck

2 tablespoons Magret-Style Dry Cure (page 229)

FOR THE COOK:

2 tablespoons olive oil

AT THE END OF THE COOK: To help crisp the skin, brush the duck with olive oil in the last 10 to 15 minutes of the cook and flip the duck over, breast side down. The duck is done when the thigh registers 155°F. Let the duck rest 10 to 15 minutes before slicing and serving.

8 TO 18 HOURS BEFORE THE COOK

Make the dry cure and set it aside.

Split the duck: Remove the backbone and break the leg/thigh joint (see the turkey on page 46 for a visual). Flip the duck over, breast-side up, and open it like a book. Using kitchen shears or a knife, cut through the middle of the breasts to split the duck in half. Reserve the neck and gizzards packaged with the duck to make stock for Classic Duck à l'Orange Sauce (page 246) or other recipes.

Score the skin: Using a small, very sharp knife, gently cut diagonal slits about 1½ inches apart across the skin and through the fat layer, slightly angling the knife to avoid piercing the meat. Turn the breast around and slice diagonal lines in the opposite direction, creating a cross-hatch diamond pattern.

Rub each duck half inside and out with 1 tablespoon of the dry cure, working the cure into the slits. Stack the duck halves together skin-to-skin and wrap them tightly in plastic wrap. Set the wrapped duck on a platter or baking sheet and refrigerate for 8 to 16 hours.

30 MINUTES BEFORE THE COOK

Remove the duck from the refrigerator and rinse it under cold running water to remove any excess cure. Pat the duck dry with paper towels.

Start a hot smoke–roast fire according to the instructions for your cooker of choice: WSM (page 35), BGE (page 35), offset (page 35), or kettle (page 36).

WSM

WHEN THE CHARCOAL is engaged in the fire ring, the water pan filled with sand is in place, and the cooker is reassembled, close the cooker and adjust the vents.

TOP VENT:	BOTTOM VENTS:
18.5-INCH MODEL: Open.	**18.5-INCH MODEL:** Open.
22.5-INCH MODEL: Open.	**22.5-INCH MODEL:** Open.

Give the temperature in the cooker 10 to 15 minutes to stabilize. If the cooker is running hotter than 350°F, close one bottom vent by one third, if you're using an 18.5-inch WSM, or by half if you're using a 22.5-inch WSM. When the temperature in the cooker has stabilized between 300°F and 350°F, place the duck halves in the middle of the top grate with the legs/thighs facing out and close the cooker.

15 MINUTES INTO THE COOK

Keep an eye on the cooker temperature and adjust the vents as needed to maintain a steady temperature between 300°F and 350°F.

30 MINUTES INTO THE COOK

Check the temperature of the duck by poking an instant-read thermometer into the thickest part of the thigh, and continue checking the duck every 10 minutes until the thigh registers 155°F.

BGE

◇◇

FIVE MINUTES AFTER adding the lit charcoal and inserting the plate setter, close the cooker and adjust the vents.

TOP VENT: **BOTTOM VENT:**

Open.   Open 2 inches.

Give the temperature in the cooker 10 to 15 minutes to stabilize. If the cooker is running hotter than 350°F, close the bottom vent by ¼ inch. When the temperature in the cooker has stabilized between 300°F and 350°F, place the duck halves in the middle of the grate with the legs/thighs facing out and close the cooker.

EVERY 15 MINUTES IN THE COOK

Keep an eye on the temperature and adjust the vents as necessary to maintain a steady temperature between 300°F and 350°F.

30 MINUTES INTO THE COOK

Check the temperature of the duck by poking an instant-read thermometer into the thickest part of the thigh, and continue checking the duck every 10 minutes until the thigh registers 155°F.

◇◇

OFFSET

◇◇

WHEN THE CHARCOAL is engaged in the firebox and the pan filled with sand is in place, close the cooker and adjust the vents.

TOP VENT:
Open.

FIREBOX VENT:
Open.

Give the temperature in the cooker 10 to 15 minutes to stabilize. If the cooker is running hotter than 350°F, close the firebox vent by one third. When the temperature in the cooker has stabilized between 300°F and 350°F, place the duck halves on the cooking grate away from the firebox with the legs/thighs facing the firebox and close the cooker.

EVERY 20 MINUTES IN THE COOK

Check the temperature. If the offset is running below 300°F, open the firebox vent to increase airflow, or add 1 full chimney of lit charcoal and 1 split of wood to the firebox if the fire is low. If the cooker is running hotter than 375°F, close the firebox vent by half. Give the cooker 10 minutes to settle into the new temperature before making another vent adjustment.

30 MINUTES INTO THE COOK

Check the temperature of the duck by poking an instant-read thermometer into the thickest part of the thigh, and continue checking the duck every 10 minutes until the thigh registers 155°F.

◇◇

KETTLE

WHEN THE CHARCOAL is engaged on the banked piles, about 5 minutes after adding the lit charcoal, close the cooker and adjust the vents.

TOP VENT:
22-INCH MODEL: Open.
26-INCH MODEL: Open.

BOTTOM VENT:
22-INCH MODEL: Close by one third.
26-INCH MODEL: Close halfway.

Give the temperature in the kettle 10 minutes to stabilize. If the cooker is running hotter than 350°F, close the top vent by one third. When the temperature in the cooker has stabilized between 300°F and 350°F, place the duck halves directly above the water pan with the legs/thighs facing out and close the cooker.

EVERY 15 MINUTES IN THE COOK

Check the temperature. If the kettle is running hotter than 350°F, close the 22-inch model's bottom vent to one half; if you're cooking on the 26-inch model, close the top vent by one half. Avoid closing the top or bottom vents on the kettle more than halfway—restricting the airflow too much could snuff the fire. Refill the water pan as needed. If the cooker temperature drops below 300°F, open the bottom vent slightly to increase airflow or restock the charcoal as needed.

30 MINUTES INTO THE COOK

Check the temperature of the duck by poking an instant-read thermometer into the thickest part of the thigh, and continue checking the duck every 10 minutes until the thigh registers 155°F.

CHICKEN WINGS
TWO WAYS

ONE OF THE things I love about cooking with charcoal is the range of flavors and textures you can achieve by simply changing the charcoal setup. Chicken wings are a great way to explore this diversity, not only because they're cheap and easy to prepare, but also because they cook quickly. Here, you'll find instructions for wings cooked two ways: hot smoke–roasted and low-and-slow style. Hot smoke–roasted wings will have crispy skin, similar to a classic Buffalo wing. Low-and-slow wings won't crisp, but you will get a deeper smoke-infused flavor. You can also dunk low-and-slow wings in 400°F oil for a minute or two if you want to make smo-fried wings. Try both methods and judge the difference. Whatever style you prefer, be prepared to make them over and over and over again. Because everybody loves a chicken wing, and these might just make you famous.

CRISPY HOT SMOKE-ROASTED CHICKEN WINGS

These are not classic Buffalo wings because they are not fried, but hot smoke-roasting achieves an equally delicious crispy-skinned wing with a bonus note of wood smoke. These marinated wings are perfect hot off the cooker without a drop of sauce.

MAKES 40 TO 60 WINGS

COOKER TEMPERATURE: 300°F to 350°F

COOK TIME: 20 to 45 minutes

FOR THE RECIPE:

5 pounds (approximately 40 to 60) chicken wings, cut into drumettes and flats (save the flats for stock)

1 recipe Chicken Wing Wet Rub (page 230) or Teriyaki Wing Marinade (page 221)

AT THE END OF THE COOK: Getting an accurate temperature read on wings is difficult because they're small and the meat is close to the bone. You're shooting for 165°F, but rely on your senses. Break a wing open to see if the meat is opaque with no translucent pink in the middle. Serve immediately.

8 TO 12 HOURS BEFORE THE COOK

Make the wet rub or marinade. Coat the wings in the rub or submerge them in the marinade in a large nonreactive container with a tight-fitting lid. Cover and refrigerate for 8 to 12 hours. Stir the wings every 1 to 2 hours to redistribute the rub or marinade.

30 MINUTES BEFORE THE COOK

Remove the wings from the marinade (if using) and let the wings sit at room temperature.

Start a hot smoke–roast fire according to the instructions for your cooker of choice: WSM (page 35), BGE (page 35), offset (page 35), or kettle (page 36).

WSM

WHEN THE CHARCOAL is engaged in the fire ring, the sand pan is in place, and the cooker is reassembled, close the cooker and adjust the vents.

TOP VENT:	BOTTOM VENTS:
18.5-INCH MODEL: Open.	**18.5-INCH MODEL:** Open.
22.5-INCH MODEL: Open.	**22.5-INCH MODEL:** Open.

Give the WSM 10 to 15 minutes for the temperature to settle in. When the temperature has stabilized, arrange the wings on the lower and top grates of the cooker. Avoid placing the wings near the outer edge of the grates, where direct heat from the fire radiates around the sand pan. Do not pile the wings. Leave room between the wings so air (and wood smoke) can flow around them.

10 MINUTES INTO THE COOK

Check the cooker temperature. If the WSM is running hotter than 350°F, close one bottom vent by one third if you're cooking on an 18.5-inch WSM or by half on a 22.5-inch WSM.

20 MINUTES INTO THE COOK

Check several wings for doneness and continue checking the meat every 5 to 10 minutes until the wings are cooked through but still juicy.

The wings on the top grate will cook slightly faster than the wings on the lower grate. When the wings on the top grate are done cooking, remove them from the cooker, move the lower wings to the top grate to finish cooking, and start a new batch of wings on the bottom grate.

Repeat the cook until you have cooked all the wings. Keep an eye on the fire and if the temperature in the cooker starts to drop below 300°F, restock the cooker as needed with 1 chimney of lit charcoal.

BGE

FIVE MINUTES AFTER adding the lit charcoal and inserting the plate setter, close the cooker and adjust the vents.

TOP VENT:
Open.

BOTTOM VENT:
Open 2 inches.

Give the BGE 10 minutes to allow the temperature to settle in. When the temperature stabilizes between 300°F and 350°F, arrange the wings on the grate. Do not pile the wings. Arrange the wings so they are not touching and air (and wood smoke) can flow around them.

10 MINUTES INTO THE COOK

Check the cooker temperature. If the BGE is running hotter than 350°F, close the bottom vent by 1 inch.

20 MINUTES INTO THE COOK

Check several wings for doneness and continue checking the meat every 5 to 10 minutes until the wings are cooked through but still juicy.

When the first batch is done, remove them from the cooker and repeat the cook with the remaining wings.

OFFSET

◇◇

WHEN THE CHARCOAL is fully engaged in the firebox and the sand pan is in place, close the cooker and adjust the vents.

TOP VENT:	FIREBOX VENT:
Open.	Open.

Give the offset 10 minutes to stabilize. When the temperature stabilizes between 300°F and 350°F, set the wings on the opposite side of the cooking grate. Do not pile the wings. Arrange the wings so they are not touching and air (and wood smoke) can flow around them.

10 MINUTES INTO THE COOK

Check the cooker temperature. If the offset is running hotter than 350°F, close the firebox vent by one third.

20 MINUTES INTO THE COOK

Check several wings for doneness and continue checking the meat every 5 to 10 minutes until the wings are cooked through but still juicy.

When the first batch is done, remove it from the cooker and repeat the cook with the remaining wings. Keep an eye on the fire; if the temperature in the cooker drops below 300°F, restock the cooker as needed with 1 chimney of lit charcoal and 1 split of wood.

◇◇

KETTLE

FIVE MINUTES AFTER pouring the lit charcoal onto the banked piles of unlit charcoal, close the cooker and adjust the vents.

TOP VENT:	**BOTTOM VENT:**
22-INCH MODEL: Open.	**22-INCH MODEL:** Close by one third
26-INCH MODEL: Open.	**26-INCH MODEL:** Close halfway

Give the kettle 5 to 10 minutes to allow the temperature to settle in. When the temperature stabilizes between 300F and 350F, arrange the wings on the cooking grate above the water pan. Do not pile the wings. Arrange the wings so they are not touching and air (and wood smoke) can flow around them.

EVERY 10 MINUTES IN THE COOK

Check the cooker temperature. If the kettle is running hotter than 350°F, close the top vent by one third. If the temperature is below 300°F and more than half of the charcoal has burned to ash, restock with ½ chimney of lit charcoal (see page 34). Refill the water pan as needed.

20 MINUTES INTO THE COOK

Check several wings for doneness and continue checking the meat every 5 to 10 minutes until the wings are cooked through but still juicy.

When the first batch is done, remove it from the grill and repeat the cook with the remaining wings. Keep an eye on the fire; if the temperature in the cooker drops below 300°F, restock the cooker as needed with ½ chimney of lit charcoal.

SMOKY LOW & SLOW WINGS

I don't like to brag, but my version of these wings—which are smoked, then fried—have been called the best in Chicago by a few reputable sources (and some disreputable ones). The zing of the buttermilk–hot sauce brine is the perfect base note and accents the smokiness of the wings in a way that, fried or not, will change everything you think you know about chicken wings. After the cook, sit back and marvel at how quickly 5 pounds of wings can disappear.

If you want the smo-fried, Buffalo wing treatment, let the smoked wings rest for 20 minutes, then dunk the wings in 400°F oil until the skin crackles, about 1 minute. Blend ½ cup melted butter with ½ cup Louisiana-style hot sauce, toss the smoke-roasted wings in the mixture to coat, and serve them with crisp celery spears and Blue Cheese Dip (page 247).

MAKES 40 TO 60 WINGS

COOKER TEMPERATURE: 225°F to 250°F

COOK TIME: 30 minutes to 1 hour

FOR THE RECIPE:

5 pounds (approximately 40 to 60) chicken wings, separated into drumettes and flats (save the flats for stock)

2 gallons Basic Buttermilk Brine (page 218)

AT THE END OF THE COOK: Getting an accurate temperature read on wings is difficult because they're small and the meat is close to the bone. You're shooting for 165°F, but rely on your senses. Break a wing open to see if the meat is opaque with no translucent pink in the middle. Serve immediately.

8 TO 12 HOURS BEFORE THE COOK

Make the brine. When the brine is fully cooled, combine the brine and wings in a large nonreactive container with a tight-fitting lid. Cover and refrigerate for 8 to 12 hours.

30 MINUTES BEFORE THE COOK

Remove the chicken wings from the refrigerator. Rinse the wings under cool running water and pat them dry with paper towels. Discard the brine.

Start a KISS method fire according to the instructions for your cooker of choice: WSM (page 26), BGE (page 29), offset (page 31), or kettle (page 33).

WSM

WHEN THE CHARCOAL is fully engaged and the cooker is reassembled, close the cooker and adjust the vents.

TOP VENT:

18.5-INCH MODEL: Open.

22.5-INCH MODEL: Open.

BOTTOM VENTS:

18.5-INCH MODEL: Close two vents by one third.

22.5-INCH MODEL: Close two vents halfway.

Give the WSM 10 to 15 minutes to allow the temperature to settle in. When the temperature stabilizes between 225°F and 250°F, arrange the wings on the lower and top grates of the cooker. Do not pile the wings. Leave room between the wings so air (and wood smoke) can flow around them.

15 MINUTES INTO THE COOK

Check the cooker temperature. The temperature should settle in somewhere between 225°F and 250°F. If the cooker is running hotter than that, close the third bottom vent by one third if you're using an 18.5-inch WSM or by half if you're using a 22.5-inch WSM. After 15 minutes, if the 22.5-inch model is still running higher than 250°F after adjusting all of the bottom vents, close the top vent by half.

30 MINUTES INTO THE COOK

Check several wings for doneness and continue checking the meat every 5 to 10 minutes until the wings are cooked through but still juicy.

The wings on the top grate will cook slightly faster than the wings on the lower grate. When the wings on the top grate are done cooking, remove them from the cooker, move the lower wings to the top grate to finish cooking, and start a new batch of wings on the bottom grate.

Repeat the cook until all of the wings are cooked. Keep an eye on the fire; if the temperature in the cooker drops below 225°F, open the vents to increase airflow or restock the cooker as needed with 1 chimney of lit charcoal.

BGE

FIVE MINUTES AFTER adding the lit charcoal and inserting the plate setter and water pan, close the cooker and adjust the vents.

TOP VENT:
Close halfway.

BOTTOM VENT:
Open 1 inch.

Give the BGE 10 minutes to allow the temperature to settle in. When the temperature stabilizes between 225°F and 250°F, arrange the wings on the grate so they are not touching and air (and wood smoke) can flow around them. Do not pile the wings. You will need to cook the wings in several batches to avoid crowding.

15 MINUTES INTO THE COOK

Check the cooker temperature. If the cooker is running hotter than 250°F, close the bottom vent by ¼ inch. If the cooker is running lower than 225°F, slightly open the top flywheel vent.

30 MINUTES INTO THE COOK

Check several wings for doneness and continue checking the meat every 5 to 10 minutes until the wings are cooked through but still juicy.

When the first batch is done, remove them from the cooker and repeat the cook with the remaining wings.

OFFSET

‹◇◇›

WHEN THE CHARCOAL is engaged in the firebox and the water pan is in place, close the cooker and adjust the vents.

TOP VENT:
Open.

FIREBOX VENT:
Close by one third.

Give the offset 10 minutes to allow the temperature to settle in. When the temperature stabilizes between 225°F and 250°F, set the wings on the opposite side of the cooking grate, away from the sand pan. Arrange the wings so they are not touching and air (and wood smoke) can flow around them. Do not pile the wings. You will need to cook the wings in several batches to avoid crowding.

15 MINUTES INTO THE COOK

Check the cooker temperature. If the cooker is running hotter than 250°F, close the firebox vent by halfway. If the cooker is running lower than 225°F, slightly open the firebox vent.

30 MINUTES INTO THE COOK

Check several wings for doneness and continue checking the meat every 5 to 10 minutes until the wings are cooked through but still juicy.

When the first batch is done, remove them from the cooker and repeat the cook with the remaining wings. Keep an eye on the fire; if the temperature in the cooker drops below 225°F, restock the firebox as needed with 1 chimney of lit charcoal.

‹◇◇›

KETTLE

WHEN THE UNLIT charcoal is engaged, about 5 minutes after adding the lit charcoal to the pile, close the cooker and adjust the vents.

TOP VENT:	**BOTTOM VENT:**
22-INCH MODEL: Open.	**22-INCH MODEL:** Close by one third.
26-INCH MODEL: Open.	**26-INCH MODEL:** Close halfway.

Give the kettle 5 minutes for the temperature to settle in, and adjust the vents as needed to stabilize the temperature below 300°F.

When the temperature is stabilized, arrange the wings on the cooking grate above the drip pan with the thickest part of the wing facing the fire. Do not pile the wings. Arrange the wings so they are not touching and air (and wood smoke) can flow around them then close the cooker. You will need to cook the wings in several batches to avoid crowding.

EVERY 15 MINUTES IN THE COOK

Check the cooker temperature. If the kettle is running hotter than 275°F, close the top vent by one third. If the temperature drops below 225°F, assess the fire. Open the bottom vent slightly if there is plenty of unengaged charcoal on the pile. If more than half of the charcoal has burned to ash, restock the cooker with ½ chimney of lit charcoal (see page 33). Refill the water pan as needed.

30 MINUTES INTO THE COOK

Check several wings for doneness and continue checking the meat every 5 to 10 minutes until the wings are cooked through but still juicy. When the first batch is done, remove it from the grill and repeat the cook with the remaining wings. Keep an eye on the fire; if the temperature in the cooker drops below 225°F, restock the cooker as needed with 1 chimney of lit charcoal.

THE MASTER CURE FOR MEATS

Curing is a straightforward process, but it takes time and the devil is in the details. Unlike rubs and brines, which are flexible in terms of ingredients and measure, a cure is an exact mix. This one is based on Michael Ruhlman's flawless basic cure in *Charcuterie* and includes measurements by weight (using a digital kitchen scale) or volume (using measuring cups/spoons).

Dextrose (aka corn sugar) has a powder-fine consistency that disperses and dissolves in cures better than table sugar, and you can buy it from an online spice store like thespicehouse.com or at a local brewing supply shop. If you can't find dextrose, you can substitute regular granulated sugar, but you must change the quantity because it has a different volume due to its coarser texture. Remember that all of my recipes use Morton's kosher salt—if you use a different brand, such as Diamond Crystal, be sure to adjust the measurement (see page 13).

All meat cures contain pink salt, which prevents certain types of bacterial growth in the meat. It goes by a few different names—curing salt, Prague powder #1, Insta Cure #1—and you can find it in many grocery stores and specialty meat shops, or buy it online. There is no substitute for pink salt in meat cures.

This recipe makes enough cure to use in several other recipes, including Duck Breast Pastrami (page 74) and Four-Pepper Bacon (page 193). When properly stored in an airtight container in a cool, dry place, this cure will keep indefinitely.

MASTER CURE WITH DEXTROSE BY WEIGHT

Makes about 5 cups

1 pound kosher salt

13 ounces dextrose

3 ounces pink salt

MASTER CURE WITH DEXTROSE BY VOLUME

Makes about 5 cups

1½ cups plus 4 tablespoons kosher salt

2⅓ cups dextrose

5 tablespoons pink salt

MASTER CURE WITH SUGAR BY WEIGHT

Makes about 5 cups

1 pound kosher salt

8 ounces granulated sugar

2 ounces pink salt

MASTER CURE WITH SUGAR BY VOLUME

Makes about 5 cups

1½ cups plus 4 tablespoons kosher salt

1 cup granulated sugar

7½ tablespoons pink salt

In a large bowl, whisk together the kosher salt, dextrose or granulated sugar, and pink salt. Store the cure in a nonreactive airtight container.

GOOSE BREAST
PASTRAMI

Americans know pastrami in its beef incarnation, but few realize that the Jewish Romanian immigrants who introduced pastrami to the United States typically made it with goose breast. Beef navel (aka belly) only replaced goose breast because it was less expensive and, at the time, more readily available in America. You can buy goose breast from specialty meat shops or online retailers; grocery stores like Whole Foods also tend to carry goose around the holidays. If you can't find goose breast, feel free to use duck breast as a substitute (see page 74 for alternate cook instructions).

SERVES 8 TO 10

COOKER TEMPERATURE: 160°F to 180°F

COOK TIME: 3-day cure, 1 to 2 hours on the cooker, plus 4 days pressed in the refrigerator

FOR THE RECIPE:

2 whole (1½- to 2½-pound) skin-on goose breasts or 4 skin-on goose breast lobes

⅓ cup Master Cure (page 68)

½ cup Pastrami Rub (page 229)

AT THE END OF THE COOK: The internal temperature of the breasts should be 160°F by the 2-hour mark, if it isn't increase the heat in the cooker to 250°F by adjusting the top and bottom vents. Check the internal temperature of the breasts every 5 minutes until they reach 160°F.

When the breasts are done, remove them from the cooker and allow the meat to cool. Wrap each breast in plastic wrap and place them in a shallow glass casserole dish. Stack 3 to 4 pounds (three or four 16–ounce cans) of weight on top of the wrapped breasts and refrigerate for 4 days. After the 4-day pressing is complete, unwrap the breasts, admire, eat, and enjoy. To serve, cut the pastrami in thin slices against the grain and serve it as an appetizer with a side of coarse, whole-grain mustard (see Smoked Creole Mustard, page 262) or Pickled Mustard Seeds (page 261). Or, serve it on toasted seedless rye bread with whole-grain mustard and grilled onions.

3 DAYS BEFORE THE COOK

Pat the goose breasts dry with paper towels and, if you have two whole breasts, cut the breasts in half to make four breast lobes. With a very sharp knife, score the skin in a crosshatch pattern, holding the knife at a slight angle to avoid piercing the flesh. Rub 1 tablespoon of the Master Cure into each breast lobe, working it into the slits. There should be a thin coat of cure sticking to the entire surface of the breast. Use more cure as necessary and shake off any excess.

Stack the lobes flesh-to-flesh and tightly wrap the breasts together in plastic wrap. Refrigerate the breasts for three days, flipping them twice per day, in the morning and at night.

30 MINUTES BEFORE THE COOK

Thoroughly rinse the goose breasts under cold, running water to completely remove the cure. Apply 2 tablespoons of Pastrami Rub to each breast, working the mixture into the skin slits. Smooth the goose breasts back into shape so the skin lays flat.

When the goose breasts are prepped, start a lower-and-slower fire according to the instructions for your cooker of choice: WSM (page 38), BGE (page 39), or offset (page 40). Adjust the vents as instructed for each cooker to stabilize the temperature between 160F and 180F.

WSM

WHEN THE CHARCOAL is engaged in the fire ring, about 5 minutes after adding the lit charcoal, reassemble the cooker with the ice pan in place. Close the cooker and adjust the vents.

TOP VENT:

18.5-INCH MODEL: Close by one third.

22.5-INCH MODEL: Close halfway.

BOTTOM VENTS:

18.5-INCH MODEL: Close all vents by one third.

22.5-INCH MODEL: Close all vents halfway.

Give the WSM 10 to 15 minutes to settle into a temperature. If the cooker is running hotter than 180°F, close two bottom vents in very slight increments. Wait 15 minutes and adjust the third bottom vent if the cooker is still running above 180°F. When the temperature in the cooker stabilizes between 160°F and 180°F, arrange the goose breasts skin-side up on the grate with the thick ends facing the outer edge and close the cooker.

EVERY 20 TO 30 MINUTES IN THE COOK

Keep an eye on the cooker temperature and adjust the vents, restock the ice pan, and restock the charcoal as needed to regulate the temperature between 160°F and 180°F. If the temperature dips below 160°F, add ½ chimney of unlit charcoal to the fire. When the pan is more than half full of water, drain and refill it with ice.

1 HOUR INTO THE COOK

Check the internal temperature of the goose by poking an instant-read thermometer into the thickest part of one breast. The breasts may take up to 2 hours to reach the target internal temperature of 160°F. This check is your reference point to gauge how much longer the breasts need to cook.

Begin checking the internal temperature every 15 to 20 minutes based on the first reading and remove the breasts when they are done.

BGE

$\diamond$

WHEN THE CHARCOAL is engaged and the plate setter and ice pan are in place, about 5 minutes after adding the lit charcoal, close the cooker and adjust the vents.

TOP VENT:

Close halfway.

BOTTOM VENT:

Open ½ inch.

Give the BGE 10 to 15 minutes to settle into a temperature. If the cooker is running hotter than 180°F, close the bottom vent ¼ inch. Wait 15 minutes and slightly close the top vent if the cooker is still running above 180°F. When the temperature in the cooker stabilizes between 160°F and 180°F, arrange the goose breasts skin-side up on the grate with the thick ends facing the outer edge and close the cooker.

EVERY 20 MINUTES IN THE COOK

Keep an eye on the cooker temperature and adjust the vents as needed to stabilize the temperature between 160°F and 180°F. When the pan is more than half full of water, drain and refill it with ice.

1 HOUR INTO THE COOK

Check the internal temperature of the goose by poking an instant-read thermometer into the thickest part of one breast. The breasts may take up to 2 hours to reach the target internal temperature of 160°F. This check is your reference point to gauge how much longer the breasts need to cook.

Begin checking the internal temperature every 15 to 20 minutes based on the first reading and remove the breasts when they are done.

$\diamond$

OFFSET

xxxxxxxxxxxxxxxxxxxxxxxxxxxxxxxxxxxxxxxxxxxxxxxxxxxxxxxxxxxxxxxxxxxxxxxxxxxxxxxxxxxx

WHEN THE CHARCOAL is engaged in the firebox and the ice pan is in place on the cooking grate, close the cooker and adjust the vents.

TOP VENT:
Close halfway.

FIREBOX VENT:
Close halfway.

Give the offset 10 to 15 minutes to settle into a temperature and adjust the vents as necessary if the cooker is too hot. You may need to close the firebox vent or top vent in very small increments to lower the temperature. When the temperature stabilizes between 160°F and 180°F, arrange the goose breasts skin-side up on the grate with the thicker ends facing the firebox and close the smoker.

EVERY 20 TO 30 MINUTES IN THE COOK

Keep an eye on the cooker temperature. When the pan is more than half full of water, drain and refill it with ice. If the temperature in the cooker drops below 160°F, assess the fire. If there is plenty of unlit charcoal in the firebox, you may need to slightly open the firebox vent to increase airflow and engage the charcoal. If the charcoal is running low but still glowing, restock the fire with ½ chimney of unlit charcoal and one small split of wood or two wood chunks.

1 HOUR INTO THE COOK

Check the internal temperature of the goose by poking an instant-read thermometer into the thickest part of one breast. The breasts may take up to 2 hours to reach the target internal temperature of 160°F. This check is your reference point to gauge how much longer the breasts need to cook.

Begin checking the internal temperature every 20 to 30 minutes based on the first reading and remove the breasts when they are done.

xxxxxxxxxxxxxxxxxxxxxxxxxxxxxxxxxxxxxxxxxxxxxxxxxxxxxxxxxxxxxxxxxxxxxxxxxxxxxxxxxxxx

DUCK BREAST PASTRAMI

IF FINDING GOOSE BREASTS PROVES DIFFICULT (OR EXPENSIVE), YOU CAN SUB-stitute duck breasts for an equally delicious riff on this pastrami. I prefer Moulard duck breasts—the same duck used to make foie gras—because they are bigger and meatier. To substitute duck, use the same instructions for curing and smoking the goose breast with the following adjustments:

1. Coat each breast with 1 tablespoon of Master Cure, or more as needed to ensure a thin, even layer over the entire surface.

2. Cure the duck breasts for 36 to 48 hours in the refrigerator, flipping the breasts once every 12 hours.

3. Apply 2 tablespoons of pastrami rub to each cured breast.

4. Smoke the breasts between 160°F and 180°F on your cooker to an internal temperature of 160°F, about 1 to 1½ hours. Start checking the internal temperature 30 minutes into the cook, then continue checking every 20 to 30 minutes based on the first temperature reading. If the breasts have not hit 160°F by the 1½-hour mark, increase the heat in your cooker by opening the bottom or firebox vents. Check the internal temperature of the breasts every 5 minutes until they reach 160°F.

5. After they are cooked to 160°F, remove the duck breasts from the cooker and let them cool to room temperature. Wrap the cooled breasts in plastic wrap and press them under weights; refrigerate for 2 days before slicing and serving.

4.

BEEF

DEAR STUDENT:

ANYONE WHO KNOWS MY BARBECUE HISTORY KNOWS ABOUT THE BRISKET epiphany I had in 1984 at Cooper's in Llano, Texas (aka where God goes when she's in the mood for brisket). Up to that point, I had been serious about barbecue for four or five years and considered myself a competent, even skilled backyard barbecue guy. My wife and I hosted barbecue parties, where everyone ate too much, drank too much, and complimented the food. But one bite of Cooper's brisket hot off the smoker changed everything. I went from approaching barbecue with heavy smoke, sauces, and secret-ingredient rubs to realizing that great barbecue is about nuance and the gentle interaction of smoke and meat. No more billowing smoke clouds, over-the-top rubs, and sticky-sweet sauces. It was a turning point that kick-started a full year of obsessive cooking. After some trial and error, I knew I'd succeeded when dinner guests stopped paying compliments and started asking questions, namely, "How'd you do it, and will you teach me?"

The brisket recipe in this chapter is the one everyone asks for because brisket is the ultimate challenge in barbecue. But there's so much more to learn. Strike awe in the hearts and bellies of dinner guests with Beef Back Ribs (page 97); and feed a small battalion of family or friends with a 7-bone Standing Rib Roast (page 110). Please the picky eaters in your life with Hot Smoke–Roasted Tri-Tip (page 121). Bask in the glory of a Smoked Corned Beef (page 102) that's better than 98 percent of the pastrami you've ever tasted. It's all here, and it's all yours.

Yours in smoke,

Gary Wiviott

MEET YOUR MEAT

The terminology and labeling of beef is tricky. Despite the USDA's best efforts, there are many variations in how some cuts are labeled and it often varies by the part of the country you live in, which can make buying the correct cut difficult. If you have a basic understanding of the primal cuts and where they are situated on a cow, you'll have an easier time talking to a butcher about the meat you want to eat. This diagram shows nine primal cuts and the subprimal cuts that are most relevant to charcoal cooking (i.e., grilling, low and slow, and hot smoke-roasting).

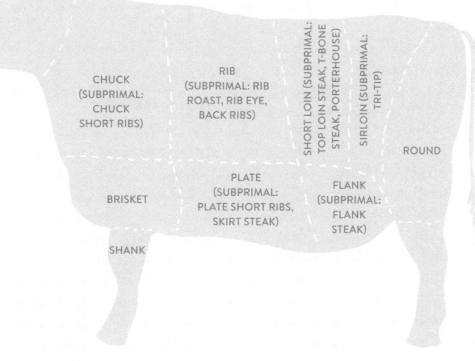

SMOKED BRISKET

I can describe my brisket methodology—and my how-to-barbecue philosophy in general—in two words: benign neglect. This might sound contradictory, particularly when you're following my step-by-step, timed instructions. Once you've smoked a brisket a few times, you'll realize this methodology isn't about completely ignoring the brisket, but ignoring it the right way. If this is your first brisket cook, the "benign neglect" philosophy is more about resisting the temptation to futz and fret to keep this cook simple. Don't use remote alarmed temperature probes to obsessively check the temperature of the meat. Don't use fans to regulate the airflow. Don't panic about whether the brisket will be ready for your 7 o'clock dinner party.

Once you've got the cooker running at the optimum temperature, this really is a low-maintenance cook. A brisket is done when it's done—it can take as little as 8 hours or as long as 12 hours depending on your cooker, the fire, and the brisket. For most of the cook, the best thing you can do for your brisket is leave it alone. If you really want to get more involved and go hardcore barbecue, surgically remove the cooked point from the brisket and whip up a batch of Burnt Ends (page 87).

SERVES 18

COOKER TEMPERATURE: 225°F to 250°F

COOK TIME: 10 to 12 hours

FOR THE RECIPE:

1 (12- to 15-pound) packer-cut brisket (see page 80 for notes on buying and trimming)

1 cup white vinegar

½ cup yellow mustard

⅔ cup Brisket Rub (page 230)

FOR THE COOK:

Aluminum foil

Tart Wash (page 15)

AT THE END OF THE COOK: Briskets typically plateau midway through a cook. Don't panic. Eventually, the temperature will start to increase. When it's done, the internal temperature of the brisket should be at the low end of the 190°F to 195°F range, but this is only one indication of doneness. The brisket is ready when a two-tined meat fork easily slides into the brisket, and the flesh has slight wobble (I call it the wabba wabba) when poked. When the brisket is ready, remove it from the cooker, tent with foil, and let it rest for 30 minutes before slicing and serving.

1 HOUR BEFORE THE COOK

Douse the brisket with the vinegar, then rinse the meat under cold running water and pat it dry with paper towels.

Slather the brisket with the mustard. Coat the meat with a generous, even layer of the rub, working it into the creases and sides of the brisket. Let the meat come to room temperature.

30 MINUTES BEFORE THE COOK

Start a KISS method fire according to the instructions for your cooker of choice: WSM (page 26), BGE (page 29), or offset (page 31).

WSM

WHEN THE CHARCOAL is engaged in the fire ring and the cooker is reassembled, place the brisket fat-side up in the middle of the top grate. Close the cooker and adjust the vents.

TOP VENT:

18.5-INCH MODEL: Open.

22.5-INCH MODEL: Open.

BOTTOM VENTS:

18.5-INCH MODEL: Open.

22.5-INCH MODEL: Open.

30 MINUTES INTO THE COOK

Adjust the bottom vents.

18.5-INCH MODEL: Close all bottom vents by one third.

22.5-INCH MODEL: Close all bottom vents halfway.

EVERY 1 TO 1½ HOURS IN THE COOK

Keep an eye on the temperature. If the cooker is running hotter than 250°F, slightly close one bottom vent if you're using an 18.5-inch WSM or close the top vent by one third if you're using a 22.5-inch WSM. If everything checks out but the cooker is running below 225°F, open one of the bottom vents to increase airflow and engage the charcoal. Keep in mind that it can take 10 to 15 minutes for a WSM to settle into a temperature after adjusting the vents, opening the cooker, or restocking the charcoal. Give the cooker time to settle before making additional vent adjustments.

Check the water pan and refill it when half of the water has evaporated. The 18.5-inch model's water pan needs to be topped off every 3 to 4 hours. The 22.5-inch model can run as long as 7 to 8 hours before refilling the water pan, but it's best to refill it after you restock the charcoal to avoid adding more weight to the center ring before you remove it.

3 HOURS INTO THE COOK

Flip the brisket fat-side down.

5 TO 6 HOURS INTO THE COOK

Restock the WSM using the instructions on page 27 (for the 18.5-inch model) or page 28 (for the 22.5-inch model). After restocking the charcoal, carefully reassemble the cooker and refill the water pan.

Flip the brisket fat-side up. To prevent the narrow end of the brisket from drying out, wrap foil around 2 to 3 inches of the tip of the flat.

8 HOURS INTO THE COOK

Check the temperature of the meat with an instant-read thermometer poked into the thickest section of the brisket. The brisket will not be done at this point (it will finish at around 190°F), but consider this check your baseline to determine how far along the brisket is.

Starting with this check, spritz the brisket with Tart Wash whenever you check the meat temperature.

9 TO 10 HOURS INTO THE COOK

Check the internal temperature of the brisket. At this stage, the temperature should start slowly increasing from the plateau point. Continue cooking and check the temperature every 20 to 30 minutes until the brisket reaches the low end of the 190°F to 195°F range and a meat fork slides easily into the meat.

BGE

<><><><><><><><><><><><><><><><><><><><><><><><><><><><><><><><><><><><><><><><>

THE BGE IS a mighty cooker, but its cooking grate is too small for a standard packer-cut brisket. The simple solution: while the charcoal is engaging in the fire ring, make a solid, baseball-size ball of aluminum foil.

Five minutes after adding the lit charcoal and inserting the plate setter and water pan, set the foil ball in the middle of the grate and lay the brisket fat-side up on top of the foil. Close the lid and adjust the vents.

TOP VENT:

Close halfway.

BOTTOM VENT:

Open ½ inch.

30 MINUTES INTO THE COOK

Check the temperature of the cooker. If the BGE is running hotter than 250°F, close the bottom vent by ¼ inch. If the BGE is running below 225°F, slightly open the top vent.

Keep in mind that it can take 10 to 15 minutes for a BGE to settle into a new temperature after adjusting the vents or opening the cooker.

EVERY 1 TO 1½ HOURS IN THE COOK

Keep an eye on the cooker temperature. At the 1-hour mark, the BGE should settle somewhere between 225°F and 250°F. If the cooker is running hotter than 275°F or drops lower than 225°F for more than 10 minutes, make very slight adjustments to the top or bottom vent. Adjust vents one at a time and wait 10 to 15 minutes before making another vent adjustment.

Check and refill the water pan as needed.

3 HOURS INTO THE COOK

Flip the brisket fat-side down. Remove the foil ball if the meat has shrunk enough to fit the grate.

Add 3 small wood chunks to the fire. (The pieces need to be small enough to fit through the gaps around the plate setter.)

6 HOURS INTO THE COOK

Flip the brisket fat-side up. To prevent the narrow end of the brisket from drying out, wrap foil around 2 to 3 inches of the tip end of the flat.

Add three small wood chunks to the fire.

8 HOURS INTO THE COOK

Check the temperature of the meat with an instant-read thermometer poked into the thickest section of the brisket. The brisket will probably not be done at this point (it will finish at around 190°F), but use this check to determine how far along the brisket is.

Starting with this check, spritz the brisket with Tart Wash whenever you check the meat.

9 TO 10 HOURS INTO THE COOK

Check the internal temperature of the brisket. At this stage, the temperature should start slowly increasing from the plateau point. Continue cooking and check the temperature every 20 to 30 minutes until the brisket reaches the low end of the 190°F to 195°F range and a meat fork slides easily into the meat.

◇◇

OFFSET

⟨⟨⟩

WHEN THE CHARCOAL is engaged in the firebox and the water pan and oven thermometer are in place on the cooking grate, set the brisket fat-side up at the far end of the cooking grate with the thicker, pointed end of the brisket facing the firebox. Close the lid and adjust the vents.

TOP VENT:	**FIREBOX VENT:**
Open.	Close by one third.

30 MINUTES INTO THE COOK

Open the firebox and set one split of wood on top of the lit charcoal. When the wood is engaged and stops billowing white smoke, after about 5 minutes, close the firebox.

EVERY HOUR IN THE COOK

Keep an eye on the grate temperature and charcoal level. If the cooker creeps higher than 275°F for more than 10 minutes, start by closing the firebox vent halfway. Give the cooker 10 to 15 minutes to settle into the temperature. If it is still running too hot, close the top vent by one third.

If the cooker temperature drops below 225°F, assess the fire. If the unlit charcoal is not engaging, open the firebox vent to increase airflow. If most of the charcoal in the pile is burned through, restock with lit charcoal. If the charcoal pile is glowing-hot, restock with unlit charcoal. (For detailed restocking instructions, see page 32.)

Add one split of wood to the charcoal at every restock from the 1-hour mark to the 5-hour mark. When the charcoal and wood stop billowing white smoke, about 5 minutes, close the firebox and continue cooking.

Check and refill the water pan as needed.

3 HOURS INTO THE COOK

Flip the brisket fat-side down.

6 HOURS INTO THE COOK

Flip the brisket fat-side up. To prevent the narrow end of the brisket from drying out, wrap foil around 2 to 3 inches of the tip end of the flat.

8 HOURS INTO THE COOK

Check the temperature of the meat with an instant-read thermometer poked into the thickest section of the brisket. The brisket will not be done at this point (it will finish at around 190°F), but use this check to determine how far along the brisket is.

Starting with this check, spritz the brisket with Tart Wash whenever you check the meat temperature.

9 TO 10 HOURS INTO THE COOK

Check the internal temperature of the brisket. At this stage, the temperature should start slowly increasing from the plateau point. Continue cooking and check the temperature every 20 to 30 minutes until the brisket reaches the low end of the 190°F to 195°F range and a meat fork slides easily into the meat.

BRISKET: BUYING & PREP GUIDE

THE #1 MISTAKE COOKS MAKE WITH BRISKET: THEY BUY THE WRONG CUT. THE small, 6- to 8-pound trimmed briskets you find in most grocery stores are not ideal for low-and-slow cooking because so much of the fat cap is trimmed away. These are also labeled "first cut" or "cap removed" briskets, and though they are fine for braising, if you cook flat or over trimmed brisket following my method, the meat will dry out and turn to shoe leather in a matter of hours on a charcoal cooker.

The correct brisket for barbecue is a full packer-cut brisket, a massive, 12- to 15-pound slab of meat covered in a hard shell of white fat on one side. (Visit LowSlowBBQ.com for illustrations of the anatomy of the correct brisket.) Knowledgeable butchers and meatpackers also know this cut as a NAMP/IMPS No. 120, which is the code used by both the National Association of Meat Purveyors and the government-issued Institutional Meat Purchase Specifications (IMPS). It is a boneless brisket with the deckle—the fat and lean between the bone and main muscle—removed. When in doubt, tell your butcher you want a Texas barbecue brisket—a cut that can withstand 10 to 12 hours in a smoker.

TO TRIM OR NOT TO TRIM

If it's your first brisket cook, don't trim the brisket. The extra inch or so of fat will protect the meat from drying out, which gives you a wider margin of error in case you have issues holding a steady temperature in your cooker. The cook will run a little longer than it would on a trimmed brisket, but it's good practice. You also get a nice hunk of spicy, crispy fat, which you can trim off and turn into Burnt Ends (page 87) or throw into the Texas Brisket Sauce (see page 248). If you've cooked a few briskets and want to refine the final hunk of meat, shaving down the rough edges and trimming away some of the fat will produce a more picturesque brisket—something you'd be proud to take a selfie with. Start with the sharpest knife in your possession and hone the blade with a steel to freshen the edge.

1. Flip the brisket fat-side down on a cutting board. Find the v-shaped wad of fad that tapers inside the brisket where the flat and the point meet. With a very sharp knife, slice along the edges of this fat and remove it. (Visit LowSlowBBQ.com for illustrated instructions on trimming a brisket).

2. Flip the brisket fat-side up. In long, even strokes, slice away strips of the fat cap but leave at least a ¼-inch-thick layer of fat on the meat. If you're unsure about how much to trim away, always err on the side of more fat—overtrimming this layer of fat will do more damage than undertrimming it. Please *always* cut away from your body when you're trimming this patch of hard fat. A sharp knife can easily slip the wrong way—think: barbecue hari kari.

BURNT ENDS

I TEND TO use the same three words in my descriptions of great barbecue, but burnt ends are the OG of fatty, crispy, and delicious barbecue. These chewy, spicy nuggets are made by cutting off and cubing the richly marbled point section of a cooked brisket, coating the nuggets in sauce, and throwing them back on the cooker to render into bite-size chunks of meaty, fatty bark.

I had my first taste of burnt ends years ago at Louie Mueller's, and the experience inspired me to research and develop my own methods for producing great burnt ends. If you own the first Low & Slow book, I highly recommend using Not Arthur Bryant's Sauce (also available at LowSlowBBQ.com), but the Texas Brisket Sauce (page 248) will work just fine, too.

CLASSIC BURNT ENDS

This is the more traditional burnt end method with my own twist, and it's for folks who are smoking a full packer-cut brisket and want to take it to the nth barbecue degree. You'll remove the point of the brisket after the cook, then cut, rub, and cook the meat twice, until the ends are dark and crispy. It only sounds like a lot of work until you eat one, and then you'll know it was worth every minute.

SERVES 10

COOKER TEMPERATURE: 225°F to 250°F

COOK TIME: 1 to 1½ hours

FOR THE RECIPE:

1 cooked brisket point

½ cup Brisket Rub (page 230),
or dry rub of your choice

½ cup Texas Brisket Sauce (page 248)

After the whole brisket cook (page 78), when the brisket is cool enough to handle, separate the point from the flat by running a sharp, 12-inch knife (a granton works best) horizontally along the fat seam that runs between the point and the flat (visit LowSlowBBQ.com for an illustrated anatomy of a brisket). Use the back of the knife to scrape away the gnarly grayish-brown patch of fat that covers this seam.

Slice the point in half horizontally. Coat the two sections in rub, with a heavier layer on the newly exposed side, about ¼ cup of rub total. Place the point sections on the grate of your cooker with the newly exposed fat–side down. Smoke in the low-and-slow temperature range (225°F to 250°F) for another 1½ to 2 hours, until the meat is crispy and dark. You're not looking for a specific internal temperature at this point—it's all about the aesthetics of a classic burnt end: fat-crisped and almost blackened.

When the point sections are dark and crisped, remove the meat from the cooker and cut the sections into 1-inch cubes. To finish, follow the remaining instructions as outlined under Burnt Ends: The Finale (page 89).

SCRATCH
BURNT ENDS

These Burnt Ends are for barbecue maniacs who want the ends alone, sans brisket, and are willing to spend 7 or 8 hours making them. The hardest part about this recipe is finding a 4- to 5-pound brisket point, which is the fattiest section cut from a whole brisket. Butchers tend to grind the point into a hamburger blend, and sell the trimmed flat separately. You'll have to ask a butcher to save a point for you, or keep an eye out for points in specialty meat markets, wholesale clubs, or restaurant suppliers like Restaurant Depot. If you find points, buy a few at a time. You can easily double or triple this recipe.

SERVES 10

COOKER TEMPERATURE: 225°F to 250°F

COOK TIME: 7 to 8 hours

FOR THE RECIPE:

1 (4- to 5-pound) brisket point

¾ cup Brisket Rub (page 230),
   or dry rub of your choice

½ cup Texas Brisket Sauce (page 248)

30 MINUTES BEFORE THE COOK

Coat the point in a heavy layer of rub, about ¼ cup or more as needed.

Start a KISS method fire for the your cooker of your choice: WSM (page 26), BGE (page 29), or offset (page 31).

When the cooker has stabilized in the low-and-slow range (225°F to 250°F), set the point fat-side up on the grate.

Follow the grate temperature checkpoints and wood/water/charcoal restocks outlined for brisket on your cooker: WSM (page 79); BGE (page 81), offset (page 83).

Smoke the point for 6 to 7 hours, until the internal temperature of the meat hits 180°F on an instant-read thermometer. When the meat is done, remove it from the cooker.

When the meat is cool enough to handle, slice the point in half horizontally with a sharp knife. Coat the sections in rub, with a heavier layer on the freshly exposed sides, about ¼ cup of rub total. Place the point sections on the grate of your cooker with the newly exposed fat-side down. Smoke the meat in the low-and-slow temperature range for another 1½ to 2 hours, until the meat is crispy and dark. You're not looking for a specific internal temperature at this point—it's all about the aesthetics of a classic burnt end: fat-crisped and dark.

When the point sections are almost blackened and crisp, remove the meat from the cooker and cut the sections into 1-inch cubes.

BURNT ENDS: THE FINALE

At this point, most barbecue guys would toss the burnt ends with ½ cup of sauce in a roasting pan, and continue cooking low and slow until the sauce bubbles and slightly caramelizes on the meat, about 10 minutes. That's Option #1.

But I'm not most barbecue guys. So here's option #2: open the vents on the cooker to increase the heat to 350°F to 375°F. Toss the burnt ends with a little more rub to coat (about 2 to 3 tablespoons), then throw the pan back on the cooker for 10 to 15 minutes. When the ends are crisped, remove the pan from the cooker, toss them with the sauce, and serve.

BEEF SHORT RIBS

Beef short ribs, aka plate short ribs, are the equivalent of pork spare ribs, but they are even bigger, tougher, and meatier. Finding these ribs may prove to be a challenge because several styles of beef ribs are labeled "short ribs." The beef short ribs you want are cut from the "shortplate" or plate section of the beef. (They're not called "short" because of their length.)

This is where a good relationship with a butcher pays off. Ask, and ye may receive. Beef plate short ribs are typically sold in 2- to 5-bone sections. Ideally, you want meaty 2-bone sections or a 4-bone section cut in half, so there are two bones per section. Having two sections optimizes the amount of smoke and rub the edges are exposed to. More smoke and rub means more crispy, spicy, and delicious meat. For this recipe, do not buy Korean or flanken-cut short ribs, which are cut in pieces or strips across the bone. You can substitute chuck short ribs in this cook. (See Meet Your Meat, page 77.)

SERVES 6 TO 8

COOKER TEMPERATURE: 225°F to 250°F
COOK TIME: 3½ to 4 hours

FOR THE RECIPES:

2 (4-bone) short plate rib sections

¼ cup yellow mustard

5 tablespoons Pitmaster Rub No. 1 (page 232)

FOR THE COOK:

1 cup Tart Wash (page 15)

AT THE END OF THE COOK: With ribs, "done" is a subjective term—the ribs are ready when they're cooked to the texture you like. Finished ribs should be in the 190°F to 200°F range, but getting an accurate read is tricky and pitmasters rarely judge ribs by temperature. Use the instant-read thermometer probe or a fork to gauge the tenderness of the meatiest section of the ribs, and pull the ribs off of the cooker when they're to your liking. The meat should be tender, with little resistance, but not cooked to the point where the meat is significantly shrinking away from the bone. If this is your first time cooking beef short ribs, pull one section when you think they're done, and keep the other set of ribs on the cooker for 20 to 30 minutes longer to judge which one you like best. The longer you cook the ribs, the more fall-off-the-bone tender they get.

30 MINUTES BEFORE THE COOK

Start a KISS method fire according to the instructions for your cooker of choice: WSM (page 26), BGE (page 29), offset (page 31), or kettle (page 33).

Cut the 4-bone rib sections in half, creating four 2-bone sections. Flip the rib sections meat-side down and slice the membranes covering the back of the rib bones vertically, from top to bottom. Score the entire membrane surface in an angled crosshatch diamond pattern, which will allow the membrane to shrink during the cook and develop a crisp, papery texture; it will also allow pockets of fat in the meat to render more effectively.

Slather the rib sections with the mustard and coat them with a solid layer of rub, about 1 tablespoon per section.

WSM

WHEN THE CHARCOAL is engaged in the fire ring and the cooker is reassembled, place the ribs meat-side up in the middle of the top grate, away from the outer edge. Close the cooker and adjust the vents.

TOP VENT:
18.5-INCH MODEL: Open.
22.5-INCH MODEL: Open.

BOTTOM VENTS:
18.5-INCH MODEL: Open.
22.5-INCH MODEL: Open.

30 MINUTES INTO THE COOK

Adjust the bottom vents.
18.5-INCH MODEL: Close two bottom vents by one third.
22.5-INCH MODEL: Close two bottom vents halfway.

EVERY HOUR IN THE COOK

Keep an eye on the temperature of the cooker. If the cooker is running hotter than 250°F or drops lower than 225°F for more than 10 minutes, troubleshoot the fire.

Check the vent closures. Two bottom vents should be closed by one third if you're using an 18.5-inch WSM or by half if you're using a 22.5-inch WSM. Be sure there are no stray pieces of charcoal blocking the bottom vents. Check and refill the water pan as needed.

If the 22.5-inch WSM continues to run hotter than 250°F, close the top vent by one third.

Keep in mind that it can take 10 to 15 minutes for a WSM to settle into a temperature after adjusting the vents, opening the cooker, or restocking the charcoal. Give the cooker time to settle into a temperature before making additional vent adjustments.

2 HOURS INTO THE COOK

Flip the ribs meat-side down.

3 HOURS INTO THE COOK

Flip the ribs meat-side up. The ribs will not be ready at this point, but give them a tug and a poke with the thermometer probe or a fork to gauge their tenderness.

Spritz the meat with Tart Wash.

3½ TO 4 HOURS INTO THE COOK

Spritz the meat with Tart Wash and check the ribs every 15 to 20 minutes until they are cooked to your desired tenderness.

BGE

FIVE MINUTES AFTER adding the lit charcoal and reassembling the cooker (plate setter, water pan, and cooking grate in place), set the ribs meat-side up on the grate, away from the outer edges. Close the cooker and adjust the vents.

TOP VENT:
Close halfway.

BOTTOM VENT:
Open ½ inch.

EVERY HOUR IN THE COOK

Check the temperature of the cooker. If the BGE is running hotter than 250°F, close the bottom vent ¼ inch. Slightly open the top vent if the cooker is running below 225°F.

Keep in mind that it can take up to 10 minutes for a BGE to settle into a new temperature after adjusting the vents or opening the cooker. Give the cooker time to settle into a temperature before making another vent adjustment.

Refill the water pan as needed.

2 HOURS INTO THE COOK

Flip the ribs meat-side down.

3 HOURS INTO THE COOK

Flip the ribs meat-side up. The ribs will not be ready at this point, but give them a tug and a poke with the thermometer probe or a fork to gauge their tenderness.

Spritz the meat with Tart Wash.

3½ TO 4 HOURS INTO THE COOK

Spritz the meat with Tart Wash and check the ribs every 15 to 20 minutes until they are cooked to your desired tenderness.

OFFSET

◇◇◇

WHEN THE CHARCOAL is engaged in the firebox and the water pan and oven thermometer are in place on the cooking grate, set the ribs meat-side up on the grate, away from the firebox. Close the lid and adjust the vents.

TOP VENT: **FIREBOX VENT:**

Open.   Close by one third.

30 MINUTES INTO THE COOK

Open the firebox and set one split of wood on top of the lit charcoal. When the wood is engaged and stops billowing white smoke, after about 5 minutes, close the firebox.

EVERY HOUR IN THE COOK

Check and refill the water pan as needed. Rotate the four sections of ribs clockwise so each section gets equal time away from the firebox.

Keep an eye on the grate temperature and charcoal level. If the cooker creeps higher than 275°F, make very slight adjustments to the vents: close the firebox vent halfway and close the top vent by one third.

If the cooker temperature drops below 225°F, assess the fire. If the unlit charcoal is not engaging, open the firebox vent to increase airflow. If most of the charcoal in the pile is burned through, restock with lit charcoal. If the pile is glowing-hot, restock with unlit charcoal. (For detailed restocking instructions, see page 32.)

Add 1 split of wood to the charcoal during the restocks at the 2-hour and 3-hour marks. When the charcoal and wood stop billowing white smoke, about 5 minutes after restocking, close the firebox.

2 HOURS INTO THE COOK

While you're checking the grate temperature and water pan, flip the ribs meat-side down.

3 HOURS INTO THE COOK

Flip the ribs meat-side up. The ribs will not be ready at this point, but give them a tug and a poke with the thermometer probe or a fork to gauge their tenderness.

Spritz the meat with Tart Wash.

3½ TO 4 HOURS INTO THE COOK

Spritz the meat with Tart Wash and check the ribs every 15 to 20 minutes until they are cooked to your desired tenderness.

KETTLE

⬦⬦⬦

AFTER POURING IN the lit charcoal, give the charcoal 5 minutes to engage and allow the billowing clouds of smoke to die down. Arrange the ribs meat-side up on the cooking grate above the drip pan with the thickest bone end facing the fire. Close the cooker and adjust the vents.

TOP VENT:	**BOTTOM VENT:**
22-INCH MODEL: Open.	**22-INCH MODEL:** Close by one third.
26-INCH MODEL: Open.	**26-INCH MODEL:** Close halfway.

EVERY 20 TO 30 MINUTES IN THE COOK

Rotate the ribs clockwise on the grate so that all sides get equal time facing the fire.

Check the temperature of the cooker. If it has dropped below 225°F, restock the cooker with ½ chimney of lit charcoal (see page 34). If the kettle is running hotter than 275°F, close the top vent by one third. Refill the water pan as needed.

1 HOUR INTO THE COOK

After you check the grate temperature, charcoal level, and water pan, flip the ribs meat-side down.

2 TO 2½ HOURS INTO THE COOK

Flip the ribs meat-side up. The ribs will not be ready at this point, but give them a tug and a poke with the thermometer probe or a fork to gauge their tenderness.

Spritz the meat with Tart Wash.

3 HOURS INTO THE COOK

Spritz the meat with Tart Wash and check the ribs every 15 to 20 minutes until they are cooked to your desired tenderness.

BEEF BACK RIBS

Beef back ribs are the equivalent of pork baby back ribs, but they are a rare, delicious find in most grocery store meat departments because this section is usually left intact for the more popular and expensive standing rib roast (page 110), or it is cut into rib-eye steaks. If you ask nicely, you can score impressive racks of 7- or 8-bone beef back ribs from a specialty meat shop or a butcher who knows you're worth the trouble. I've also spotted them in restaurant supply stores, like Restaurant Depot.

Although you can cook back ribs low and slow (225°F to 250°F) in 3 to 4 hours, I often prefer to hot smoke roast back ribs at around 350°F. This method produces a more toothsome rib with a spicier, crispier bark in about half the time. A note for kettle users: you will not be able to fit two full racks of beef back ribs on the grate. Either cut the recipe in half, or cook one rack at a time.

SERVES 6 TO 8

COOKER TEMPERATURE: 325°F to 350°F

COOK TIME: 1½ to 2 hours

FOR THE RECIPE:

2 (7- to 8-bone) racks of beef back ribs

¼ cup yellow mustard

½ cup Gary Wiviott's Beef Rub (page 232)

FOR THE COOK:

1 cup Tart Wash (page 15)

AT THE END OF THE COOK: The ribs are ready when the bark is crispy and the meat feels firm when you poke it with the thermometer probe. When in doubt, slice off a rib and conduct a very scientific taste test. Bite into it and decide: Will another 10 minutes on the cooker improve the texture or risk drying it out? If you need a temperature, aim for 170°F to 175°F.

30 MINUTES BEFORE THE COOK

Start a hot smoke–roast fire according to the instructions for your cooker of choice: WSM (page 35), BGE (page 35), offset (page 35) or kettle (page 36).

Flip the racks meat-side down and slice the membrane covering the rib bones, from top to bottom. Score the membrane in an angled crosshatch diamond pattern, which will allow the membrane to shrink during the cook and develop a crisp, papery texture; it will also allow pockets of fat in the meat to render more effectively.

Slather the racks with the mustard and coat them with a solid layer of rub, about ¼ cup per rack, or more to taste.

WSM

WHEN THE CHARCOAL is engaged in the fire ring, the water pan filled with sand is in place, and the cooker is reassembled, place the ribs meat-side up in the middle of the top grate, away from the outer edge. Close the cooker and adjust the vents.

TOP VENT:

18.5-INCH MODEL: Open.

22.5-INCH MODEL: Open.

BOTTOM VENTS:

18.5-INCH MODEL: Open.

22.5-INCH MODEL: Open.

20 TO 30 MINUTES INTO THE COOK

Check the cooker temperature. If the WSM is running hotter than 350°F, adjust the bottom vents. Close one bottom vent by one third if you're using an 18.5-inch WSM or by half if you're using a 22.5-inch WSM.

Wait 10 to 15 minutes for the temperature to settle in after the vent adjustment. If the cooker is still running too hot, close a second bottom vent by one third if you're using an 18.5-inch WSM or by half if you're using a 22.5-inch WSM.

1 HOUR INTO THE COOK

Open the cooker and check the ribs with the probe of an instant-read thermometer. The ribs won't be ready at this point, but this check gives you a temperature to judge how close the ribs are to being ready.

Spritz the meat with Tart Wash and continue cooking.

1½ HOURS INTO THE COOK

Spritz the meat with Tart Wash and check the ribs every 5 to 10 minutes until they are cooked to your desired tenderness.

BGE

FIVE MINUTES AFTER adding the lit charcoal and inserting the plate setter, set the ribs meat-side up in the middle of the grate. Close the cooker and adjust the vents.

TOP VENT:
Open.

BOTTOM VENT:
Open 2 inches.

30 MINUTES INTO THE COOK

Check the cooker temperature. If the BGE is running hotter than 350°F, close the bottom vent by ½ inch. If the temperature doesn't drop within 10 to 15 minutes, close the bottom vent in ¼-inch increments until the temperature decreases.

1 HOUR INTO THE COOK

Open the cooker and check the ribs with the probe of an instant read thermometer. The ribs won't be done at this point, but this check gives you a temperature to judge how close the ribs are to being ready.

Spritz the meat with Tart Wash and continue cooking.

1½ HOURS INTO THE COOK

Spritz the meat with Tart Wash and check the ribs every 5 to 10 minutes until they are cooked to your desired tenderness.

OFFSET

WHEN THE CHARCOAL is engaged in the firebox and the water pan and oven thermometer are in place on the cooking grate, set the ribs meat-side up on the grate, with the thickest sides facing the firebox. Close the cooker and adjust the vents.

TOP VENT:
Open.

FIREBOX VENT:
Open.

20 MINUTES INTO THE COOK

Check the cooker temperature. If the offset is running hotter than 350°F, close the firebox vent by one third.

45 MINUTES INTO THE COOK

Check the cooker temperature. If the offset is running below 300°F, add 1 full chimney starter of lit charcoal and 1 split of wood to the firebox. When the charcoal engages and the fire stops billowing white smoke, after about 5 minutes, close the firebox. If the offset is running hotter than 375°F, close the firebox vent halfway.

1 HOUR INTO THE COOK

Open the cooker and check the ribs with the probe of an instant-read thermometer. The ribs won't be ready at this point, but this check gives you a temperature to judge how close the ribs are to being ready.

Spritz the meat with Tart Wash and continue cooking.

1½ HOURS INTO THE COOK

Spritz the meat and check the ribs every 5 to 10 minutes until they are cooked to your desired tenderness.

KETTLE

◇◇

WHEN THE CHARCOAL is engaged on the banked piles, about 5 minutes after adding the lit charcoal, place the ribs meat-side up on the grate, directly above the water pan. Close the cooker and adjust the vents.

TOP VENT:

22-INCH MODEL: Open.

26-INCH MODEL: Open.

BOTTOM VENT:

22-INCH MODEL: Open.

26-INCH MODEL: Open.

EVERY 20 MINUTES IN THE COOK

Flip the racks. Check the temperature of the cooker. If the cooker temperature spikes above 350°F, close the bottom vent by one third. If the temperature dips below 300°F, restock the cooker with ½ chimney of lit charcoal.

Check and refill the water pan as needed.

1 HOUR INTO THE COOK

Open the cooker and check the ribs with the probe of an instant-read thermometer. The ribs may not be ready at this point, but this check gives you a temperature to judge how close the ribs are to being ready.

Spritz the meat and check the ribs every 10 to 15 minutes until they are cooked to your desired tenderness.

◇◇

SMOKED CORNED BEEF

Think of this as a shortcut way of making pastrami. It's something like a cheat in barbecue, but if you do it right, it perfectly mimics the smoky, fatty, spicy, old-fashioned pastrami people line up for at legendary delis. That sentence alone should make you drool a little.

Beef pastrami is typically made by curing a brisket, then smoking and steaming it. My method starts with a raw packer cut corned beef, which is a wet-cured or brined brisket. So, we're cutting out the curing step. And because a long low-and-slow cook will concentrate the meat's saltiness, I soak the corned beef for at least 48 hours (and up to 72 hours) to leach most of the curing salt out of the meat. If you don't soak the corned beef, you'll end up with a salty, dried-out brick of meat. The corning process (even after the soak) prevents the meat from ever achieving the fall-apart tender texture of a low-and-slow brisket, but it also means this cook is much shorter—the meat is done in 6 or 7 hours. Be sure to use a full, packer cut corned beef, not a corned beef flat, which is too lean and will turn to shoe leather in a smoker. My Smoked Corned Beef Rub is based on traditional pastrami seasonings, but for an exotic twist, check out the Pakistani-style Hunter Beef Rub (page 234).

SERVES 16 TO 18

COOKER TEMPERATURE: 225°F to 250°F

COOK TIME: 6 to 7 hours

FOR THE RECIPE:

1 (10- to 12-pound) raw corned beef brisket

¾ cup Smoked Corned Beef Rub (page 233)

FOR THE COOK:

Large plastic food-safe container

Aluminum foil

AT THE END OF THE COOK: The target internal temperature is around 180°F. A piece of meat this size can plateau between 150°F and 175°F and hold the temperature for several hours—so be patient. When you think the corned beef is ready, stick a two-tined fork in the middle to test the texture. There will be some resistance—remember, this isn't a tender low-and-slow brisket, but the fork should slide in easily. When the meat is done, remove it from the cooker, wrap it in foil, and let it rest for at least 30 minutes before slicing. If you want a more tender, moist pastrami-style texture, follow the steaming directions on page 109.

2 TO 3 DAYS BEFORE THE COOK

Rinse the corned beef under cold running water and pat it dry with paper towels. Trim away the excess fat the same way you would trim a packer-cut brisket (see page 85), leaving at least ¼ inch of fat. Or, you can keep the fat cap intact to protect the meat from drying out.

Place the corned beef in a plastic, food-safe container large enough to fit the meat and fill the container with enough cold water to completely submerge the meat. Set a dinner plate or platter on top of the corned beef to keep it submerged.

Cover and refrigerate the meat for at least 48 hours or up to 72 hours. Every 12 to 24 hours, completely drain the water and add fresh cold water. Change the water at least three or four times during the soaking process.

1 HOUR BEFORE THE COOK

Remove the corned beef from the water and set it on a rimmed baking sheet. Pat the meat dry with paper towels and generously season both sides with the Smoked Corned Beef Rub. Allow the meat to reach room temperature.

30 MINUTES BEFORE THE COOK

Start a KISS method fire according to the instructions for your cooker of choice: WSM (page 26), BGE (page 29), or offset (page 31).

WSM

xxxxxxxxxxxxxxxxxxxxxxxxxxxxxxxxxxxxxxxxxxxxxxxxxxxxxxxxxxxxxxxxxxxxxxxxxx

WHEN THE CHARCOAL is engaged in the fire ring and the cooker is reassembled, place the corned beef fat-side up in the middle of the cooking grate. Close the cooker and adjust the vents.

TOP VENT:

18.5-INCH MODEL: Open.

22.5-INCH MODEL: Open.

BOTTOM VENTS:

18.5-INCH MODEL: Open.

22.5-INCH MODEL: Open.

30 MINUTES INTO THE COOK

Adjust the bottom vents.

18.5-INCH MODEL: Close all three bottom vents by one third.

22.5-INCH MODEL: Close all three bottom vents halfway.

EVERY HOUR IN THE COOK

Keep an eye on the temperature. If the cooker is running hotter than 250°F or drops below 225°F for more than 10 minutes, check the vent closures. Be sure there are no stray pieces of charcoal blocking the bottom vents. If the cooker is running below 225°F, open one bottom vent. If the 22.5-inch WSM continues to run hotter than 250°F, close the top vent by one third.

Check and refill the water pan as needed.

2 HOURS INTO THE COOK

Flip the corned beef fat-side down.

4 HOURS INTO THE COOK

Flip the corned beef fat-side up. Wrap aluminum foil around 2 to 3 inches of the tapered edge of the flat.

Add 2 wood chunks to the fire, and while you're in there, assess the fire. If it looks like the fire will need a boost to run for 2 or 3 more hours, or if you just want to play it safe, light a chimney starter full of charcoal and follow the instructions for restocking the 18.5-inch WSM (page 27) or the 22.5-inch WSM (page 28).

5 HOURS INTO THE COOK

Check the temperature of the meat with an instant-read thermometer poked in several places (flat, middle, and point). This check is a reference point to see how close the meat is to 180°F.

For a chef's treat, slice off a piece of the fatty point. This crunchy, salty, fatty, smoky-with-a-hint-of-spice bite should reassure you that everything is going fine with the cook.

6 HOURS INTO THE COOK

Start checking the temperature of the meat every 20 to 30 minutes until it reaches 180°F and a meat fork slides in with slight resistance.

BGE

xxxxxxxxxxxxxxxxxxxxxxxxxxxxxxxxxxxxxxxxxxxxxxxxxxxxxxxxxxxxxxxxxxxxxxxxxxxxx

FIVE MINUTES AFTER adding the lit charcoal and reassembling the cooker (plate setter, water pan, and cooking grate in place), lay the corned beef on the grate fat-side up. If the meat is too large to fit the grate, crumple a large sheet of aluminum foil into a baseball-size ball, set it in the middle of the grate, and lay the corned beef over the foil ball. Close the cooker and adjust the vents.

TOP VENT:

Close halfway.

BOTTOM VENT:

Open ½ inch.

30 MINUTES INTO THE COOK

Check the temperature of the cooker. If the BGE is running hotter than 250°F, close the bottom vent by ¼ inch.

EVERY HOUR IN THE COOK

Keep an eye on the cooker temperature. If the BGE is running hotter than 250°F, slightly close the top or bottom vent. Check and refill the water pan as needed.

2 HOURS INTO THE COOK

Add 3 small wood chunks to the fire. (The pieces need to be narrow enough to fit through the gaps around the plate setter.)

Flip the corned beef fat-side down. Remove the foil ball if the meat has shrunk enough to fit the grate.

4 HOURS INTO THE COOK

Add 2 small wood chunks to the fire. (The wood needs to be narrow enough to fit through the gaps around the plate setter.)

Flip the corned beef fat-side up. Wrap foil around 2 to 3 inches of the tapered edge of the flat.

5 HOURS INTO THE COOK

Check the temperature of the meat with an instant-read thermometer poked in several places (flat, middle, and point). This check is a reference point to see how close the meat is to 180°F.

For a chef's treat, slice off a piece of the fatty point. This crunchy, salty, fatty, smoky-with-a-hint-of-spice bite should reassure you that everything is going fine with the cook.

8 HOURS INTO THE COOK

Start checking the temperature of the meat every 20 to 30 minutes until it reaches 180°F and a meat fork slides in with slight resistance.

◇◇◇

OFFSET

WHEN THE CHARCOAL is engaged in the firebox and the water pan and oven thermometer are in place on the cooking grate, set the corned beef fat-side up in the middle of the grate with the thicker, point end of the brisket facing the firebox. Close the lid and adjust the vents.

TOP VENT:

Open.

FIREBOX VENT:

Close by one third.

30 MINUTES INTO THE COOK

Open the firebox and set 1 split of wood on top of the lit charcoal. When the wood is engaged and stops billowing white smoke, after about 5 minutes, close the firebox.

EVERY HOUR IN THE COOK

Check and refill the water pan as needed.

Keep an eye on the grate temperature and charcoal level. If the cooker creeps higher than 275°F, make very slight adjustments to the vents. Close the firebox vent halfway or close the top vent by one third.

If the cooker temperature drops below 225°F, assess the fire. If the unlit charcoal is not engaging, open the firebox vent to increase airflow. If the charcoal is running low, restock the cooker with 1 chimney of lit or unlit charcoal, depending on the status of the fire. (For detailed restocking instructions, see page 32.)

Add 1 split of wood to the charcoal during the restocks at the 2-hour and 3-hour marks. When the charcoal and wood stop billowing white smoke, about 5 minutes after restocking, close the firebox and continue cooking.

2 HOURS INTO THE COOK

Flip the corned beef fat-side down.

4 HOURS INTO THE COOK

Flip the corned beef fat-side up. Gently wrap foil around 2 to 3 inches of the tapered edge of the flat.

STEAMING SMOKED CORNED BEEF

I PREFER THE SLICEABLE TEXTURE OF THE SMOKED CORNED BEEF AS IS, BUT others like the tenderness of classic, steamed pastrami. If you want to hold the meat a few hours before serving or achieve tenderness of classic pastrami after the meat has been refrigerated, you'll need to steam it in a roasting pan.

Preheat the oven to 250°F. Place the meat on a rack set inside a roasting pan above 1 to 2 cups of liquid (water, stock, or beer). Cover the roasting pan tightly with foil. Place the covered roasting pan in the oven and steam the meat for up to 2 hours. If you are reheating meat that has been refrigerated, steam it until it reaches an internal temperature of 160°F.

5 HOURS INTO THE COOK

Check the temperature of the meat with an instant-read thermometer poked in several places (flat, middle, and point). This check is a reference point to see how close the meat is to 180°F.

For a chef's treat, slice off a piece of the fatty point. This crunchy, salty, fatty, smoky-with-a-hint-of-spice bite should reassure you that everything is going fine with the cook.

6 HOURS INTO THE COOK

Start checking the temperature of the meat every 20 to 30 minutes until it reaches 180°F and a meat fork slides in with slight resistance.

STANDING RIB ROAST

Ask anyone who knows me what my favorite vegetable is, and they'll all say the same thing: 7-bone standing rib roast. This piece of meat is a beauty—the kind of showstopper that causes a hush in the room when it is presented whole on a platter. You may know this gorgeous cut as "prime rib," but I find the term confusing and misleading because it isn't necessarily USDA Prime grade beef. This cut comes from the rib primal section (see Meet Your Meat, page 77), and rib-eye steaks are cut from the roast.

Cooking the meat at hot smoke–roast temperatures with my wet rub slathered on thick gives the roast a crunchy, spicy, caramelized, juicy, meaty, fatty, rich, smoky, fat-in-the-fire riot of flavors that, in case you can't tell by the description, I really love. There are a few tricks to achieving this carnivorous delight, which I'll outline in bullet points so there's no confusion.

* *Do not, under any circumstances, let your butcher pretty the rib roast up—French the bones, trim the fat, tie it up in a bow. You want the whole hunk of meat as is.*
* *If you can't find a 7-bone roast or you're feeding a smaller crowd, a 4-bone roast is equally delicious and cooks in about half the time. Start your meat temperature checks around the 1-hour mark.*

SERVES 10 TO 12

COOKER TEMPERATURE: 300°F to 350°F

COOK TIME: 2 to 3 hours

FOR THE RECIPE:

1 (12- to 15-pound) 7-bone standing rib roast

¾ cup Standing Rib Roast Wet Rub (page 233)

AT THE END OF THE COOK: The worst mistake you can make in this dead-simple cook is over-cooking such a gorgeous hunk of meat. The meat is done when an instant-read thermometer poked in the center reads 125°F. Let the meat rest for 30 minutes before slicing into it, and carry-over cooking will continue to increase the temperature to bull's-eye rare in the center. The meat will be more well done toward the outer slices—perfect when you're feeding a group that likes meat at different degrees of doneness.

UP TO 2 HOURS BEFORE THE COOK

Lightly score the fat cap in a crosshatch pattern using a very sharp knife. Angle the knife slightly to avoid piercing the meat. Slather the roast with the wet rub, cover it with plastic wrap, and let it marinate in the refrigerator for at least 30 minutes or up to 2 hours before cooking.

30 MINUTES BEFORE THE COOK

Remove the roast from the refrigerator and allow the meat to sit at room temperature.

Start a hot smoke–roast fire according to the instructions for your cooker of choice: BGE (page 35), offset (page 35), or kettle (page 36).

If you are cooking on a WSM, make these modifications to the hot smoke–roast setup (page 35): Remove the water pan and lower grate from the center ring (the fire is far enough away from the top grate, where the roast will cook, and will not burn the meat). Fill the fire ring three-quarters full of charcoal and top the charcoal with 3 wood chunks. Pour 1 chimney of lit charcoal over the unlit charcoal. When the charcoal engages and stops billowing white smoke, add 3 wood chunks to the fire.

WSM

◇◇

WHEN THE CHARCOAL is engaged in the fire ring and the cooker is reassembled, close the cooker and adjust the vents.

TOP VENT:	**BOTTOM VENTS:**
18.5-INCH MODEL: Open.	**18.5-INCH MODEL:** Open.
22.5-INCH MODEL: Open.	**22.5-INCH MODEL:** Open.

Give the cooker 10 to 15 minutes to settle into a temperature. If the WSM is running hotter than 300°F to 325°F, close one bottom vent by one third if you're using an 18.5-inch WSM or by half if you're using a 22.5-inch WSM. You may need to close a second bottom vent by the same amount, but give the cooker 10 to 15 minutes to settle in before making additional vent adjustments.

When the cooker temperature stabilizes around 300°F to 325°F, set the rib roast fat-side up in the middle of the top grate and close the cooker.

EVERY 25 TO 30 MINUTES IN THE COOK

Flip the rib roast.

If the cooker is running hotter than 325°F, slightly close one of the bottom vents.

2 HOURS INTO THE COOK

Check the internal temperature of the meat with an instant-read thermometer poked into the center of the roast. This is your checkpoint to see how far along the roast is. On a WSM at 300°F, a 7-bone rib roast typically takes 2½ to 3 hours to hit the 120°F to 125°F internal temperature range. Check the internal temperature every 15 to 20 minutes until it hits the target temperature.

◇◇

BGE

XXXXXXXXXXXXXXXXXXXXXXXXXXXXXXXXXXXXXXXXXXXXXXXXXXXXXXXXXXXXXXXXXX

FIVE MINUTES AFTER adding the lit charcoal and inserting the plate setter, close the cooker and adjust the vents.

TOP VENT:
Open.

BOTTOM VENT:
Open 2 inches.

Give the cooker 10 to 15 minutes to settle into a temperature. If the BGE is running hotter than 350°F, close the bottom vent by ½ inch. Close the bottom vent in ¼-inch increments as needed, but give the cooker 10 to 15 minutes to settle in before making additional vent adjustments.

When the cooker temperature stabilize, set the roast fat-side up in the middle of the grate and close the cooker.

EVERY 25 TO 30 MINUTES IN THE COOK

Flip the rib roast. Keep an eye on the cooker temperature and adjust the vents as necessary.

2 HOURS INTO THE COOK

Check the temperature of the meat with an instant-read thermometer poked into the center of the roast. This is your checkpoint to see how far along the roast is. On a BGE at 350°F, a 7-bone rib roast typically takes around 2½ hours to hit the 120°F to 125°F internal temperature range. Check the temperature every 15 to 20 minutes until it hits the target temperature.

XXXXXXXXXXXXXXXXXXXXXXXXXXXXXXXXXXXXXXXXXXXXXXXXXXXXXXXXXXXXXXXXXX

OFFSET

◇◇

WHEN THE CHARCOAL is engaged in the firebox and the oven thermometer is in place, close the cooker and adjust the vents.

TOP VENT:
Open.

FIREBOX VENT:
Open.

Give the cooker 10 minutes to settle into a temperature. If the cooker is running hotter than 350°F, close the firebox vent by one third. When the cooker temperature stabilizes, set the roast fat-side up in the middle of the grate and close the cooker.

EVERY 30 TO 40 MINUTES IN THE COOK

Flip the roast and rotate the side facing the firebox away from the heat.

Keep an eye on the grate temperature and make vent adjustments as needed. Close the firebox vent by up to half if the cooker is running hotter than 350°F. When the charcoal runs low or the cooker starts dipping closer to 300°F, add 1 chimney of lit charcoal and 1 split of wood to the firebox. When the charcoal engages and the fire stops billowing white smoke, about 5 minutes after restocking, close the firebox.

2 HOURS INTO THE COOK

Check the temperature of the meat with an instant-read thermometer poked into the center of the roast. This is your checkpoint to see how far along the roast is. On an offset smoker at 350°F, a 7-bone rib roast typically takes around 2½ hours to hit the 120°F to 125°F internal temperature range. Check the temperature every 15 to 20 minutes until it hits the target temperature.

◇◇

KETTLE

WHEN THE CHARCOAL is engaged on the banked piles, about 5 minutes after adding the lit charcoal, place the roast fat-side up on the grate directly above the water pan. Close the cooker and adjust the vents.

TOP VENT:

22-INCH MODEL: Open.

26-INCH MODEL: Open.

BOTTOM VENT:

22-INCH MODEL: Open.

26-INCH MODEL: Open.

EVERY 20 TO 25 MINUTES IN THE COOK

Check the cooker temperature. If the kettle is running hotter than 350°F, close the bottom vent by one third. If the temperature starts dipping closer to 300°F, restock the piles with ½ chimney of lit charcoal.

Flip the roast and rotate it 90 degrees on the grate so that each side of the roast gets equal time away from the fire.

Check and refill the water pan as needed.

1½ HOURS INTO THE COOK

Check the temperature of the meat with an instant-read thermometer poked into the center of the roast. This is your checkpoint to see how far along the roast is. On a kettle grill at 350°F, a 7-bone rib roast typically takes 2 to 2½ hours to hit the 120°F to 125°F internal temperature range. Check the temperature every 15 to 20 minutes until it hits the target temperature.

SMOKE-ROASTED BALTIMORE PIT BEEF

Pit beef is Baltimore's answer to barbecue: a lean hunk of meat cooked hot and fast to a pink-rare center. Think of it as a distinct regional variation of roast beef—one that is "marinated" in a dry rub and comes off the cooker with a crusty, almost blackened exterior. Traditional Baltimore pit beef doesn't include the nuanced flavor of wood smoke, but naturally, my riff does.

The one strict rule about pit beef is how it is served: shaved paper-thin against the grain, preferably with a rotating meat slicer. Thicker cuts will be chewier. If you don't have a meat slicer, ask the deli counter clerk at a local grocery to slice it for you, or do your best shaving slices with the sharpest knife in your quiver. Serve it on a fluffy Kaiser roll or seeded rye bread with slices of sweet onion and Horseradish Sauce (page 247).

SERVES 12 TO 14

COOKER TEMPERATURE: 350°F

COOK TIME: 45 minutes to 1 hour

FOR THE RECIPE:

1 (5-pound) top round roast

⅓ cup Baltimore Pit Beef Rub (page 235), divided

1¼ cup Horseradish Sauce (page 247)

AT THE END OF THE COOK: Medium-rare is ideal for this cut, so shoot for an internal temperature between 130°F and 135°F. Remember: carryover cooking will increase the internal temperature a few degrees as the meat rests. Don't go too rare—anything below 125°F will be extremely chewy. When the meat is done, tent the roast loosely with foil and let it rest for up to 20 minutes before slicing.

UP TO 48 HOURS BEFORE THE COOK

Coat the beef roast with ¼ cup of the rub. Wrap the meat in plastic wrap and refrigerate it for 24 to 48 hours, flipping once every 10 to 12 hours.

1 HOUR BEFORE THE COOK

Remove the roast from the refrigerator and sprinkle it with more rub, about 2 tablespoons. Let the meat sit at room temperature.

30 MINUTES BEFORE THE COOK

Start a hot smoke–roast fire according to the instructions for your cooker of choice: WSM (page 35), BGE (page 35), offset (page 35), or kettle (page 36).

If you are cooking on a WSM or offset, remove the sand pan. This roast benefits from the sizzle of semidirect heat, and the fire is far enough away from the meat to prevent flare-ups.

WSM

WHEN THE CHARCOAL is engaged in the fire ring and the cooker is reassembled, set the roast in the middle of the top grate. Close the cooker and adjust the vents

TOP VENT:	BOTTOM VENTS:
18.5-INCH MODEL: Open.	**18.5-INCH MODEL:** Open.
22.5-INCH MODEL: Open.	**22.5-INCH MODEL:** Open.

20 MINUTES INTO THE COOK

Check the cooker temperature. If the cooker is running hotter than 350°F, close one bottom vent by one third if you're using an 18.5-inch WSM or by half if you're using a 22.5-inch WSM.

Wait 10 minutes for the temperature to settle in after the vent adjustment. If the cooker is still running too hot, close a second bottom vent by the same amount.

45 MINUTES INTO THE COOK

Check the temperature of the meat with an instant-read thermometer poked into the center of the roast. If the internal temperature is below 130°F, continue cooking and check the internal temperature every 10 to 15 minutes until the meat is done.

BGE

FIVE MINUTES AFTER adding the lit charcoal and inserting the plate setter, set the roast in the middle of the grate. Close the cooker and adjust the vents.

TOP VENT:
Open.

BOTTOM VENT:
Open 2 inches.

20 MINUTES INTO THE COOK

Check the cooker temperature. If the BGE is running hotter than 350°F, close the bottom vent by ½ inch. If the temperature doesn't drop within 10 minutes, continue to close the bottom vent in ¼-inch increments until the temperature decreases, giving the cooker 10 minutes to settle into the temperature before making another vent adjustment.

45 MINUTES INTO THE COOK

Check the temperature of the meat with an instant-read thermometer poked into the center of the roast. If the internal temperature is below 130°F, continue cooking and check the internal temperature every 10 to 15 minutes until the meat is done.

OFFSET

WHEN THE CHARCOAL is engaged in the firebox and the oven thermometer is in place, set the roast on the grate at least 10 inches away from the firebox. Close the cooker and adjust the vents.

TOP VENT:
Open.

FIREBOX VENT:
Open.

20 MINUTES INTO THE COOK

Check the grate temperature. If the cooker is running hotter than 350°F, close the firebox vent by one third. If the cooker is running below 300°F, add 1 chimney of lit charcoal and 1 split of wood to the firebox. When the charcoal engages and the fire stops billowing white smoke, about 5 minutes after restocking, close the firebox.

45 MINUTES INTO THE COOK

Check the temperature of the meat with an instant-read thermometer poked into the center of the roast. If the internal temperature is below 130°F, continue cooking and check the internal temperature every 10 to 15 minutes until the meat is done.

KETTLE

<><><><><><><><><><><><><><><><><><><><><><><><><><><><><><><><><><><><><><><><><><><><>

WHEN THE CHARCOAL is engaged on the banked piles, about 5 minutes after adding the lit charcoal to the cooker, place the roast on the grate directly above the water pan. Close the cooker and adjust the vents.

TOP VENT:

22-INCH MODEL: Open.

26-INCH MODEL: Open.

BOTTOM VENT:

22-INCH MODEL: Open.

26-INCH MODEL: Open.

EVERY 10 TO 15 MINUTES IN THE COOK

Check the cooker temperature. If the kettle is running hotter than 350°F, close the bottom vent by one third. If the temperature dips below 300°F, restock the piles with ½ chimney of lit charcoal.

Flip and rotate the meat so that all sides of the roast get equal time facing the fire.

45 MINUTES INTO THE COOK

Check the temperature of the meat with an instant-read thermometer poked into the center of the roast. If the internal temperature is below 130°F, continue cooking and check the temperature every 10 to 15 minutes until the meat is done.

<><><><><><><><><><><><><><><><><><><><><><><><><><><><><><><><><><><><><><><><><><><><>

HOT SMOKE-ROASTED TRI-TIP

Once upon a time, this tender, triangular roast was chopped into ground beef or stew meat. Then, in the 1950s, a California butcher named Bob Schutz gave it a name and promoted its rich, beefy flavor. The cut became the cornerstone of Santa Maria "barbecue," a distinct regional style from this coastal town in Central California. (I use quotations because it is cooked hot and fast, which some might argue isn't barbecue at all.)

It took a while for the rest of the country to catch up, but these days, you can find tri-tip at places like Costco, as well as good meat markets. The roasts, which are cut from the bottom sirloin where the round meets the flank (see Meet Your Meat, page 77), typically weigh 1½ to 2½ pounds each and can feed up to 6 people. I am especially partial to the Garlic-Rosemary Marinade or, try the Fiery Harissa Marinade (page 224) if you like a little heat..

SERVES 4 TO 6

COOKER TEMPERATURE: 325°F to 350°F

COOK TIME: 30 minutes to 1 hour

FOR THE RECIPE:

1 (1½- to 2½-pound) tri-tip

¾ cup Garlic-Rosemary Marinade (page 223)

AT THE END OF THE COOK: Tri-tips should never be cooked past medium-rare because they get tough and chewy. Pull the meat off of the cooker when it reaches an internal temperature between 125°F and 130°F; carryover cooking increases the temperature a few more degrees as it rests. Tent the meat loosely with foil and let it rest for 15 minutes before slicing it against the grain and serving.

UP TO 4 HOURS BEFORE THE COOK

Combine the marinade and tri-tip in a 1-gallon zip-top bag. Squeeze and roll the bag so the meat is thoroughly coated in the marinade. Seal the bag and refrigerate it for 2 to 4 hours, flipping the bag every hour to redistribute the marinade.

30 MINUTES BEFORE THE COOK

Remove the bag from the refrigerator and allow the meat to come to room temperature.

Start a hot smoke–roast fire according to the instructions for your cooker of choice: WSM (page 35), BGE (page 35), offset (page 35), or kettle (page 36).

WSM

WHEN THE CHARCOAL is engaged in the fire ring, the water pan filled with sand is in place, and the cooker is reassembled, close the cooker and adjust the vents.

TOP VENT:	BOTTOM VENTS:
18.5-INCH MODEL: Open.	**18.5-INCH MODEL:** Open.
22.5-INCH MODEL: Open.	**22.5-INCH MODEL:** Open.

Give the cooker 10 to 15 minutes to settle into a temperature. If the WSM is running hotter than 350°F, close one bottom vent by one third if you're using an 18.5-inch WSM or by half if you're using a 22.5-inch WSM. When the cooker temperature stabilizes, set the tri-tip in the middle of the top grate and close the cooker.

20 MINUTES INTO THE COOK

Check the temperature of the tri-tip with an instant-read thermometer poked into the thickest end of the meat. The target internal temperature is 125°F to 130°F, and a smaller tri-tip may be ready at this checkpoint. If it's not ready, start checking the meat every 5 to 10 minutes until the meat is done.

BGE

◇◇◇

FIVE MINUTES AFTER adding the lit charcoal and inserting the plate setter, close the cooker and adjust the vents.

TOP VENT: **BOTTOM VENT:**

Open.   Open 2 inches.

Give the cooker 10 minutes to settle into a temperature. If the BGE is running hotter than 350°F, close the bottom vent by ½ inch. If the temperature doesn't drop within 10 minutes, continue to close the bottom vent in ¼-inch increments until the temperature decreases. When the cooker temperature stabilizes, set the tri-tip in the middle of the grate and close the cooker.

20 MINUTES INTO THE COOK

Check the temperature of the tri-tip with an instant-read thermometer poked into the thickest end of the meat. The target internal temperature is 125°F to 130°F, and a smaller tri-tip may be ready at this checkpoint. If it's not ready, start checking the meat every 5 to 10 minutes until the meat is done.

◇◇◇

OFFSET

◇◇◇

When the charcoal is engaged in the firebox and the sand pan and oven thermometer are in place, close the cooker and adjust the vents.

TOP VENT:
Open.

FIREBOX VENT:
Open.

Give the cooker 10 to 15 minutes to settle into a temperature. If the cooker is running hotter than 350°F, close the firebox vent by one third. When the cooker temperature stabilizes, set the tri-tip on the far side of the grate away from the firebox and close the cooker.

20 MINUTES INTO THE COOK

Check the temperature of the tri-tip with an instant-read thermometer poked into the thickest end of the meat. The target internal temperature is 125°F to 130°F, and a smaller tri-tip may be ready at this checkpoint. If it's not ready, start checking the meat every 5 to 10 minutes until the meat is done.

◇◇◇

KETTLE

When the charcoal is engaged on the banked piles, about 5 minutes after adding the lit charcoal, close the cooker and adjust the vents.

TOP VENT:
22-INCH MODEL: Open.
26-INCH MODEL: Open.

BOTTOM VENT:
22-INCH MODEL: Open.
26-INCH MODEL: Open.

Give the cooker five minutes to settle into a temperature. If the cooker temperature is running hotter than 350°F, close the bottom vent by one third. When the cooker temperature stabilizes, set the tri-tip on the grate directly above the water pan and close the cooker.

20 MINUTES INTO THE COOK

Check the temperature of the tri-tip with an instant-read thermometer poked into the thickest end of the meat. The target internal temperature is 125°F to 130°F, and a smaller tri-tip may be ready at this checkpoint. If it's not ready, start checking the meat every 5 to 10 minutes until the meat is done.

SMOKE-ROASTED BEEF TENDERLOIN

Beef tenderloin is perfect for fancy dinner parties, and it's a dead-simple cook. I crank one out whenever my wife, Ellen, hosts a ladies luncheon or baby shower because, let's face it, there are occasions that call for something a little more dainty and refined than beef ribs and brisket.

Buy a whole trimmed (5-pound) or untrimmed (7-plus-pound) tenderloin—you'll find them at specialty meat shops and in big box stores like Costco. If you buy it untrimmed, you must remove the "chain" (a long, fatty rope of meat), the tough silverskin, and any big chunks of fat running along the roast. Throw the chain on the smoker for a nice chef's treat while you're cooking, or reserve it to use for stock.

You can serve the meat warm, after letting it rest, or you can cool the tenderloin, wrap it in plastic wrap, and refrigerate it for a few hours before slicing and serving it cold. For Ellen's parties, I like to arrange the chilled, sliced tenderloin on a bed of watercress or arugula, dot the salad with halved cherry tomatoes, and serve it with a simple, punchy Horseradish Sauce (page 247) and cocktail rye or small rolls.

SERVES 10 TO 12

COOKER TEMPERATURE: 325°F to 350°F
COOK TIME: 1 to 1½ hours

FOR THE RECIPE:

1 (5- to 6-pound) trimmed whole beef tenderloin

¼ cup Beef Tenderloin Rub (page 236)

AT THE END OF THE COOK: Pull the meat off the cooker when it reaches an internal temperature between 130°F and 135°F for medium-rare; carryover cooking will increase the temperature a few more degrees as it rests. Tent the meat loosely with foil and let it rest for 15 minutes before slicing and serving or wrapping to refrigerate.

1 HOUR BEFORE THE COOK

Coat the tenderloin in the rub and let the meat reach room temperature.

30 MINUTES BEFORE THE COOK

Start a hot smoke–roast fire according to the instructions for your cooker of choice: WSM (page 35), BGE (page 35), offset (page 35), or kettle (page 36).

WSM

WHEN THE CHARCOAL is engaged in the fire ring, the sand pan is in place, and the cooker is reassembled, set the tenderloin in the middle of the top grate. Close the cooker and adjust the vents.

TOP VENT:

18.5-INCH MODEL: Open.
22.5-INCH MODEL: Open.

BOTTOM VENTS:

18.5-INCH MODEL: Close one vent by one third.
22.5-INCH MODEL: Close one vent halfway.

15 MINUTES INTO THE COOK

Check the cooker temperature. If the cooker is running hotter than 350°F, adjust the bottom vents.

Wait 10 minutes for the temperature to settle in after the vent adjustment. If the cooker is still running too hot, close a second bottom vent by one third if you're using an 18.5-inch WSM or by half if you're using a 22.5-inch WSM.

45 MINUTES INTO THE COOK

Check the temperature of the tenderloin with an instant-read thermometer poked into the thickest part of the meat. If it registers below 130°F, start checking the meat every 5 to 10 minutes until it hits the target internal temperature.

BGE

◇◇◇

FIVE MINUTES AFTER adding the lit charcoal and inserting the plate setter, set the tenderloin in the middle of the grate. Close the cooker and adjust the vents.

TOP VENT:
Open.

BOTTOM VENT:
Open 2 inches.

15 MINUTES INTO THE COOK

Check the cooker temperature. If the BGE is running hotter than 350°F, close the bottom vent by ½ inch. If the temperature doesn't drop within 10 to 15 minutes, continue to close the bottom vent in ¼-inch increments until the temperature decreases, giving the cooker 10 minutes to settle in between each vent adjustment.

45 MINUTES INTO THE COOK

Check the temperature of the tenderloin with an instant-read thermometer poked into the thickest part of the meat. If it registers below 130°F, start checking the meat every 5 to 10 minutes until it hits the target internal temperature.

◇◇◇

TOP: *Goose Breast Pastrami (page 68);* **BOTTOM:** *Smoked Turkey (page 45)*

Smoked Brisket (page 78)

TOP: *Beef Short Ribs (page 90);* **BOTTOM:** *Hush Puppies with Charred Jalapeños (page 209)*

Standing Rib Roast (page 110)

Smoke-Roasted Leg of Lamb (page 165)

Smoked Snapper (page 133)

naster Porchetta (page 181)

TOP: *Neapolitan-Style Pizza (page 198);* **BOTTOM:** *BBQ-Baked Potatoes (page 211) and Smoked Elotes (page 206)*

OFFSET

WHEN THE CHARCOAL is engaged in the firebox and the sand pan and oven thermometer are in place, set the tenderloin on the grate at least 10 inches away from the firebox, with the thickest end facing the firebox. Close the cooker and adjust the vents.

TOP VENT:
Open.

FIREBOX VENT:
Open.

20 MINUTES INTO THE COOK

Check the grate temperature. If the cooker is running hotter than 350°F, close the firebox vent by one third. If the cooker is running below 300°F, add 1 chimney of lit charcoal and 1 split of wood to the firebox. When the charcoal engages and the fire stops billowing white smoke, about 5 minutes after restocking, close the firebox.

45 MINUTES INTO THE COOK

Check the temperature of the tenderloin with an instant-read thermometer poked into the thickest part of the meat. If it registers below 130°F, start checking the meat every 5 to 10 minutes until it hits the target internal temperature.

KETTLE

◇◇◇

WHEN THE CHARCOAL is engaged on the banked piles, about 5 minutes after adding the lit charcoal, place the tenderloin on the grate directly above the water pan. Close the cooker and adjust the vents.

TOP VENT:

22-INCH MODEL: Open.

26-INCH MODEL: Open.

BOTTOM VENT:

22-INCH MODEL: Open.

26-INCH MODEL: Open.

EVERY 10 TO 15 MINUTES IN THE COOK

Flip the tenderloin.

Check the cooker temperature. If the kettle is running hotter than 350°F, close the bottom vent by one third. If the temperature dips below 300°F, restock the piles with ½ chimney of lit charcoal. Check and refill the water pan as needed.

30 MINUTES INTO THE COOK

Check the temperature of the tenderloin with an instant-read thermometer poked into the thickest part of the meat. If it registers below 130°F, start checking the meat every 5 to 10 minutes until it hits the target internal temperature.

◇◇◇

5.

FISH
&
SEAFOOD

DEAR STUDENT:

TRUE STORY: THIS BARBECUE THING I DO, THE OBSESSION THAT BECAME MY calling, it all started because my wife, Ellen, wanted smoked salmon. So she bought me a WSM. I'd been grilling over charcoal for years, but this smoker introduced me to an entirely new dimension of flavor and cooking with charcoal. From that point on, the smoked fish my lovely bride wanted often took a backseat to my experimenting with beef ribs, pulled pork, and brisket. She's a patient, incredibly sweet woman who has put up with me for reasons I still can't imagine, although I suspect it has something to do with the recipes you'll find in this chapter.

Since you've mastered the classics—the ribs, brisket, pork shoulders, and other barnyard animals in barbecue—fish and seafood may seem like a breeze. The cooks are quick, but this doesn't make it easier. Fish and seafood are far less forgiving than other meats. A fillet of salmon or a pound of shrimp can dry out or absorb too much smoke in the blink of an eye. In this chapter, you'll learn the essentials for infusing fish and seafood with smoke flavor and keeping the meat moist without overcooking.

If you've followed the program closely, you'll notice I make an occasional exception in this chapter and use wood chips in some of the cooks to give the fish a quick, initial blast of smoke. This isn't a necessity, but it's a good technique to use when you want to infuse small, lean, fast-cooking foods with smoke flavor. Just remember, you can easily oversmoke it. Try the wood chips and see how the flavor suits you. If you want to dial back the smokiness, one or two small wood chunk slivers will create a whisper of smoke on whole fish, fish fillets, and smaller seafood.

Enjoy!

Gary Wiviott

SMOKED WHOLE FISH

This is the perfect recipe for people who think they can't cook fish. The fish stays moist; wood smoke gives it a rustic, campfire note; and it makes a striking presentation on a platter. The steps and cooking instructions outlined here are meant to be a template—one you can use on most fresh, quality, whole fish. Flaky, lean whole fish (think: snapper, trout, flounder) is less likely to dry out and will pick up more smoke flavor in a low-and-slow cook. However, if you're cooking a fattier whole fish like salmon or mahi mahi, you can run the cook at hot smoke–roast temperatures and cut the cook time by 15 to 20 minutes.

The cook works best on 1½- to 2-pound whole fish, and you can easily fit two whole fish this size on all of the cookers except the smaller 22-inch kettle grill. In my experience, bigger fish are easier to overcook and, more importantly, flipping a heavier whole fish is much more difficult. Use the biggest, widest spatula in your kitchen, or double up with two spatulas to flip the fish. Using tongs will absolutely destroy a whole fish.

To serve, use a sharp fillet knife to cut along the backbone of the fish, starting just behind the head. Use two spatulas to gently lift and support the top fillet as you pull it away from the spine. Then gently lift and remove the tail and spine together, using a knife or spatula as needed to separate it from the bottom fillet. Inspect the fillets and remove any remaining bones.

SERVES 4 TO 6

COOKER TEMPERATURE: 225°F to 250°F

COOK TIME: 40 to 60 minutes

FOR THE RECIPES

1 (1½- to 2-pound) whole fish, scaled and gutted

½ gallon Basic 24-Hour Brine (page 217), using granulated sugar instead of brown sugar

1 tablespoon whole black peppercorns, crushed

2 tablespoons Lemon Oil Wet Rub (page 237)

2 teaspoons Lemon Oil (page 237)

AT THE END OF THE COOK: To avoid overcooking, judge doneness by the look and feel of the flesh. Use the tip of a paring knife to peek inside the thickest section of the fish. The center should be just opaque and even slightly translucent. The flesh shouldn't "flake" (a sign it's overcooked) but should gently resist the knife. The target internal temperature for whole fish is around 140°F, but I recommend removing most whole fish when it reaches an internal temperature around 135°F. Carryover cooking will increase the internal temperature by a few degrees after the fish is removed from the cooker. When the fish is done, let it rest for up to 10 minutes and drizzle it with a thin streak of strained Lemon Oil before serving.

1 TO 2 HOURS BEFORE THE COOK

Cut slits into both sides of the fish at an angle, from the backbone to the belly, about 1 inch apart.

Pour the Basic 24-Hour Brine into a nonreactive container large enough to fit the whole fish without the brine overflowing. When the brine is completely cooled, add the peppercorns and fish to the container. Cover the container and refrigerate for at least 1 or up to 2 hours.

30 MINUTES BEFORE THE COOK

Remove the fish from the brine and pat it dry with paper towels. Smear both sides of the fish with the wet rub, working the mixture into the slits.

Start a KISS method fire according to the instructions for your cooker of choice: WSM (page 26), BGE (page 29), offset (page 31), or kettle (page 33).

IMPORTANT NOTE: With a full KISS load of charcoal, the WSM and BGE will run for hours longer than it takes to smoke a whole fish. Start the cook with half the amount of unlit charcoal to reduce the cooker's running time. Or, use the initial running time to smoke ingredients for side dishes.

WSM

◇◇

WHEN THE CHARCOAL is engaged in the fire ring and the cooker is reassembled with the water pan in place, close the cooker and adjust the vents.

TOP VENT:
18.5-INCH MODEL: Open.

22.5-INCH MODEL: Open.

BOTTOM VENTS:
18.5-INCH MODEL: Close two vents by one third.

22.5-INCH MODEL: Close two vents halfway.

When the temperature in the cooker stabilizes between 225°F and 250°F, set the whole fish on the grate and close the cooker.

Keep an eye on the cooker temperature throughout the cook. If the cooker is running hotter than 250°F, close the third bottom vent by one third if you're using an 18.5-inch WSM or by half if you're using a 22.5-inch WSM. If the 22.5-inch WSM continues to run hotter than 250°F, close the top vent by one third. Give the WSM 10 to 15 minutes to settle into the new temperature before making additional vent adjustments.

15 TO 20 MINUTES INTO THE COOK
Carefully flip the fish using a very large spatula or two spatulas to hold the fish together.

30 MINUTES INTO THE COOK
Check the internal temperature of the fish with an instant-read thermometer poked into the thickest section, and continue checking for doneness every 10 to 15 minutes until it registers 135°F.

◇◇

BGE

WHEN THE CHARCOAL is engaged and the plate setter and water pan are in place, close the cooker and adjust the vents.

TOP VENT:
Close halfway.

BOTTOM VENT:
Open ½ inch.

When the temperature stabilizes between 225°F and 250°F, place the fish on the grate and close the cooker.

15 TO 20 MINUTES INTO THE COOK

Carefully flip the fish using a very large spatula or two spatulas to hold the fish together.

Keep an eye on the cooker temperature throughout the cook. If the cooker is running hotter than 250°F, close the bottom vent in ¼-inch increments, giving the BGE 10 to 15 minutes to settle in between vent adjustments.

30 MINUTES INTO THE COOK

Check the internal temperature of the fish with an instant-read thermometer poked into the thickest section, and continue checking for doneness every 10 to 15 minutes until it registers 135°F.

OFFSET

◇◇

WHEN THE CHARCOAL is engaged in the firebox, and the water pan and oven thermometer are in place on the cooking grate, close the cooker and adjust the vents.

TOP VENT:
Open.

FIREBOX VENT:
Close by one third.

When the temperature stabilizes between 225°F and 250°F, arrange the fish vertically on the grate with the thick spine side facing the firebox. Close the firebox and cooker.

15 TO 20 MINUTES INTO THE COOK

Carefully flip the fish using a very large spatula or two spatulas to hold the fish together.

Keep an eye on the cooker temperature throughout the cook. If the temperature in the cooker is running hotter than 250°F, close the firebox vent halfway. Give the cooker 10 minutes to settle in between vent adjustments, and if it continues to run too hot, close the top vent by one third.

30 MINUTES INTO THE COOK

Check the internal temperature of the fish with an instant-read thermometer poked into the thickest section, and continue checking for doneness every 10 to 15 minutes until it registers 135°F.

◇◇

KETTLE

◇◇

WHEN THE CHARCOAL is engaged and the water pan is in place, close the cooker and adjust the vents.

TOP VENT:
22-INCH MODEL: Open.
26-INCH MODEL: Open.

BOTTOM VENT:
22-INCH MODEL: Close by one third.
26-INCH MODEL: Close halfway.

When the temperature stabilizes between 225°F and 300°F, gently pour the wood chips over the ignited charcoal. Place the fish on the grate opposite the water pan with the spine facing the fire and close the cooker.

15 TO 20 MINUTES INTO THE COOK

Carefully flip the fish using a very large spatula or two spatulas to hold the fish together.

Keep an eye on the temperature throughout the cook. If the cooker is running hotter than 300°F, close the top vent by one third if you're using the 22-inch kettle or by half if you're using the 26-inch kettle.

30 MINUTES INTO THE COOK

Check the internal temperature of the fish with an instant-read thermometer poked into the thickest section, and continue checking for doneness every 10 to 15 minutes until it registers 135°F.

◇◇

FISH & SEAFOOD
INTERNAL TEMPERATURES

TASTINESS IS NOT THE GOAL OF THE FEDERAL AGENCY THAT SETS SAFE MINI-mum internal temperatures. Food safety is their only concern, and they say that 145°F is the safe internal temperature for pretty much all finfish and most seafood. The problem is, this recommendation doesn't leave much leeway for the variations in density and oiliness of different fish and seafood, and these factors affect cook times and carryover cooking, which continues to cook fish after it is removed from the heat. A fresh piece of ahi tuna cooked to 145°F would be dry and flavorless—you may as well eat canned tuna. But if you pull it off the cooker around 125°F, carryover cooking will bring it to a perfect rare to medium-rare as it rests.

My guideline for fish and seafood internal temperatures hinges on good common sense. Buy the freshest fish you can find from a reputable source and keep the fish refrigerated on a bed of ice. Fish should have a fresh, clean, ocean scent. If it smells overly fishy, appears slimy or discolored, or feels mushy, don't buy it. Consider your fellow diners and do not serve rare or raw fish or seafood to the elderly or very young, pregnant women, or anyone with a compromised immune system. If you plan to eat it raw or very rare, as in ceviche or rare-in-the-middle tuna, buy "sushi-grade" fish. Although there are no U.S. laws regulating this quality designation, it generally means that the fish has been frozen and stored at a temperature of -4°F or less for a minimum of 7 days, effectively killing most parasites.

SMOKED SALMON

A thick fillet of hot-smoked salmon is right up there with brisket and ribs on the list of most-requested smoker recipes. It's a relatively quick cook, and the oiliness and density of the fish is perfectly suited for smoking.

This cook also works on just about any medium to firm, skin-on fish fillet up to 2 inches thick. If you can't find salmon or if you luck into a few pounds of fresh tuna instead, you can easily substitute. I like to use herbes de Provence or Old Bay seasoning on most fish and seafood, but feel free to experiment with other fish-friendly rubs.

You can also dabble with the cooker temperature and wood when smoking fish fillets. For a lighter smoke or a quicker cook, run a KISS setup between 225°F and 250°F. For a heavier smoke flavor, use wood chips instead of chunks. Fish fillet and small seafood (think: oysters and shrimp) cooks are the rare exception I make for using wood chips because these meats cook quickly and the intense initial blast of smoke from fast-burning chips produces more smoke flavor. Use one wood chunk instead of the chips if you want a lighter smoke flavor.

You can serve the salmon warm or chilled. To serve the salmon chilled, cool the fillet to room temperature, wrap it tightly in plastic wrap, and refrigerate for at least 1 hour before serving. Garnish the fish with dill or slices of lemon, and serve it with creamy Horseradish Sauce (page 247) and buttery crackers or crostini.

SERVES 2 TO 4

COOKER TEMPERATURE: 160°F to 180°F

COOK TIME: 45 minutes to 1 hour

FOR THE RECIPE:

1 (2- to 3-pound) center-cut salmon fillet, skin on

½ gallon Basic 24-Hour Brine (page 217)

2 tablespoons plus ½ teaspoon Herbes de Provence Rub (page 228) or Old Bay seasoning, divided

FOR THE COOK:

Aluminum foil

1 teaspoon olive oil or nonstick cooking spray

1 wood chunk or 2 cups wood chips

AT THE END OF THE COOK: To avoid overcooking, judge the fish's doneness by the look and feel of the flesh. Use the tip of a paring knife to peek at the center of the fish. It should be just opaque and even slightly translucent at the thickest center of the fillet. The flesh shouldn't "flake" (a sign that it's overcooked) but should gently resist the knife. Shoot for an internal temperature of

135°F—carryover cooking will increase the temperature after it is removed from the cooker. Let the fillet rest for up to 15 minutes before serving.

UP TO 3 HOURS BEFORE THE COOK

Run your fingers along the center of the salmon fillet to feel for small pin bones. Remove any bones with a clean pair of tweezers or needle-nose pliers.

Pour the Basic 24-Hour Brine into a nonreactive container large enough to fit the fish fillet without the brine overflowing. When the brine has cooled completely, stir in 2 tablespoons of the Herbes de Provence Rub or Old Bay seasoning. Add the fillet to the brine, cover the container, and refrigerate for at least 1 hour or up to 3 hours.

30 MINUTES BEFORE THE COOK

Remove the salmon from the brine and pat the fillet completely dry with paper towels. Slice off the thin, narrow belly flap to make the width and thickness of the fillet uniform. (This flap piece will go on the cooker, too. It cooks faster, and I consider it a chef's treat or *amuse bouche* for anyone hanging around.) Sprinkle the salmon with the remaining ½ teaspoon of the same rub or seasoning you used in the brine.

Start a lower-and-slower fire, using wood chunks or chips as desired, according to the instructions for your cooker of choice: WSM (page 38), BGE (page 39), or offset (page 40). If you're cooking on a kettle, start a KISS fire (page 33) and fill the water pan with ice.

Tear off a long, rectangular piece of aluminum foil and fold it to form a disposable baking sheet large enough to fit the salmon. Smear a light coat of olive oil or cooking spray on the foil.

WSM

WHEN THE CHARCOAL is engaged in the fire ring and the cooker is reassembled with the ice pan in place, close the cooker and adjust the vents.

TOP VENT:
18.5-INCH MODEL: Close
22.5-INCH MODEL: Close

BOTTOM VENTS:
18.5-INCH MODEL: Close all vents by one third.
22.5-INCH MODEL: Close all vents halfway.

When the cooker temperature stabilizes between 160°F and 180°F, place the salmon fillet and belly flap skin-side down on the prepared foil sheet and set the sheet on the grate. If you are using wood chips, open the side door and carefully pour the wood chips over the ignited charcoal.

EVERY 15 MINUTES IN THE COOK

Check the cooker temperature. If the WSM is running below 160°F, open the top vent. Close two of the bottom vents in very slight increments if the cooker is running hotter than 180°F. Give the WSM 10 to 15 minutes to settle into the new temperature after each vent adjustment. If it is still running hotter than 180°F, adjust the third bottom vent as needed.

Restock the water pan with ice as needed. When the pan is more than half full of water, drain and refill it with ice.

30 MINUTES INTO THE COOK

Check the belly flap for doneness. If the meat is opaque, remove it from the cooker and consider this piece an official taste test.

45 MINUTES INTO THE COOK

Check the thickest section of the fillet for doneness. If the meat is opaque or barely translucent, or registers 135°F on an instant-read thermometer, remove it from the cooker. If the fish is not ready, start checking the fillet every 10 to 15 minutes until it is done.

BGE

WHEN THE CHARCOAL is engaged and the plate setter and ice pan are in place, close the cooker and adjust the vents.

TOP VENT:
Close halfway.

BOTTOM VENT:
Open ½ inch.

When the cooker temperature stabilizes between 160°F and 180°F, place the salmon fillet and belly flap skin-side down on the prepared foil sheet and set the sheet on the grate. If you are using wood chips, carefully pour 1 cup of wood chips around the plate setter, over the ignited charcoal, before you set the salmon on the grate.

EVERY 15 MINUTES IN THE COOK

Check the cooker temperature. Slightly open the top vent if the cooker is running below 160°F. If the cooker is running hotter than 180°F, close the bottom vent in ¼-inch increments. Give the BGE 10 to 15 minutes to settle into the new temperature before making another adjustment.

Restock the water pan with ice as needed. When the pan is more than half full of water, drain and refill it with ice.

30 MINUTES INTO THE COOK

Check the belly flap for doneness. If the meat is opaque, remove it from the cooker and consider this piece an official taste test.

45 MINUTES INTO THE COOK

Check the thickest section of the fillet for doneness. If the meat is opaque or barely translucent, or registers 135°F on an instant-read thermometer, remove it from the cooker. If the fish is not ready, start checking the fillet every 10 to 15 minutes until it is done.

OFFSET

◇◇◇

When the charcoal is engaged in the firebox and the ice pan and oven thermometer are in place on the cooking grate, close the cooker and adjust the vents.

TOP VENT:
Close halfway.

FIREBOX VENT:
Close halfway.

When the cooker temperature stabilizes between 160°F and 180°F, place the salmon fillet and belly flap skin-side down on the prepared foil sheet and set the sheet on the grate with the thicker side of the salmon fillet facing the firebox. If you are using wood chips, open the firebox and carefully pour wood chips over the ignited charcoal.

EVERY 15 MINUTES IN THE COOK

If the temperature on the cooker begins to drop below 160°F, slightly open the top vent. If the fire is too low, restock the cooker with ½ chimney of unlit charcoal. If the temperature spikes above 180°F, slightly close the firebox vent.

Restock the water pan with ice as needed. When the pan is more than half full of water, drain and refill it with ice.

30 MINUTES INTO THE COOK

Check the belly flap for doneness. If the meat is opaque, remove it from the cooker and consider this piece an official taste test.

45 MINUTES INTO THE COOK

Check the thickest section of the fillet for doneness. If the meat is opaque or barely translucent, or registers 135°F on an instant-read thermometer, remove it from the cooker. If the fish is not ready, start checking the fillet every 10 to 15 minutes until it is done.

◇◇◇

KETTLE

◇◇

ABOUT 5 MINUTES after pouring the lit charcoal onto the banked pile of charcoal, fill the ice pan with ice, close the cooker, and adjust the vents.

TOP VENT:

22-INCH MODEL: Open.

26-INCH MODEL: Open.

BOTTOM VENT:

22-INCH MODEL: Close by one third.

26-INCH MODEL: Close halfway.

When the cooker temperature stabilizes below 250°F, place the salmon fillet and belly flap skin-side down on the prepared foil sheet and set the sheet on the grate. If you are using wood chips, pour the wood chips over the ignited charcoal before placing the fillet on the grate.

EVERY 15 MINUTES IN THE COOK

Check the cooker temperature. If the cooker is running hotter than 250°F, close the top vent by one third if you're using a 22-inch kettle or by half if you're using a 26-inch kettle.

Rotate the salmon so the side that was facing the fire is now turned to the outer edge of the grate, away from the fire. (This prevents one side from overcooking.)

Check the belly flap for doneness. If the meat is opaque, remove it from the cooker and consider this piece an official taste test.

Restock the water pan with ice as needed. When the pan is more than half full of water, drain and refill it with ice.

30 MINUTES INTO THE COOK

Check the thickest section of the fillet for doneness. If the meat is opaque or barely translucent, or registers 135°F on an instant-read thermometer, remove it from the cooker. If the fish is not ready, start checking the fillet every 5 to 10 minutes until it is done. You may need to add ½ chimney (or less) of unlit charcoal to the pile to maintain the fire if it starts to burn out.

◇◇

DRY-CURED SMOKED SALMON

If you want to take smoked salmon to the next level, this method adds a few steps to my usual technique and the results are outstanding. The process is sometimes referred to as kippering: the fillet is dry cured, then air-dried under a fan, then smoked at the lower-and-slower cooking temperature. Dry curing sucks out some of the moisture in the salmon, which creates a slightly firmer texture. As it air-dries, the dry-cured salmon develops a pellicle, a sticky protein coating that forms on the surface and allows more smoke flavor to "stick" to the fish. A pellicle may also discourage proteins in the fish from bubbling out. (If you've cooked enough salmon, you know the white stuff I'm talking about.) This method produces a buttery, bronzed slab of salmon that you'll need to approach elbows-out to fend off the hungry hordes.

I've hot smoked salmon with and without the pellicle, and both methods produce entirely edible, delicious smoked salmon. For the sake of self-discovery, I suggest buying two fillets and trying it both ways—brined (page 140) or cured, pellicle or no pellicle—then deciding which way you like it best.

FOR THE RECIPE:

1 (2- to 3-pound) center-cut salmon fillet, skin on

¼ cup Salmon Dry Cure (page 238)

FOR THE COOK:

2 glass nesting baking dishes

Aluminum foil

1 teaspoon olive oil or nonstick cooking spray

5 TO 6 HOURS BEFORE THE COOK

Place the fillet in the largest baking dish and coat the salmon with a thin, packed layer of the dry cure, pressing the mixture into the surface and sides of the fillet. (You may need to use more cure if the fillet is large.) Cover the salmon lightly with plastic wrap. Place the smaller baking dish on top of the covered fillet and add 2 to 3 pounds of weight (think: canned goods, clean bricks) to the dish to press the salmon down. (This helps the dry cure work by forcing moisture out of the salmon as it cures.) Refrigerate the weighted salmon for 4 hours.

At the 4-hour mark, you should see sticky liquid pooling around the salmon. Remove the salmon from the refrigerator and rinse it thoroughly under cold running water, gently wiping away any spices sticking to the fillet. Pat the fillet completely dry with paper towels.

Set the salmon on a cooling rack set inside a baking sheet to allow airflow around the fish. Place this setup in a cool, dry, dark place, and aim a fan set on low directly at the fish. Air-dry the fish for 1 hour or until you see a translucent sheen across the surface of the fillet. The flesh will look shiny and may feel slightly tacky to the touch. (You can also air-dry the fillet in the refrigerator, but it can take 2 hours or more to develop the pellicle.)

30 MINUTES BEFORE THE COOK

Follow the instructions for starting a lower-and-slower fire on your cooker of choice: WSM (page 38), BGE (page 39), or offset (page 39). If you're cooking on a kettle, start a KISS fire (page 33) and fill the waterpan with ice. Follow the cook instructions for Smoked Salmon (page 142).

---

5 FISH CATEGORIES

Access to fresh, quality fish and seafood varies so much depending on geography, proximity to water, and time of year. In case you need to substitute one fish for another, based on availability, it helps to know the general category of fish grouped by the density, color, and oiliness of the flesh.

DARK and oily: Anchovies, bluefin tuna, herring, mackerel, salmon, sardines, skipjack tuna

WHITE, lean, and firm: Pollock, catfish, grouper, haddock, Pacific cod, Pacific halibut, rockfish, sole, striped bass, swordfish

MEDIUM color and oily: amberjack, arctic char, coho salmon, mahi mahi, marlin, pompano, sockeye salmon, wahoo, yellowfin tuna

WHITE, lean, and flaky: Croaker, black sea bass, branzino, flounder, red snapper, tilapia, rainbow trout, whiting

WHITE, firm, and oily: albacore tuna, bluefish, Chilean sea bass, cobia, lake trout, escolar, white sturgeon

---

SMOKED SHRIMP

If I'm serving a full spread with five or six different dishes, this shrimp is always the first to disappear. You can serve this shrimp cocktail style with the Seafood Cocktail Sauce (page 252) or the Pitmaster Remoulade Sauce (page 253). Or, toss the peeled shrimp with the zippy Smoked Tomato Vinaigrette (page 264) and serve them with ripe tomatoes, pickled okra, and pickled green beans on a bed of fresh greens.

SERVES 6 TO 8

COOKER TEMPERATURE: 225°F to 250°F

COOK TIME: 15 to 30 minutes

FOR THE RECIPE:

½ gallon Basic 24-Hour Brine (page 217)

2 pounds shell-on jumbo (16/20-count) shrimp, deveined

AT THE END OF THE COOK: When the meat is slightly firm and opaque with a light orange or pink cast, the shrimp are done. If the center is still translucent or gray, continue cooking and check for doneness every 5 minutes or less. Carryover cooking will increase the temperature of the shrimp after you remove them from the cooker. It is better to pull the shrimp off of the grate when they are just barely done or slightly underdone.

1 HOUR BEFORE THE COOK

Pour the brine into a nonreactive container large enough to hold the shrimp. When the brine has cooled completely, add the shrimp. Cover the container and refrigerate for at least 30 minutes or up to 1 hour.

30 MINUTES BEFORE THE COOK

Remove the shrimp from the brine and rinse them under cold running water. Pat them dry with paper towels and return the shrimp to the refrigerator.

Start a KISS method fire according to the instructions for your cooker of choice, using half the amount of unlit charcoal and two small wood chunks or one split of wood to start: WSM (page 26), BGE (page 29), offset (page 31), or kettle (page 33).

If you are cooking on a kettle, stock the water pan with ice to help moderate the temperature on this quick cook.

WSM

◇◇

When the charcoal is engaged in the fire ring and the cooker is reassembled with the water pan in place, close the cooker and adjust the vents.

TOP VENT:

18.5-INCH MODEL: Open.

22.5-INCH MODEL: Open.

BOTTOM VENTS:

18.5-INCH MODEL: Close two vents by one third.

22.5-INCH MODEL: Close two vents halfway.

When the cooker temperature stabilizes between 225°F and 250°F, arrange the shrimp on the top grate and close the cooker.

15 MINUTES INTO THE COOK

Check the shrimp for doneness. Continue cooking if the center is still translucent or gray, but check the shrimp every 3 to 5 minutes until the meat is slightly firm and opaque.

◇◇

BGE

WHEN THE CHARCOAL is engaged, reassemble the cooker (insert the plate setter, water pan, and grate), close the lid, and adjust the vents.

TOP VENT:
Close halfway.

BOTTOM VENT:
Open ½ inch.

When the temperature stabilizes between 225°F and 250°F, arrange the shrimp on the grate and close the cooker.

15 MINUTES INTO THE COOK

Check the shrimp for doneness. Continue cooking if the center is still translucent or gray, but check the shrimp every 3 to 5 minutes until the meat is slightly firm and opaque.

OFFSET

WHEN THE CHARCOAL is engaged in the firebox and the water pan and oven thermometer are in place on the cooking grate, close the cooker and adjust the vents.

TOP VENT:
Open.

FIREBOX VENT:
Close by one third.

When the temperature stabilizes between 225°F and 250°F, arrange the shrimp on the grate and close the cooker.

15 MINUTES INTO THE COOK

Check the shrimp for doneness. Continue cooking if the center is still translucent or gray, but check the shrimp every 3 to 5 minutes until the meat is slightly firm and opaque.

KETTLE

◇◇

WHEN THE CHARCOAL is engaged in the firebox and the ice pan is in place on the cooking grate, close the cooker and adjust the vents.

TOP VENT

22-INCH MODEL: Open.

26-INCH MODEL: Open.

FIREBOX VENT:

22-INCH MODEL: Close by one third.

26-INCH MODEL: Close by one third.

When the temperature stabilizes between 225°F and 250°F, drain and restock the ice pan and arrange the shrimp on the top grate and close the cooker.

10 MINUTES INTO THE COOK

Check the shrimp for doneness. Continue cooking if the center is still translucent or gray, but check the shrimp every 3 to 5 minutes until the meat is slightly firm and opaque.

◇◇

SMOKED NEW ORLEANS-STYLE BARBECUE SHRIMP

Liuzza's by the Track is a ramshackle bar/restaurant in my coauthor's neighborhood in New Orleans, beloved for its frosty schooners of beer, bracing Bloody Marys on Jazz Fest mornings, and the signature BBQ Shrimp Po-Boy that inspired this recipe. One bite and we instantly reimagined the flavors through the prism of wood smoke.

Like a handful of other fish and seafood recipes, this is one of the few cooks where I sanction the use of wood chips. Both the sauce and the shrimp need an intense initial blast of smoke from fast-burning chips to pick up the flavor. This is a two-stage recipe. First, you'll smoke the buttery "barbecue" sauce over a lower-and-slower fire for about 30 minutes to infuse it with wood smoke. Then you'll add peeled jumbo (16/20-count) shrimp to the sauce and another handful or two of wood chips to the fire to get another blast of smoke. You can use bigger or smaller shrimp—just be sure to adjust the cook time accordingly. It will only take about 15 to 20 minutes to cook large (31/35-count) shrimp; add another 10 to 15 minutes to cook colossal (13/15-count) shrimp.

If you're using a kettle, you'll cook the sauce and shrimp over a low-and-slow fire (225°F to 250°F) for a shorter period of time. Because butter has a relatively low smoke point (as low as 265°F, depending on the brand), keep a close eye on the cooker temperature. Adjust the vents and restock the ice pan whenever the temperature starts to rise.

SERVES 6 TO 8

COOKER TEMPERATURE: 160°F to 180°F

COOK TIME: 1 hour

FOR THE BRINE:

½ gallon Basic 24-Hour Brine (page 217)

2 pounds peeled, deveined jumbo (16/20-count) shrimp

FOR THE SAUCE:

¼ cup dry white wine

3 tablespoons Worcestershire sauce

3 tablespoons minced garlic

2 tablespoons Dijon mustard

2 tablespoons freshly squeezed lemon juice

1 tablespoon crab or seafood boil, such as Zatarain's or Old Bay Seasoning

1 tablespoon Louisiana hot sauce

1 tablespoon freshly ground black pepper

1½ teaspoons guajillo chili powder

½ teaspoon dried basil

½ teaspoon dried thyme

½ teaspoon dried oregano

2 bay leaves

1 pound unsalted butter

FOR THE COOK:

4 cups wood chips, divided

3-quart disposable aluminum pan

AT THE END OF THE COOK: Remove the pan from the cooker just before the shrimp are completely done (carryover heat from the hot butter sauce will continue cooking the shrimp). When in doubt about doneness, cut one shrimp in half and inspect the center of the meat. If it is opaque white, the shrimp are done. If the center is still translucent or gray, continue cooking.

1 TO 2 HOURS BEFORE THE COOK

Pour the brine into a nonreactive container large enough to hold the shrimp. When the brine has cooled completely, add the shrimp. Cover the container and refrigerate for at least 30 minutes or up to 2 hours.

30 MINUTES BEFORE THE COOK

Omit the wood chunks (because you're using wood chips) and start a lower-and-slower fire according to the instructions for you cooker of choice: WSM (page 38), BGE (page 39), or offset (page 40).

If you're cooking on a kettle, omit the wood chunks (because you're using wood chips), and start a KISS fire (page 33) and stock the water pan with ice to help moderate the temperature for this quick cook. You do not need the "drip" pan with this cook.

WSM

WHEN THE CHARCOAL is engaged in the fire ring and the cooker is reassembled with the ice pan in place, close the cooker and adjust the vents.

TOP VENT:
18.5-INCH MODEL: Close by one third.
22.5-INCH MODEL: Close.

BOTTOM VENTS:
18.5-INCH MODEL: Close by one third.
22.5-INCH MODEL: Close halfway.

When the cooker temperature stabilizes between 160°F and 180°F, restock the pan with ice. Set the pan with the sauce on the grate and close the cooker. Open the side door and carefully pour 2 cups of wood chips over the ignited charcoal.

EVERY 15 TO 20 MINUTES IN THE COOK

Keep an eye on the cooker temperature throughout the cook. If the cooker is running below 160°F, open the top vent. Close two of the bottom vents in very slight increments if the cooker is running hotter than 180°F. Give the WSM 10 to 15 minutes to settle into the new temperature after each vent adjustment. If it is still running hotter than 180°F, adjust the third bottom vent.

When the ice pan is more than half full of water, drain and refill it with more ice.

30 MINUTES INTO THE COOK

Open the cooker and gently whisk the melted butter and sauce seasonings to blend in the aluminum pan.

Carefully pour the shrimp into the smoked butter sauce and close the cooker.

Open the side door and carefully pour the remaining 2 cups of wood chips over the ignited charcoal.

45 MINUTES TO 1 HOUR INTO THE COOK

Check the shrimp: if they are still translucent or gray, use a pair of tongs to flip them. Continue cooking and check the shrimp every 5 to 10 minutes until the shrimp are done.

BGE

WHEN THE CHARCOAL is engaged, reassemble the cooker (insert the plate setter and ice pan), close the cooker, and adjust the vents.

TOP VENT:
Close halfway.

BOTTOM VENT:
Open ½ inch.

When the temperature stabilizes between 160°F and 180°F, restock the pan with ice and carefully pour 2 cups of wood chips through the gaps around the plate setter. Set the aluminum pan with the sauce on the grate and close the cooker.

EVERY 20 MINUTES IN THE COOK

Keep an eye on the cooker temperature. Slightly open the top vent if the cooker drops below 160°F. If the temperature starts climbing higher than 180°F, close the bottom vent in ¼-inch increments. Give the BGE 10 to 15 minutes to settle into the new temperature after each vent adjustment.

When the ice pan is more than half full of water, drain and refill it with more ice.

30 MINUTES INTO THE COOK

Open the cooker. Carefully remove the pan and grate and set them on a heatproof surface. Pour the remaining 2 cups of wood chips through the gaps around the plate setter.

Return the grate and the pan to the cooker. Gently whisk the melted butter and sauce seasonings to blend. Carefully pour the shrimp into the smoked butter sauce and close the cooker.

45 MINUTES TO 1 HOUR INTO THE COOK

Check the shrimp: if they are still translucent or gray, use a pair of tongs to flip them. Continue cooking and check the shrimp every 5 to 10 minutes until the shrimp are done.

OFFSET

WHEN THE CHARCOAL is engaged in the firebox and the ice pan and oven thermometer are in place on the cooking grate, close the cooker and adjust the vents.

TOP VENTS:

Close halfway.

FIREBOX VENTS:

Close halfway.

When the temperature stabilizes between 160°F and 180°F, place the aluminum pan with the sauce in the cooker on the opposite end of the grate, away from the firebox. Close the cooker. Open the firebox and pour 2 cups of wood chips over the ignited charcoal.

EVERY 20 MINUTES IN THE COOK

Keep an eye on the cooker temperature. If it drops below 160°F, slightly open the top and firebox vents. If the temperature spikes above 180°F, slightly close the firebox vent.

When the ice pan is more than half full of water, drain and refill it with more ice.

30 MINUTES INTO THE COOK

Open the cooker and gently whisk the melted butter and sauce seasonings to blend. Carefully pour the shrimp into the smoked butter sauce. Close the cooker. Open the firebox and pour the remaining 2 cups of wood chips over the ignited charcoal.

45 MINUTES TO 1 HOUR INTO THE COOK

Check the shrimp: if they are still translucent or gray, use a pair of tongs to flip them. Continue cooking and check the shrimp every 5 to 10 minutes until the shrimp are done.

KETTLE

When the charcoal is engaged and the cooker is reassembled, with the ice pan in place, close the cooker and adjust the vents.

TOP VENT:

22-INCH MODEL: Open.

26-INCH MODEL: Open.

BOTTOM VENT:

22-INCH MODEL: Close by one third.

26-INCH MODEL: Close halfway.

When the temperature stabilizes between 225°F and 250°F, pour 1 cup of wood chips over the fire. Drain and restock the pan with ice. Set the aluminum pan with the sauce on the grate away from the fire, opposite the ice pan. Close the cooker.

EVERY 15 TO 20 MINUTES IN THE COOK

Keep an eye on the cooker temperature. If the cooker is running hotter than 250°F, close the top vent by one third (if you're using a 22-inch kettle) or by half (if you're using a 26-inch kettle).

Rotate the baking pan so the side facing the fire is turned to the outer edge of the grate, away from the fire.

When the ice pan is more than half full of water, drain and refill it with more ice.

30 MINUTES INTO THE COOK

Open the cooker and gently whisk the melted butter and sauce seasonings to blend. Carefully pour the shrimp into the smoked butter sauce. Pour 1 cup of wood chips over the ignited charcoal and close the cooker.

45 MINUTES INTO THE COOK

Check the shrimp: if they are still translucent or gray, use a pair of tongs to flip them. Continue cooking and check the shrimp every 5 to 10 minutes until the shrimp are done.

HOT SMOKE-ROASTED SOFT-SHELL CRABS

When soft-shell crabs are in season, I keep my bride happy by hot smoke-roasting them on the cooker. It's a rare treat in the Midwest, but if you live near a coast, you'll find fresh soft-shell crabs in abundance in late spring and early summer. Most recipes call for battering and deep-frying them, but I like the more straightforward approach; brush the crabs with a flavored oil or butter and hot smoke-roast them until they're bright red and crackly around the edges. The light dose of smoke contrasts beautifully with and enhances the sweetness of the crab.

You can serve the soft-shell crabs as is, with a side of grilled or smoke-roasted vegetables like asparagus, zucchini, or green beans lightly dressed in vinaigrette. I also like a smoke-roasted soft-shell crab sandwich on plain white bread. Brush the bread with the flavored oil or butter, lightly toast it, then dress the sandwich with crisp lettuce, a slice of tomato, and a slather of Old Bay Tartar Sauce (page 253).

SERVES 2 TO 4

COOKER TEMPERATURE: 325°F to 350°F
COOK TIME: 15 to 20 minutes

FOR THE RECIPEE:
6 prime (4½- to 5-inch) soft-shell crabs, cleaned

½ cup Lemon Oil Wet Rub (page 237)
or Old Bay Butter Sauce (page 254)

AT THE END OF THE COOK: When the shells are bright red, the crabs are done.

30 MINUTES BEFORE THE COOK

Start a hot smoke–roast fire according to the instructions for your cooker of choice: WSM (page 35), BGE (page 35), offset (page 35), or kettle (page 36).

WSM

WHEN THE CHARCOAL is engaged in the fire ring and the cooker is reassembled with the sand pan in place, close the cooker and adjust the vents.

TOP VENT:

18.5-INCH MODEL: Open.

22.5-INCH MODEL: Open.

BOTTOM VENTS:

18.5-INCH MODEL: Close one vent by one third.

22.5-INCH MODEL: Close one vent halfway.

Give the WSM 10 to 15 minutes to settle into a temperature. If it is running hotter than 350°F, close a second bottom vent by one third if you're using an 18.5-inch WSM or by half if you're using a 22.5-inch WSM.

When the temperature stabilizes between 300°F and 350°F, place the soft-shell crabs shell-side up on the grate and close the cooker.

10 MINUTES INTO THE COOK

Flip the crabs shell-side down and brush them with some of the Lemon Oil Wet Rub or Old Bay Butter Sauce.

15 MINUTES INTO THE COOK

Flip the crabs shell-side up and brush them again with the Lemon Oil Wet Rub or Old Bay Butter Sauce. Check for doneness and continue cooking until the shells are bright red.

BGE

◇◇◇

WHEN THE CHARCOAL is engaged and the plate setter is in place, close the cooker and adjust the vents.

TOP VENT:
Open.

BOTTOM VENT:
Open 2 inches.

Give the BGE 10 minutes to settle into a temperature. If the cooker is running hotter than 350°F, close the bottom vent by ½ inch. If the temperature doesn't drop within 10 to 15 minutes, continue to close the bottom vent in ¼-inch increments until it decreases.

When the temperature stabilizes between 300°F and 350°F, place the crabs shell-side up on the grate and close the cooker.

10 MINUTES INTO THE COOK

Flip the crabs shell-side down and brush them with some of the Lemon Oil Wet Rub or Old Bay Butter Sauce.

15 MINUTES INTO THE COOK

Flip the crabs shell-side up and brush them again with the Wet Rub or sauce. Check for doneness and continue cooking until the shells are bright red.

◇◇◇

OFFSET

WHEN THE CHARCOAL is engaged in the firebox and the sand pan and oven thermometer are in place, close the cooker and adjust the vents.

TOP VENT:
Open.

FIREBOX VENT:
Open.

Give the cooker 10 minutes to settle into a temperature. If the cooker is running hotter than 350°F, close the firebox vent by one third. If the cooker is running below 300°F, add 1 chimney of lit charcoal to the firebox.

When the temperature stabilizes between 300°F and 350°F, place the crabs shell-side up on the far end of the grate, away from the firebox, and close the cooker.

10 MINUTES INTO THE COOK

Flip the crabs shell-side down and brush them with some of the Lemon Oil Wet Rub or Old Bay Butter Sauce.

15 MINUTES INTO THE COOK

Flip the crabs shell-side up and brush them again with the Wet Rub or sauce. Check for doneness and continue cooking until the shells are bright red.

KETTLE

WHEN THE CHARCOAL is engaged on the banked piles, about 5 minutes after adding the lit charcoal, close the cooker and adjust the vents.

TOP VENT:
22-INCH MODEL: Open.
26-INCH MODEL: Open.

BOTTOM VENT:
22-INCH MODEL: Open.
26-INCH MODEL: Open.

When the temperature in the cooker has stabilized below 350°F, open the cooker and place the crabs shell-side up on the grate directly above the water pan and close the cooker.

10 MINUTES INTO THE COOK

Flip the crabs shell-side down and brush them with some of the Lemon Oil Wet Rub or Old Bay Butter Sauce.

15 MINUTES INTO THE COOK

Flip the crabs shell-side up and brush them again with the Wet Rub or sauce. Check for doneness and continue cooking until the shells are bright red.

8.

LAMB

DEAR STUDENT,

IF BEEF IS KING, THEN LAMB, DECADENT AND SUCCULENT, IS THE QUEEN OF meats to cook on a charcoal fire. Lamb elevates a backyard cookout to dining *al fresco*, so put away the paper plates and napkins—you'll want linens and china when serving a smoke-roasted rack or leg of lamb.

Cooking lamb reminds me of a point in my barbecue history when I realized that teaching is even more rewarding than being the backyard barbecue guy who can make a mean rack of ribs. I walked my friend Steve Zaransky, a great home cook and terrific barbecue guy, through the paces of hot smoke-roasting a leg of lamb on his WSM. Steve's wife is Greek, but Steve is not. If you know anything about Greeks and lamb, you understand the magnitude of this endeavor—one he willingly and voluntarily submitted to. Let's just say, Steve's first leg of lamb didn't meet the rigorous standards of a Greek woman who loves lamb. But like a true master-in-the-making, Steve cooked leg of lamb repeatedly after his first attempt, honing and refining the flavors and technique to a degree that his lamb eventually passed muster with the toughest critic and the only one who mattered. This is the joy of teaching.

If you're following the program chapter to chapter, you should be feeling a sense of familiarity with the cooks. You may view it as repetitive, and that is exactly the point. I am drilling into your system the techniques for building and maintaining airflow and a clean-burning fire on just about any type of cooker you'll ever run across in a backyard setting. What feels like repetition now will evolve into a reflex.

Keep at it.

Gary Wiviott

SMOKE-ROASTED
LEG OF LAMB

Smoke-roasted leg of lamb is one of those harbingers of spring I look forward to every year because, to me, it means the months of Midwestern snowstorms and butt-busting ice are almost over. That, and prime barbecue season is just around the corner. A leg of lamb is a rich and tender piece of meat that doesn't require a long, low-and-slow cook. It cooks quickly and is best served medium-rare. Hot smoke-roasting bathes the leg in a light layer of smoke and just enough heat to render and crisp the fat.

My favorite way to prepare a leg of lamb is to borrow techniques and flavors from a variety of ethnic cuisines and recipes. I cut small slits into the leg and turn them into spice pockets filled with aromatics anchovies and fresh herbs that infuse the meat with flavor. (You won't taste anchovy. It melts and gives the lamb a mysteriously delicious pop of umami flavor that can remain our secret.)

SERVES 12 TO 14

COOKER TEMPERATURE: 325°F to 350°F

COOK TIME: 2 to 2½ hours

FOR THE RECIPE:

1 (9- to 10-pound) leg of lamb

1 (2-ounce) tin anchovies in oil

10 garlic cloves

2 sprigs fresh rosemary

¼ cup olive oil

3 tablespoons freshly squeezed lemon juice

1 tablespoon kosher salt

1 tablespoon freshly ground black pepper

AT THE END OF THE COOK: For rare to medium-rare, pull the meat off of the cooker when the internal temperature hits 130°F to 135°F. Carryover cooking results in a final resting temperature around 140°F. Let the meat rest for 20 minutes and remove the sprigs of rosemary before slicing and serving.

1 HOUR BEFORE THE COOK

Check the length of the leg on the cooker you are using. If the leg is too long to fit the grate, use a serrated saw to cut the leg bone to fit.

Using a sharp paring knife, cut about ten deep, ½-inch-wide slits around the leg. Poke your finger into the slits to widen and loosen the pockets. Slice the anchovy fillets into thirds. Slip one garlic clove, a piece of anchovy, and several rosemary needles into each pocket. Drizzle the leg with the olive oil and lemon juice, then season it with the salt and pepper.

30 MINUTES BEFORE THE COOK

Start a hot smoke–roast fire according to the instructions for your cooker of choice: WSM (page 35), BGE (page 35), offset (page 35), or kettle (page 36).

WSM

◇◇

WHEN THE CHARCOAL is engaged in the fire ring, the water pan filled with sand is in place, and the cooker is reassembled, set the leg in the middle of the top grate. Close the cooker and adjust the vents.

TOP VENT:

18.5-INCH MODEL: Open.

22.5-INCH MODEL: Open.

BOTTOM VENTS:

18.5-INCH MODEL: Close one bottom vent by one third.

22.5-INCH MODEL: Close one bottom vent halfway.

30 MINUTES INTO THE COOK

Check the temperature of the cooker. If it is running hotter than 325°F, close a second bottom vent by one third if you're using an 18.5-inch WSM or by half if you're using a 22.5-inch WSM. Give the cooker 10 to 15 minutes to settle into the new temperature before making another vent adjustment.

EVERY 20 TO 30 MINUTES IN THE COOK

Flip the leg on the grate and keep an eye on the temperature in the cooker. Adjust the vents as needed to maintain a temperature between 300°F and 325°F.

2 HOURS INTO THE COOK

Check the temperature of the lamb with an instant-read thermometer poked into the thickest part of the meat without touching the bone. If the meat registers below the 130°F to 135°F range, continue cooking and check the internal temperature every 5 to 10 minutes until it is done.

◇◇

BGE

FIVE MINUTES AFTER adding the lit charcoal and inserting the plate setter, set the lamb in the middle of the grate. Close the cooker and adjust the vents.

TOP VENT:
Open.

BOTTOM VENT:
Open 2 inches.

EVERY 20 TO 30 MINUTES IN THE COOK

Flip the leg on the grate and keep an eye on the cooker temperature. Adjust the vents as needed to maintain a temperature between 300°F to 325°F in the cooker. If the BGE is running hotter than 325°F, close the bottom vent by ½ inch. If the temperature doesn't drop within 10 to 15 minutes, continue to close the bottom vent in ¼-inch increments, allowing 15 minutes between adjustments to allow the temperature to resettle.

2 HOURS INTO THE COOK

Check the temperature of the lamb with an instant-read thermometer poked into the thickest part of the meat without touching the bone. If the meat registers below the 130°F to 135°F range, continue cooking and check the internal temperature every 5 to 10 minutes until it is done.

OFFSET

<><><><><><><><><><><><><><><><><><><><><><><><><><><><><><><><><><><><><><>

WHEN THE CHARCOAL is engaged in the firebox and the water pan filled with sand and oven thermometer are in place, set the leg on the grate with the thickest, widest end facing the firebox. Close the cooker and adjust the vents.

TOP VENT:

Open.

FIREBOX VENT:

Open.

EVERY 20 TO 30 MINUTES IN THE COOK

Flip the leg on the grate and keep an eye on the temperature in the cooker. Adjust the vents and restock the fire as needed to maintain a temperature between 300°F and 325°F in the cooker. If the offset is running hotter than 325°F, close the firebox vent by one third. If the cooker is running below 300°F, add 1 chimney of lit charcoal and 1 split of wood to the firebox. When the charcoal engages and the fire stops billowing white smoke, about 5 minutes after restocking the cooker, close the firebox.

2 HOURS INTO THE COOK

Check the temperature of the lamb with an instant-read thermometer poked into the thickest part of the meat without touching the bone. If the meat registers below the 130°F to 135°F range, continue cooking and check the internal temperature every 5 to 10 minutes until it is done.

<><><><><><><><><><><><><><><><><><><><><><><><><><><><><><><><><><><><><><>

KETTLE

◇◇

WHEN THE CHARCOAL is engaged on the banked piles, about 5 minutes after adding the lit charcoal to the cooker, add 1 wood chunk to each pile. Set the leg on the grate directly above the water pan. Close the cooker and adjust the vents.

TOP VENT:

22-INCH MODEL: Open.

26-INCH MODEL: Open.

BOTTOM VENT:

22-INCH MODEL: Open.

26-INCH MODEL: Open.

EVERY 15 TO 20 MINUTES IN THE COOK

Rotate the leg on the grate so that all sides of the meat are exposed to the fire for an equal amount of time.

Keep an eye on the cooker temperature throughout the cook. If the cooker temperature spikes above 350°F, close the bottom vent by one third. When the coals start to burn down and the temperature in the cooker begins to drop, restock the piles with ½ chimney of lit charcoal.

1½ HOURS INTO THE COOK

Check the temperature of the lamb with an instant-read thermometer poked into the thickest part of the meat without touching the bone. If the meat registers below the 130°F to 135°F range, continue cooking and check the internal temperature every 5 to 10 minutes until it is done.

◇◇

LAMB BREAST
(AKA LAMB SPARE RIBS)

You don't see lamb breast often, but I think it's one of the better-suited meats for a smoker, and it's a relatively inexpensive cut of lamb. The name tends to throw people off. A lamb breast is the exact same cut as pork spare ribs. If you cut the breastbone (or tips) off, the trimmed 6- to 8-bone rack is called a Denver cut—just like trimmed pork spare ribs are called St. Louis style.

I treat lamb breast exactly as I do pork ribs: with a rinse of vinegar, a slather of yellow mustard, and a fairly aggressive rub to balance the fattiness of the meat.

SERVES 4 TO 6

COOKER TEMPERATURE: 225°F to 250°F

COOK TIME: 2½ to 3 hours

FOR THE RECIPE:

2 (6- to 8-bone) racks Denver-cut lamb

½ cup white vinegar

¼ cup yellow mustard

¼ cup Five Pepper Lamb Rub (page 238)

2 tablespoons olive oil

2 tablespoons freshly squeezed lemon juice

1 garlic clove, chopped

½ teaspoon kosher salt

½ teaspoon freshly ground black pepper

AT THE END OF THE COOK: Denver-cut lamb breast can take up to 3½ hours to reach the 190°F to 195°F internal temperature range, but it's tough to get an accurate temperature read on ribs because the meat is so close to the bone. To test for doneness, pick up one end of the rack with tongs, holding the rack about two ribs in. If the rack flexes and the meat splits or breaks when you bend it, the ribs are done. Brush the meat with a mix of olive oil, crushed garlic, lemon juice, salt, and freshly ground black pepper.

30 MINUTES BEFORE THE COOK

Start a KISS method fire according to the instructions for your cooker of choice: WSM (page 26), BGE (page 29), offset (page 31), or kettle (page 33).

While the charcoal is engaging, douse the lamb with the vinegar, then rinse it under cold running water. Pat the lamb dry with paper towels. Slather the lamb with mustard and coat it with an even layer of rub, about 2 tablespoons per side.

In a plastic squeeze bottle, combine the oil, lemon juice, garlic, salt, and pepper and shake vigorously to blend.

WSM

◇◇◇

WHEN THE CHARCOAL is engaged in the fire ring and the cooker is reassembled, place the racks meat-side up on the top grate, away from the outer edge. Close the cooker and adjust the vents.

TOP VENT:
18.5-INCH MODEL: Open.
22.5-INCH MODEL: Open.

BOTTOM VENTS:
18.5-INCH MODEL: Open.
22.5-INCH MODEL: Open.

15 MINUTES INTO THE COOK

Adjust the bottom vents.
18.5-INCH MODEL: Close two bottom vents by one third.
22.5-INCH MODEL: Close two bottom vents halfway.

EVERY HOUR IN THE COOK

Keep an eye on the cooker temperature. If the cooker is running hotter than 250°F, close the third bottom vent by one third if you're using an 18.5-inch WSM or by half if you're using a 22.5-inch WSM. If the 22.5-inch WSM continues to run hotter than 250°F, close the top vent by one third. It can take 10 to 15 minutes for a WSM to settle into a temperature after adjusting the vents, opening the cooker, or restocking the charcoal. Give the cooker time to settle in before making additional vent adjustments.

Check and refill the water pan as needed.

1½ HOURS INTO THE COOK

Flip the ribs meat-side down.

2½ HOURS INTO THE COOK

Flip the ribs meat-side up. Spritz the ribs with the lemon-garlic oil mixture.

Bend and flex the racks with a pair of tongs to check for doneness. The ribs will probably not be done at this point, but this check will give you an idea of how close they are. Continue cooking and start checking and spritzing the ribs every 15 to 20 minutes until they are done.

◇◇◇

BGE

<><><><><><><><><><><><><><><><><><><><><><><><><><><><><><><><><><><><><><><><><><><><><><>

FIVE MINUTES AFTER adding the lit charcoal and reassembling the cooker (plate setter, water pan, and cooking grate in place), place the racks meat-side up on the grate, away from the outer edges. Close the cooker and adjust the vents.

TOP VENT:

Close halfway.

BOTTOM VENT:

Open ½ inch.

EVERY HOUR IN THE COOK

Check the cooker temperature. If the cooker is running hotter than 250°F, close the bottom vent ¼ inch. Slightly open the top vent if the cooker is running below 225°F. Keep in mind that it can take up to 10 minutes for a BGE to settle into a new temperature after adjusting the vents or opening the cooker. Give the cooker time to settle in before making another vent adjustment.

Check and refill the water pan as needed.

1½ HOURS INTO THE COOK

Flip the ribs meat-side down.

2½ HOURS INTO THE COOK

Flip the ribs meat-side up. Spritz the ribs with the lemon-garlic oil mixture.

Bend and flex the racks with a pair of tongs to check for doneness. The ribs will probably not be done at this point, but this check will give you an idea of how close they are. Continue cooking and start checking and spritzing the ribs every 15 to 20 minutes until they are done.

<><><><><><><><><><><><><><><><><><><><><><><><><><><><><><><><><><><><><><><><><><><><><><>

OFFSET

WHEN THE CHARCOAL is engaged in the firebox and the water pan and oven thermometer are in place on the cooking grate, set the racks meat-side up in the middle of the grate. Close the lid and adjust the vents.

TOP VENT:
Open.

FIREBOX VENT:
Close by one third.

30 MINUTES INTO THE COOK

Open the firebox and set 1 split of wood on top of the lit charcoal. When the wood is engaged and stops billowing white smoke, after about 5 minutes, close the firebox.

EVERY HOUR IN THE COOK

Check and refill the water pan as needed. Swap and rotate the position of the racks so each side gets equal time away from the firebox.

Keep an eye on the grate temperature and charcoal level. If the cooker creeps higher than 275°F, make very slight adjustments to the vents: close the firebox vent halfway or close the top vent by one third.

If the cooker temperature drops below 225°F, restock the charcoal. (For detailed instructions on restocking an offset cooker, see page 32.)

1½ HOURS INTO THE COOK

While you're checking the grate temperature and water pan, flip the ribs meat-side down.

2½ HOURS INTO THE COOK

Flip the ribs meat-side up. Spritz the ribs with the lemon-garlic oil mixture.

Bend and flex the racks with a pair of tongs to check for doneness. The ribs will probably not be done at this point, but this check will give you an idea of how close they are. Continue cooking and start checking and spritzing the ribs every 15 to 20 minutes until they are done.

KETTLE

AFTER POURING LIT charcoal onto the banked pile of unlit charcoal, arrange the racks meat-side up on the cooking grate above the drip pan with the thickest bone side facing the fire. Close the cooker and adjust the vents.

TOP VENT:

22-INCH MODEL: Open.

26-INCH MODEL: Open.

BOTTOM VENT:

22-INCH MODEL: Close by one third.

26-INCH MODEL: Close halfway.

EVERY 20 TO 30 MINUTES IN THE COOK

Rotate the racks on the grate so that all sides get equal time facing the fire.

Check the cooker temperature. If the cooker temperature has dropped below 225°F, restock the cooker with ½ chimney of lit charcoal (see page 34). If the kettle is running hotter than 275°F, close the top vent by one third. Refill the water pan as needed.

1½ HOURS INTO THE COOK

After you check the grate temperature, charcoal level, and water pan, flip the ribs meat-side down.

2 HOURS INTO THE COOK

Flip the ribs meat-side up. Spritz the ribs with the lemon-garlic oil mixture.

Bend and flex the racks with a pair of tongs to check for doneness. The ribs will probably not be done at this point, but this check will give you an idea of how close they are. Continue cooking and start checking and spritzing the ribs every 15 to 20 minutes until they are done.

RACK OF LAMB

The most tender meat on a lamb is, without a doubt, the 7- or 8-bone rib section cut between the shoulder and the loin. It is rich but delicately flavored, and a hot smoke–roasted rack of lamb is one of those dead-simple, quick cooks you can pull off at the last minute with very little prep. The only real decision you have to make for this cook is: American, Australian, or New Zealand rack of lamb? Domestic rack of lamb tends to be grain-fed, fattier, and less gamey, but it is also about double the price of lamb from New Zealand or Australia. Your dinner, your call.

Whatever you choose, I recommend buying a Frenched rack of lamb, with the meat, fat, and membrane between the bones removed. Two or 3 inches of individual bones will be cleaned and visible, and it makes for a fancy, Queen of England presentation when you slice and serve it.

For the cook, you'll edge into the higher end of the hot smoke–roast range, cooking between 350°F and 375°F to ensure that there's a good bit of browned, crispy caramelization happening on the surface. To serve, slice the rack into small "lollipop" chops and drizzle with with Mint Salsa Verde (page 260). The contrast of the rich, tender lamb, the fat-crisped exterior, and the zing of this sauce is powerful and delicious.

SERVES 4

COOKER TEMPERATURE: 350°F to 375°F

COOK TIME: 25 to 30 minutes

FOR THE RECIPE:

1 (8-bone) rack of lamb

¼ cup Dijon mustard

½ teaspoon kosher salt

½ teaspoon freshly ground black pepper

2 tablespoons dried parsley

2 tablespoons chopped garlic

AT THE END OF THE COOK: For rare lamb, pull the rack off the cooker when the meat reaches 125°F to 130°F on an instant-read thermometer. For medium-rare to medium, pull it off the cooker when the meat registers around 135°F on an instant-read thermometer, and carryover cooking will bring it to about 140°F after resting. When the lamb is done, allow it to rest for 10 to 15 minutes before slicing and serving.

30 MINUTES BEFORE THE COOK

Start a hot smoke–roast fire according to the instructions for your cooker of choice: WSM (page 35), BGE (page 35), offset (page 35), or kettle (page 36).

Coat the lamb with the Dijon mustard and season it with the salt, pepper, parsley, and garlic.

WSM

WHEN THE CHARCOAL is engaged in the fire ring, the sand pan is in place, and the cooker is reassembled, close the cooker and adjust the vents.

TOP VENT:
18.5-INCH MODEL: Open.
22.5-INCH MODEL: Open.

BOTTOM VENTS:
18.5-INCH MODEL: Open.
22.5-INCH MODEL: Open.

Give the WSM 20 minutes to settle into a temperature and adjust the vents to run the cooker between 350°F and 375°F. If the cooker is running hotter than 375°F, close one bottom vent by one third if you're using an 18.5-inch WSM or by half if you're using a 22.5-inch WSM. When the temperature is stabilized, place the rack of lamb in the middle of the grate and close the cooker.

20 MINUTES INTO THE COOK

Check the temperature of the lamb with an instant-read thermometer poked into the meatiest section without touching bone. If the meat registers below the 130°F to 135°F range, continue cooking and checking the rack every 5 minutes until it is done.

BGE

FIVE MINUTES AFTER adding the lit charcoal and inserting the plate setter, close the cooker and adjust the vents.

TOP VENT:
Open.

BOTTOM VENT:
Open 2 inches.

Give the BGE 15 minutes to settle into a temperature, and then adjust the vents to run the cooker between 350°F and 375°F. If the cooker is running hotter than 375°F, close the bottom vent by ½ inch. Give the cooker 10 to 15 minutes to settle into the temperature, and then adjust the bottom vent in ¼-inch increments as needed. When the temperature is stabilized, place the rack of lamb in the middle of the grate and close the cooker.

20 MINUTES INTO THE COOK

Check the temperature of the lamb with an instant-read thermometer poked into the meatiest section without touching bone. If the meat registers below the 130°F to 135°F range, continue cooking and checking the rack every 5 minutes until it is done.

OFFSET

WHEN THE CHARCOAL is engaged in the firebox and the water pan and oven thermometer are in place, close the cooker and adjust the vents.

TOP VENT:
Open.

FIREBOX VENT:
Open.

Give the offset 15 minutes to settle into a temperature and adjust the firebox vent as needed to run the cooker between 350°F and 375°F. If the cooker is running hotter than 375°F, close the firebox vent by one third. Give the cooker 10 minutes to settle into the temperature, and then close the firebox vent halfway if the cooker is still running too hot. When the temperature is stabilized, place the rack of lamb in the middle of the grate and close the cooker.

20 MINUTES INTO THE COOK

Check the temperature of the lamb with an instant-read thermometer poked into the meatiest section without touching bone. If the meat registers below the 130°F to 135°F range, continue cooking and checking the rack every 5 minutes until it is done.

KETTLE

◇◇

WHEN THE CHARCOAL is engaged on the banked piles, about 5 minutes after adding the lit charcoal, add 1 wood chunk to each pile. Close the cooker and adjust the vents.

TOP VENT:

22-INCH MODEL: Open.

26-INCH MODEL: Open.

BOTTOM VENT:

22-INCH MODEL: Open.

26-INCH MODEL: Open.

Give the kettle 10 minutes to settle into a temperature, then adjust the bottom vent as needed to run the cooker between 350°F and 375°F. If the cooker is running hotter than 375°F, close the bottom vent by one third. If the cooker is still too hot, slightly close the top vent. When the temperature is stabilized, place the rack of lamb in the middle of the grate and close the cooker.

15 MINUTES INTO THE COOK

Check the temperature of the lamb with an instant-read thermometer poked into the meatiest section without touching the bone. If the meat registers below the 130°F to 135°F range, continue cooking and checking the rack every 5 minutes until it is done.

◇◇

7.
LAGNIAPPE

DEAR STUDENT,

NOW, IT'S TIME TO SHOW OFF. THESE ARE THE "LAGNIAPPE"—RECIPES WITH A little something extra to help you that will flex your skills and teach you new techniques that should inspire you to fire up your cooker on a weekly basis. I have one word for you: bacon. It's in here. There's also a Neapolitan-style pizza with a crackly, blistered crust so good, you'll want to devote a month of weekends to perfecting your technique. (I know I did.) And fair warning: the porchetta, a rolled pork belly roast, is so gorgeous and delicious that you'll post pictures of it like it was your first born. In all, these are a few blow-your-mind cooks you never imagined you or your cooker would be capable of.

Enjoy!

Gary Wiviott

Gary Wiviott

PITMASTER PORCHETTA

When you've been playing with fire and barbecue as long as I have, it's always a treat to work up a unique dish that hits every note in a pitch-perfect pork symphony. This is that dish—a low-and-slow reconfiguration of porchetta, the traditional Italian rolled and stuffed pork roast. Every bite is a commotion of texture and flavor: the spicy, crackly outer shell of pork belly gives way to a juicy, herb-wrapped tenderloin, and the whole package is wrapped in a light layer of smoke.

When adapted for charcoal cooking, porchetta is not a set-it-and-forget-it kind of cook, and there's a bit of handiwork involved in preparing the roast. You'll dry cure the skinless pork belly for up to 24 hours, brine the tenderloin, then roll and tie the two into a meat torpedo. In the final stage, after a low-and-slow cook, you'll pull the meat off the cooker at just the right point, then blast the roast in a 450°F oven to finish rendering and crisping the belly.

There are too many variables that can make the skin chewy instead of crispy, so I recommend using a skinless belly, which crisps beautifully. You'll find inexpensive, whole pork bellies at the meat counter in many Asian and ethnic markets; gourmet markets or butcher shops generally sell trimmed bellies at a higher price. If you buy a whole belly, ask the butcher to cut one piece of the belly into a neat, 12-inch rectangle and remove the skin. You can use the remaining piece of skin-on belly to make bacon (page 193).

Don't even think about serving this dish without Salsa Verde (page 259) on the side—it's a must. Just be sure you're sitting down when you take the first bite. It's a knockout.

SERVES 12 TO 14

COOKER TEMPERATURE: 225°F to 250°F
COOK TIME: 3½ to 4 hours

FOR THE RECIPE:

1 (12-inch) pork belly section, skin removed

⅓ cup plus 6 tablespoons Porchetta Spice Rub (page 239), divided

½ gallon Basic 24-Hour Brine (page 217)

1 (1- to 2-pound) pork tenderloin

⅓ cup roughly chopped fresh flat-leaf parsley

2 tablespoons roughly chopped fresh rosemary

FOR THE COOK:

1 metal cooling rack

1 large, rimmed baking sheet

Kitchen twine

Roasting rack

AT THE END OF THE COOK: When the temperature at the center of the tenderloin hits the 140°F to 145°F range, remove the meat from the cooker and place it on a roasting rack set in the baking sheet. Transfer this setup to the center rack of the preheated oven and roast until the skin is deeply browned and crisp, about 20 minutes. Keep a close eye on the roast as it crisps to avoid burning the skin.

Remove the roast from the oven and let it rest for 15 to 20 minutes before slicing. To serve, carefully slice the roast into ½-inch rounds using a serrated knife, and drizzle with Salsa Verde.

12 TO 24 HOURS BEFORE THE COOK

Set the belly fat-side up on a clean work surface. Using a sharp paring knife, score the fat in a ¼-inch-deep diamond crosshatch pattern, with the slits 1 to 1½ inches apart. Cut deep into the fat, but avoid cutting too close to the layer of meat.

Sprinkle both sides of the pork belly with ⅓ cup of the rub and work the rub into the slits. Lay the belly fat-side up on a cooling rack set inside a large, rimmed baking sheet to allow airflow around the belly. Refrigerate, uncovered, to air-dry the belly for up to 24 hours.

2 HOURS BEFORE THE COOK

Pour the Basic 24-Hour Brine into a medium nonreactive container. Stir in 3 tablespoons of rub to infuse the brine. When the brine has cooled completely, add the tenderloin. Cover the container and refrigerate for up to 2 hours.

1 HOUR BEFORE THE COOK

Remove the tenderloin and pork belly from the refrigerator. Rinse the tenderloin under cold running water and pat it dry with paper towels. Lay the pork belly fat-side down on a clean work surface. Sprinkle the meat side of the belly with an even layer of the parsley and rosemary. Place the tenderloin vertically at one end of the belly, and roll the belly tightly around the tenderloin. Using kitchen twine, tie butcher's knots at ½-inch intervals along the roast. Trim any excess twine. Sprinkle the outside of the roast with the remaining 3 tablespoons of rub.

Let the roast sit at room temperature for up to 1 hour.

30 MINUTES BEFORE THE COOK

Start a KISS method fire according to the instructions for your cooker of choice: WSM (page 26), BGE (page 29), offset (page 31), or kettle (page 33).

WSM

WHEN THE CHARCOAL is engaged in the fire ring and the cooker is reassembled, place the tied roast seam-side down on the top grate. Close the cooker and adjust the vents.

TOP VENT:
18.5-INCH MODEL: Open.
22.5-INCH MODEL: Open.

BOTTOM VENTS:
18.5-INCH MODEL: Open.
22.5-INCH MODEL: Open.

20 MINUTES INTO THE COOK

Adjust the bottom vents.
18.5-INCH MODEL: Close all bottom vents by one third.
22.5-INCH MODEL: Close all bottom vents halfway.

EVERY HOUR IN THE COOK

Keep an eye on the cooker temperature. If the WSM is running hotter than 250°F or drops below 225°F for more than 10 minutes, troubleshoot the fire. Check the vent closures—all three bottom vents should be closed by one third if you're using an 18.5-inch WSM or by half if you're using a 22.5-inch WSM. Be sure there are no stray pieces of charcoal blocking the bottom vents.

If the 22.5-inch WSM continues to run hotter than 250°F, close the top vent by one third. Before you adjust the vents again, give the cooker 10 to 15 minutes to settle into a temperature.

Check the water pan and refill it whenever half of the water has evaporated.

3 HOURS INTO THE COOK

Check the temperature of the roast with an instant-read thermometer poked into the middle of the meat at the center of the tenderloin. This check is to establish how close the tenderloin is to the 140°F to 145°F range. Start checking the meat every 10 to 20 minutes until it is done.

About 20 minutes before the roast is ready, preheat the oven to 450°F with an oven rack in the middle position.

BGE

◇◇

WHEN THE CHARCOAL is engaged and the plate setter and water pan are in place, set the roast seam-side down in the middle of the grate. Close the lid and adjust the vents.

TOP VENT:	**BOTTOM VENT:**
Close halfway.	Open ½ inch.

30 MINUTES INTO THE COOK

Check the cooker temperature. If the BGE is running hotter than 250°F, close the bottom vent in ¼-inch increments to lower the temperature in the cooker. If it is running below 225°F, slightly open the top vent.

It can take up to 10 minutes for a BGE to settle into a new temperature after adjusting the vents or opening the cooker. Give the cooker time to settle before making another vent adjustment.

EVERY HOUR IN THE COOK

Keep an eye on the cooker temperature. At the 1-hour mark, the BGE should settle somewhere between 225°F and 250°F, and stay there for the remainder of the cook. If the cooker creeps higher than 250°F or drops lower than 225°F for more than 10 minutes, make very slight adjustments to the top or bottom vent. Adjust vents one at a time and wait 10 to 15 minutes before adjusting another vent to give the cooker time to settle in.

Check and refill the water pan as needed.

3 HOURS INTO THE COOK

Check the temperature of the roast with an instant-read thermometer poked into the center of the tenderloin. This check is to establish how close the tenderloin is to the 140°F to 145°F range. Start checking the meat every 10 to 20 minutes until it is done.

About 20 minutes before the roast is ready, preheat the oven to 450°F with an oven rack in the middle position.

OFFSET

XXXXXXXXXXXXXXXXXXXXXXXXXXXXXXXXXXXXXXXXXXXXXXXXXXXXXXXXXXXXXXXXXXXXXXX

WHEN THE CHARCOAL is engaged in the firebox and the water pan and oven thermometer are in place on the cooking grate, set the roast vertically on the far end of the cooking grate, seam-side down, away from the firebox. Close the lid and adjust the vents.

TOP VENT:
Open.

FIREBOX VENT:
Close by one third.

30 MINUTES INTO THE COOK

Open the firebox and set 1 split of wood on top of the lit charcoal. When the wood is engaged and stops billowing white smoke, after about 5 minutes, close the firebox.

EVERY HOUR IN THE COOK

Roll the roast in quarter turns on the grate so that all sides spend an equal amount of time facing the firebox.

Keep an eye on the grate temperature and charcoal level. If the offset creeps higher than 275°F for more than 10 minutes, close the firebox vent halfway or close the top (damper) vent by one third. If the cooker temperature drops below 225°F, assess the fire. If the unlit charcoal is not engaging, you may need to slightly open the firebox vent to increase airflow. Or, you may need to restock the charcoal. (For detailed instructions on restocking an offset cooker, see page 32.)

Add 1 split of wood to the charcoal at every restock from the 1-hour mark to the 2-hour mark. When the charcoal and wood are engaged and stop billowing white smoke, about 5 minutes after each restock, close the firebox.

Check and refill the water pan as needed.

3 HOURS INTO THE COOK

Check the temperature of the roast with an instant-read thermometer poked into the center of the tenderloin. This check is to establish how close the tenderloin is to the 140°F to 145°F range. Start checking the meat every 10 to 20 minutes until it is done.

About 20 minutes before the roast is ready, preheat the oven to 450°F with an oven rack in the middle position.

KETTLE

WHEN THE CHARCOAL is engaged, about 5 minutes after pouring lit charcoal onto the pile, set the roast on the cooking grate above the drip pan, seam-side down. Close the cooker and adjust the vents.

TOP VENT:

22-INCH MODEL: Open.

26-INCH MODEL: Open.

BOTTOM VENT:

22-INCH MODEL: Close by one third.

26-INCH MODEL: Close halfway.

EVERY 30 TO 45 MINUTES IN THE COOK

Roll the roast in quarter turns on the grate so that all sides spend equal time facing the fire.

Check the cooker temperature. If the kettle temperature has dropped below 225°F, restock with ½ chimney of lit charcoal (see page 34) and 1 wood chunk if the wood has burned out. If the kettle is running hotter than 275°F, close the top vent by one third. Refill the water pan as needed.

2½ HOURS INTO THE COOK

Check the temperature of the roast with an instant-read thermometer poked into the center of the tenderloin. This check is to establish how close the tenderloin is to the 140°F to 145°F range. Start checking the meat every 10 to 20 minutes until it is done.

About 20 minutes before the roast is ready, preheat the oven to 450°F with an oven rack in the middle position.

SMOKED FRESH HAM

Fresh or "green" ham is uncured and uncooked, and if you've only ever eaten the precooked variety, get ready for a sliced ham binge. A light layer of smoke paired with a flavorful wet rub really transforms this ham. For the wet rub, I suggest using either the Lemon-Rosemary (page 240) or the Chinese Five-Spice (page 240).

The most common fresh hams are cut from two parts of the pig: the classic ham (aka rump or butt), which is cut from the top end of the back leg, and the front-end "picnic" ham, which is cut from the shoulder. For my time and money, I prefer a 7- to 8-pound skinless, bone-in picnic ham because it has more fat on it, but a similar size butt ham will work for this cook, too. If your ham has skin on it, you can cook it as is, but the low-and-slow temperature isn't conducive to crisping skin. You'll need to score it, then remove it after the cook. If you're ambitious, reseason the trimmed skin and crackle it on a baking sheet at 350°F in an oven or on your cooker.

If you're worried about the ham drying out, or if you want to amp up the flavor, brine the ham for 12 to 24 hours in the Basic 24-Hour Brine (page 217) supplemented with ¼ cup of ingredients that echo the rub you use. Or, toss other ham-friendly herbs and spices into the brine, like cloves, thyme, bay leaf, Dijon mustard, or soy sauce. For a sweeter, more classic flavor, you can substitute honey for sugar in the brine.

SERVES 12 TO 14

COOKER TEMPERATURE: 225°F to 250°F

COOK TIME: 6 to 7 hours

FOR THE RECIPE:

1 (7- to 8-pound) fresh picnic ham

½ cup cider vinegar

⅓ cup wet rub of your choice (pages 225 to 240)

AT THE END OF THE COOK: The smoked ham is done when the internal temperature hits 170°F on an instant-read thermometer and a two-tined meat fork slides into the meat with little resistance.

UP TO 24 HOURS BEFORE THE COOK

Douse the ham with the cider vinegar, then rinse it in cold water. Using a sharp paring knife, score the ham all over in a crosshatch diamond pattern. Coat the meat evenly with the wet rub, and work the rub deep into the scored slits. Cover the ham and keep it in the refrigerator until 30 minutes before the cook.

30 MINUTES BEFORE THE COOK

Remove the ham from the refrigerator to allow it to reach room temperature.

Start a KISS method fire according to the instructions for your cooker of choice: WSM (page 26), BGE (page 29), offset (page 31), or kettle (page 33).

WSM

◇◇◇

WHEN THE CHARCOAL is engaged in the fire ring and the cooker is reassembled, place the ham in the middle of the top grate with the thickest layer of fat facing up. Close the cooker and adjust the vents.

TOP VENT:	BOTTOM VENTS:
18.5-INCH MODEL: Open.	**18.5-INCH MODEL:** Open.
22.5-INCH MODEL: Open.	**22.5-INCH MODEL:** Open.

30 MINUTES INTO THE COOK

Adjust the bottom vents.

18.5-INCH MODEL: Close all bottom vents by one third.

22.5-INCH MODEL: Close all bottom vents halfway.

EVERY HOUR IN THE COOK

Keep an eye on the cooker temperature. If the WSM is running hotter than 250°F or drops below 225°F for more than 10 minutes, troubleshoot the fire. Check the vent closures are correct. Be sure there are no stray pieces of charcoal blocking the bottom vents.

If the 22.5-inch WSM continues to run hotter than 250°F, close the top vent by one third. Give the cooker 10 to 15 minutes to settle into a temperature after adjusting the vents, opening the cooker, or restocking the charcoal.

Check and refill the water pan whenever half of the water in the pan has evaporated. The 18.5-inch model's water pan needs to be topped off every 3 to 4 hours. The 22.5-inch model can run for as long as 6 to 7 hours with one pan of water.

3 HOURS INTO THE COOK

Flip the ham fat-side down.

5½ HOURS INTO THE COOK

Flip the ham fat-side up. Check the temperature of the ham with an instant-read thermometer poked deep into the meat without touching the bone. This checkpoint is your reference to see how close the meat is to 170°F.

6 HOURS INTO THE COOK

Start checking the meat every 20 to 30 minutes and remove the ham from the cooker when the internal temperature hits 170°F.

BGE

WHEN THE CHARCOAL is engaged and the plate setter and water pan are in place, set the ham in the middle of the grate with the thickest layer of fat facing up. Close the lid and adjust the vents.

TOP VENT:

Close halfway.

BOTTOM VENT:

Open ½ inch.

30 MINUTES INTO THE COOK

Check the cooker temperature. If the BGE is running hotter than 250°F, close the bottom vent in ¼-inch increments. If it's running below 225°F, slightly open the top vent. It can take up to 10 minutes for a BGE to settle into a new temperature after adjusting the vents or opening the cooker. Give the cooker time to settle before making another vent adjustment.

EVERY HOUR IN THE COOK

Keep an eye on the cooker temperature. By the 1-hour mark, the BGE should settle somewhere between 225°F and 250°F, and it should stay there for the remainder of the cook. If the cooker creeps higher than 250°F or drops lower than 225°F for more than 10 minutes, make very slight adjustments to the top or bottom vent. Adjust vents one at a time and wait 10 to 15 minutes before adjusting another vent to give the cooker time to settle in.

Check and refill the water pan as needed.

3 HOURS INTO THE COOK

Flip the ham fat-side down.

5½ HOURS INTO THE COOK

Flip the ham fat-side up. Check the temperature of the ham with an instant-read thermometer poked deep into the ham without touching the bone. This checkpoint is your reference to see how close the meat is to 170°F.

6 HOURS INTO THE COOK

Start checking the meat every 20 to 30 minutes and remove the ham from the cooker when the internal temperature hits 170°F.

OFFSET

◇◇

WHEN THE CHARCOAL is engaged in the firebox and the water pan and oven thermometer are in place on the cooking grate, set the ham on the far end of the cooking grate away from the firebox, with the thickest layer of fat facing up and the thickest side facing the heat. Close the lid and adjust the vents.

TOP VENT:
Open.

FIREBOX VENT:
Close by one third.

30 MINUTES INTO THE COOK

Open the firebox and set 1 split of wood on top of the lit charcoal. When the wood is engaged and stops billowing white smoke, after about 5 minutes, close the firebox.

EVERY HOUR IN THE COOK

Keep an eye on the grate temperature and charcoal level. If the cooker creeps higher than 275°F for more than 10 minutes, close the firebox vent halfway or close the top (damper) vent by one third. If the cooker temperature drops below 225°F, assess the fire. If the unlit charcoal is not engaging, you may need to slightly open the firebox vent to increase airflow. Or, you may need to restock the charcoal. (For detailed instructions on restocking an offset cooker, see page 32.)

Add 1 split of wood to the charcoal at every restock between the 1-hour mark and the 3-hour mark. When the charcoal and wood stop billowing white smoke, about 5 minutes after each restock, close the firebox.

Check and refill the water pan as needed.

3 HOURS INTO THE COOK

Flip the ham fat-side down.

5½ HOURS INTO THE COOK

Flip the ham fat-side up. Check the temperature of the ham with an instant-read thermometer poked deep into the meat without touching the bone. This checkpoint is your reference to see how close the meat is to 170°F.

6 HOURS INTO THE COOK

Start checking the meat every 20 to 30 minutes and remove the ham from the cooker when the internal temperature hits 170°F.

KETTLE

◇◇

WHEN THE CHARCOAL is engaged, about 5 minutes after pouring lit charcoal onto the pile, set the ham on the cooking grate directly above the drip pan, with the thickest layer of fat facing up. Close the cooker and adjust the vents.

TOP VENT:

22-INCH MODEL: Open.

26-INCH MODEL: Open.

BOTTOM VENT:

22-INCH MODEL: Close by one third.

26-INCH MODEL: Close halfway.

EVERY 30 TO 45 MINUTES IN THE COOK

Keep an eye on the temperature. If the cooker drops below 225°F, restock with ½ chimney of lit charcoal and 1 wood chunk if the wood is burned out. If the kettle is running hotter than 275°F, close the top vent by one third.

Refill the water pan as needed.

Rotate the ham on the grate so that the three meatiest, thick sides of the ham alternate time facing the fire.

2 HOURS INTO THE COOK

Flip the ham fat-side down.

4½ HOURS INTO THE COOK

Flip the ham fat-side up. Check the temperature of the ham with an instant-read thermometer poked deep into the meat without touching the bone. This checkpoint is your reference to see how close the meat is to 170°F.

5 HOURS INTO THE COOK

Start checking the meat every 20 to 30 minutes and remove the ham from the cooker when the internal temperature hits 170°F.

◇◇

FOUR-PEPPER CURED BACON

What can be said about bacon that hasn't already been said before? I could tell you about the smoky, fatty, spicy, peppery perfection of this bacon, and how it is better than any thick-cut, high-quality bacon you've ever spent too much money on. But here's something you don't often hear about making your own bacon: it is incredibly and embarrassingly easy. This process fits my "benign neglect" philosophy to a tee. You'll rub a pork belly with cure and spices, practically ignore it in the refrigerator for one week, then smoke it for a few hours at a lower-and-slower temperature. Slice it, pan-fry it, and boom, you're done.

The pepper rub is my favorite blend for bacon because I like the contrast of heat, spice, and the unusual, bright note of coriander—it's one of those can't-put-your-finger-on-it flavors that makes this bacon unique. But you are free to mess around with the rub elements to suit your taste. Your bacon, your call. I aim for about ¼ cup to ⅓ cup of rub seasonings per belly, or less if the herbs or spices are very pungent.

The bacon will cure in 6 to 8 days, depending on the thickness of the pork belly. A thin, inexpensive pork belly will cure faster than a thick, "gourmet" belly you buy at a specialty meat market. When you poke the belly and it feels stiff instead of spongy or soft, the belly is cured and ready to smoke. I rarely recommend a specific type of wood for smoking, but I do prefer apple or hickory wood for this cook to give it that classic, smoky bacon flavor.

MAKES 3 TO 5 POUNDS

COOKER TEMPERATURE: 160°F to 180°F
COOK TIME: 2½ to 3 hours

FOR THE RECIPE:

1 (4- to 5-pound) pork belly with skin attached

⅓ cup Master Cure (page 68)

1½ teaspoons freshly ground black pepper

1½ teaspoons red pepper flakes

1 teaspoon ground coriander

1 teaspoon coarsely ground Szechuan pepper

½ teaspoon cayenne pepper

2 tablespoons pure maple syrup (preferably grade B)

AT THE END OF THE COOK: The bacon is done smoking when the internal temperature hits 150°F. While the bacon is still warm but cool enough to handle, carefully remove the tough, outer skin with a very sharp knife. When the meat has cooled, wrap the bacon tightly in plastic wrap and chill it completely in the refrigerator or freezer before slicing.

1 WEEK BEFORE THE COOK

Place the belly skin-side up on a cutting board. Score the skin in a 2-inch diamond crosshatch pattern with a very sharp paring knife. Cut all the way through the tough outer skin and slightly into the layer of fat under the skin, but avoid slicing into the meat.

Spread the Master Cure in a light, even layer over both sides of the belly, pressing the mixture into the slits in the skin and sides of the belly. Be sure that all exposed surfaces of the belly are evenly coated in a layer of the cure. In a small bowl, combine the black pepper, red pepper flakes, coriander, Szechuan pepper, and cayenne, and whisk to blend. Coat both sides of the belly with the spice mix and work it into the slits. Drizzle and rub the maple syrup on both sides of the belly.

Place the meat in a zip-top bag that is just big enough to fit the belly. It should lay flat in the bag with minimal excess space and easily zip closed to seal. Refrigerate the belly for 6 to 8 days, flipping the bag daily so that both sides are exposed to the cure solution.

1 TO 2 DAYS BEFORE THE COOK

Poke the belly and assess the level of curing. If the belly is still soft and pliable, allow it to cure for another day or two. For comparison, "soft and pliable" is what it feels like when you poke the fleshy part of your palm at the base of your thumb when your hand and fingers are loose and resting. Poke the same spot when your hand and fingers are extended taut. This is what "cured" feels like.

When the belly is cured, remove it from the bag and rinse it thoroughly under cold running water. Pat the belly completely dry with paper towels. At this point, if you're not ready to smoke the pork belly, you can place it on a cooling rack set inside a rimmed baking sheet and let it air-dry in the refrigerator, uncovered, for 2 or 3 days. The extra day or so of air-drying gives the belly a stickier surface for smoke to adhere to, like the pellicle on Dry-Cured Smoked Salmon (page 146). Or, you can smoke it immediately.

30 MINUTES BEFORE THE COOK

Start a lower-and-slower fire according to the instructions for your cooker of choice: WSM (page 38), BGE (page 39), or offset (page 40). The bacon will last up to 10 days wrapped in the refrigerator, or up to 3 months in the freezer.

WSM

<><><><><><><><><><><><><><><><><><><><><><><><><><><><><><><><><><><><><><><>

WHEN THE CHARCOAL is engaged in the fire ring and the cooker is reassembled with the ice pan in place, close the cooker and adjust the vents.

TOP VENT:

18.5-INCH MODEL: Close.

22.5-INCH MODEL: Close.

BOTTOM VENTS:

18.5-INCH MODEL: Close all vents by one third.

22.5-INCH MODEL: Close all vents halfway.

When the cooker temperature stabilizes between 160°F and 180°F, set the cured belly skin-side up on the grate and close the cooker.

EVERY HOUR IN THE COOK

Keep an eye on the cooker temperature. If the cooker is running below 160°F, open the top vent. Close two of the bottom vents in very slight increments if the cooker is running hotter than 180°F. Give the WSM 10 to 15 minutes to settle into a temperature after vent adjustments. If it is still running above 180°F, adjust the third bottom vent.

Restock the pan with ice as needed. When the pan is more than half full of water, drain and refill it with more ice.

2 HOURS INTO THE COOK

Add 2 wood chunks to the fire.

Check the temperature of the pork belly with an instant-read thermometer poked into the middle of the meat. This checkpoint is your reference to see how close the meat is to the target internal temperature of 150°F.

Check the charcoal level. This charcoal setup should run steady for up to 3 hours, but you may need to restock the fire if the charcoal is running low or if the temperature in the cooker is dropping. If the fire needs restocking, add 2 wood chunks and ½ chimney of unlit charcoal to the fire ring. Give the fire and wood 10 minutes to engage the charcoal before reassembling or closing the cooker.

2½ HOURS INTO THE COOK

Start checking the internal temperature every 20 to 30 minutes based on your first reading, and remove the bacon from the cooker when it registers 150°F.

BGE

◇◇

WHEN THE CHARCOAL is engaged and the plate setter and ice pan are in place, close the cooker and adjust the vents.

TOP VENT:	**BOTTOM VENT:**
Close halfway.	Open ½ inch.

When the cooker temperature stabilizes between 160°F and 180°F, set the cured pork belly skin-side up on the grate and close the cooker.

EVERY HOUR IN THE COOK

Keep an eye on the cooker temperature and adjust the vents as needed to maintain the heat between 160°F and 180°F. Slightly open the top vent if the cooker is running below 160°F. If the cooker is running hotter than 180°F, close the bottom vent ¼ inch. Give the BGE 10 to 15 minutes to settle into a new temperature before making another adjustment.

When the ice pan is more than half full of water, drain and refill it with more ice.

2 HOURS INTO THE COOK

Add 3 to 4 wood chunk slivers to the fire. (The pieces need to be small enough to fit through the gaps around the plate setter.)

Check the temperature of the pork belly with an instant-read thermometer poked into the center of the meat. This checkpoint is your reference to see how close the meat is to the target temperature of 150°F.

2½ HOURS INTO THE COOK

Start checking the internal temperature every 20 to 30 minutes based on your first reading, and remove the bacon from the cooker when it registers 150°F on an instant-read thermometer.

OFFSET

∞∞∞

WHEN THE CHARCOAL is engaged in the firebox and the ice pan and oven thermometer are in place on the cooking grate, close the cooker and adjust the vents.

TOP VENT:
Close halfway.

FIREBOX VENT:
Close halfway.

When the cooker temperature stabilizes between 160°F and 180°F, set the pork belly skin-side up at the far end of the cooking grate away from the firebox and close the cooker.

EVERY 30 TO 45 MINUTES IN THE COOK

Keep an eye on the cooker temperature and adjust the vents as needed to maintain the heat between 160°F and 180°F. If the cooker temperature spikes above 180°F, slightly close the firebox vent. If the cooker temperature drops below 160°F, assess the fire. If the unlit charcoal isn't engaging, you may need to slightly open the firebox vent to increase airflow. If most of the charcoal is glowing or burned through, restock the fire with ½ chimney of unlit charcoal and 1 small split of wood (or 2 wood chunks). Give the fire 5 to 10 minutes to engage after restocking with unlit charcoal before closing the firebox.

2 HOURS INTO THE COOK

Check the temperature of the pork belly with an instant-read thermometer poked into the center of the meat. This checkpoint is your reference to see how close the meat is to the target temperature of 150°F.

2½ HOURS INTO THE COOK

Start checking the internal temperature every 20 to 30 minutes based on your first reading, and remove the bacon from the cooker when it registers 150°F on an instant-read thermometer.

∞∞∞

NEAPOLITAN-STYLE PIZZA

If you want to master Neapolitan-style pizza on a charcoal cooker, you must devote yourself to it. It takes a lot of practice and more than a few burned pies to get the hang of it. To achieve my pizza nirvana breakthrough, it only took about 100 pies. When it happened, time slowed down. I could feel the interaction of the individual ingredients. The heat of the fire, the heft of the cornmeal-speckled dough, the acidity and viscosity of the sauce, the precision and ratio of toppings to crust. It all finally clicked. And, my friends, once you have that breakthrough moment, you'll know what I mean. You will be rewarded with blistered, crackly-crusted pizzas that could threaten the top dog status of your perfectly-smoked brisket.

A word of caution about toppings: there's a fine line between delicious and excessive. These thin-crust pizzas are difficult to handle and will collapse under the weight of too many toppings. Err on the side of less (around ¼ cup of toppings total), and choose high-quality ingredients that pack a lot of flavor.

Your success with this cook hinges on two things: your ability to make a great pizza dough and your ability to build and maintain a searing-hot 500°F charcoal fire on the BGE. (As a brisket is on a kettle, this task is more difficult and prone to disaster on any other cooker.) Follow the steps, follow your instincts, and don't give up.

MAKES 6 TO 7 10-INCH PIZZAS

COOKER TEMPERATURE: 500°F to 525°F

COOK TIME: 4 to 6 minutes

FOR THE RECIPE:

1 recipe Pizza Dough (recipe follows)

½ cup cornmeal, divided

2 cups Red Sauce of your choice, recipe follows

Pizza toppings of your choice

Olive oil, for brushing the crust

FOR THE COOK:

Long-handled pizza peel

1 damp kitchen towel

Long-handled metal tongs

Cooling rack

1 large rimmed baking sheet

Pizza stone

30 MINUTES BEFORE THE COOK

Prepare and light one full chimney of charcoal. While the charcoal is engaging, fill the BGE firebox and fire ring with charcoal—you want to fit as much charcoal as you can in the cooker, filling it just below the grooves for the plate setter.

When the charcoal in the chimney is fully engaged, carefully pour it into the fire ring. Keep the cooker open for about 5 minutes to give the fire time to engage. Wearing a pair of heavy-duty heatproof gloves, set the plate setter inside the cooker with the "feet" down, resting in the grooves on the fire ring. Place the pizza stone on top of the plate setter.

Close the cooker and adjust the vents.

DAMPER VENT:
Open.

BOTTOM VENT:
Open.

When the cooker temperature hits 500°F, close the bottom vent by 1 inch. You'll need to stabilize the temperature between 500°F and 525°F, which will require some tinkering with the bottom and damper vents. Give the cooker 10 minutes to settle into a new temperature before making additional adjustments, then open or close the vents in ¼-inch increments as needed to increase or decrease the heat. The more open the vents are, the hotter the BGE will burn.

IMPORTANT SAFETY NOTE: HOW TO BURP YOUR BGE

When the BGE is running over 400°F, a quick blast of air can cause a major backdraft or flare-up when you open the cooker. Any time your BGE is running at a high temperature, such as when you are making pizzas, before you open the lid completely you must first burp the cooker by slightly opening and shutting the lid several times (just an inch or two) to allow air slowly into the cooker.

10 TO 15 MINUTES BEFORE THE COOK

While the cooker is getting to the pizza-hot zone, prepare the first pie. Sprinkle the pizza peel with 1 tablespoon cornmeal. Gently transfer your first disk of stretched dough onto the pizza peel. Smear the pizza with ¼ cup (or less) of sauce, then dot it with your toppings of choice. (Be careful not to overload the pie with sauce and toppings, or it will buckle under the weight.) Brush the crust with olive oil.

When the temperature in the cooker is stabilized, burp the BGE (see sidebar). Quickly wipe the pizza stone with the wet towel, then scatter about 1 tablespoon of cornmeal over the pizza stone. Carefully shake the pizza from the peel onto the stone. The cornmeal should act like tiny ball bearings to roll the pie onto the stone. Once the pie is on the stone, close the cooker immediately. It should take 5½ to 6 minutes to cook the pizza at 500°F to 525°F. Check the pie at the 4-minute mark to see how close it is and whether the dough is cooking evenly. If one side is cooking faster, use the tongs to rotate the pie.

When the pizza is ready, use the tongs to pull the pizza onto the prepared cooling rack/baking sheet setup. (If you drop a smoking-hot pie onto a cutting board or plate, the crust you just spent at least 24 hours working on will get soggy. You want airflow around the pie so that it cools evenly.) As soon as the pizza is cool enough to handle, use a pair of sharp scissors or a rolling cutter to slice it.

Repeat the process with the remaining dough and toppings.

PIZZA DOUGH

It is my pseudo-scientific observation that beginners will burn one in four pies. Like the first pancake on a hot griddle, the first pizza on a hot pizza stone is the worst, but they get progressively better as you go. That's why this recipe makes enough dough for six or seven pies. You've got enough dough to burn a few and nail a few. You can also refrigerate leftover dough for up to 5 days, or freeze it for future use. Or, cut the dough recipe in half as you improve your technique.

For this dough, I use a cold rise method, which allows the yeast in the dough to ferment at a slower rate. A longer fermentation improves the texture and structure of the dough tremendously. The second rise/proofing takes about 2 hours—remember to factor this into your cook plan. Make the dough in the morning if you want pizza for dinner, or give it a full 24 to 48 hours in the fridge. The dough keeps for up to 5 days in the refrigerator.

MAKES 6 TO 7 10-INCH PIZZA CRUSTS

FOR THE RECIPE:

2 cups warm water

2 (¼-ounce) packages active dry yeast

4½ to 5 cups unbleached all-purpose flour, divided

¼ cup olive oil, plus more for brushing

1 teaspoon kosher salt

⅓ cup cornmeal

Combine the water, yeast, and 3 cups of the flour in the bowl of an upright stand mixer fitted with the paddle attachment. Mix until the ingredients are well combined.

Scrape the paddle clean and replace it with the dough hook attachment. With the mixer running on low, add the oil, salt, and cornmeal.

Gradually add the remaining 1½ to 2 cups flour in small amounts until the dough forms a mass that hardly sticks to the bowl as it kneads. Occasionally scrape down the sides of the bowl to release any dough that is sticking. If the dough gets too sticky, add 1 tablespoon of flour at a time. You might not need to use all of the flour. Add it slowly, and err on the side of using less flour and producing a wetter dough. Knead the dough with the hook for approximately 5 minutes after the dough ball has formed.

Place the dough on a lightly floured surface and continue kneading it with your hands until the dough begins to turn smooth and silky. If the dough becomes sticky while you are kneading it, sprinkle it with ½ teaspoon of flour and continue kneading.

Knead the dough for about 10 minutes, until the dough feels smooth and bouncy, then form the mass into a large ball. Hold the ball at shoulder height and slam it on the work surface. Reform the ball and repeat this dough "thunking" 7 to 8 times or until the ball has a glossy, silky texture. (This may seem like an odd technique, but slamming the dough on the work surface helps to develop the gluten. Gluten makes the dough smoother and more elastic, which makes it less prone to tearing when you're forming it into pizza rounds.)

After kneading, once the dough takes on a noticeably glossy, silky appearance, transfer the dough to a lightly oiled bowl or two-gallon zip-top bag. Cover the bowl with plastic wrap or seal the bag, and refrigerate the dough for at least 10 hours, or up to 5 days.

About 2 hours before you plan to make the pizzas, remove the dough from the refrigerator. Transfer the dough to a lightly floured work surface and dust the top with additional flour. Using a dough scraper, divide the dough into uniform pieces, about 6 ounces each or the size of a baseball. Shape each piece into a ball, tucking the dough under at the bottom. If the dough begins to stick, dust your hands with flour.

If you do not plan to use all of the dough, return the extra dough balls to the oiled plastic bag or covered bowl and refrigerate. The dough will last for up to 5 days in the refrigerator, or up to 2 months in the freezer in a heavy-duty zip-top bag.

Brush the top of each dough ball with olive oil, and place in separate oiled bowls. Cover each bowl tightly with plastic wrap and allow the dough to rise at room temperature for 1½ to 2 hours. (The dough should almost double in size.)

When the dough has risen, transfer it to a lightly floured work surface and dust the top with flour. Flatten the ball with the palm of your hand, then carefully stretch the dough into a 10-inch circle with your fingertips. Remember to leave the edges slightly thicker than the center to form the crust.

If the dough contracts as you're stretching it, it is too elastic to handle. Let the dough sit longer, about 10 minutes, before you continue stretching it. I don't recommend the palm-to-palm twist and toss stretching you see pizzeria guys doing. This is a different type of dough, and you risk overworking it and tearing holes in the disc. Stretch the dough until you create a 10-inch disk.

Transfer the dough disk to the prepared pizza peel and follow the instructions at 10 to 15 minutes before the Cook (page 199).

RED SAUCE

It doesn't get any more basic than this sauce—it's the perfect balance of light, bright acidity and aromatic herbs with just a pinch of heat. If it's too mild, bump up the amount of garlic, oregano, or pepper to taste. You can also add one or two peeled, puréed smoked tomatoes (page 263). Use about ¼ cup of sauce per 10-inch pie.

MAKES 6 CUPS

FOR THE RECIPE:

2 (28-ounce) cans tomato purée

2 teaspoons dried oregano

2 large garlic cloves, minced

8 fresh basil leaves

½ teaspoon red pepper flakes

½ teaspoon granulated sugar

1 bay leaf

Combine all of the ingredients in a large, heavy, nonreactive saucepan over medium-high heat. Cover the pan and bring the mixture to a boil. As soon as the sauce boils, uncover the saucepan, reduce the heat to low, and simmer the sauce for 30 minutes, stirring occasionally.

Store the sauce in an airtight container for up to 1 week in the refrigerator, or for up to 2 months in the freezer.

8.

SIDE DISHES

DEAR STUDENT,

ALTHOUGH THE FOCUS OF THIS BOOK IS PRIMARILY ON MEAT, SMOKE, AND FIRE control, you can't make a meal of only perfectly smoked brisket or smoke-roasted leg of lamb (although it would be tasty). This collection of sides is a glimpse into the dishes I like to serve whenever I fire up a cooker. Many of the recipes include smoked ingredients, and I think of smoke as an ingredient itself. It is a wonderful flavoring agent, but you can have too much of a good thing. Err on the side of light and subtle when you are looking for dishes to serve with smoked meats. Even if you're not using smoked ingredients in a side dish, take advantage of the fire while it's burning to smoke onions, tomatoes, peppers, spices, oils, and other ingredients you can use in future meals and recipes.

Enjoy!

Gary Wiviott

GRILLED CORN

Summer in the Midwest means fresh sweet corn, and in my world, the corn is best grilled. Cooked over hot coals, shucked corn on the cob chars and produces mouthfuls of crispy, sweet, and nutty kernels all in one bite. Only buy it when it's in season (grilling will make old or out-of-season corn very tough), and always buy more than you think you and your guests can possibly eat. The leftovers (if there are any) can be cut and milked from the cob and used in Macque Choux with Smoked Tomatoes & Corn (page 207).

MAKES 6 EARS, ABOUT 4 CUPS OF CUT KERNELS

FOR THE RECIPE:

6 ears of fresh corn

2 tablespoons olive oil

Remove the husks and silk from the corn. Rinse the corn and let it soak in a pot of cold water until you are ready to cook. Before grilling, rub each ear of corn with a thin layer of oil.

Set up your cooker for direct-heat grilling and let the coals burn down until they are glowing and covered in ash. Place 1 wood chunk on the hottest glowing coals in the fire. When the wood engages and the billowing clouds of smoke die down, after about 5 minutes, place the corn on the grate above the fire. Rotate and turn the corn frequently to prevent burning, but allow the fire to char the corn in some places. The corn will be cooked in 3 to 5 minutes.

If you are eating it on the cob, hot off the grill, sprinkle each ear with a pinch of salt or the rub of your choice. If you are using the corn in another recipe, wait until it is cool enough to handle, then, using a sharp knife, shave the kernels off of the cob into a bowl. Use the back of the knife to scrape the corn cob over the bowl to extract the milk and pulp.

SMOKED ELOTES

This is decadent Mexican street food at its best: creamy, spicy, cheesy, and messy. Serve it alongside light, citrusy seafood dishes, like Smoked Whole Fish (page 133). You can serve it on the cob (cut the cobs in half for appetizer portions), or shave the kernels off of the cob and toss the corn with the crumbly cheese and a dressing made with crema, lime juice, chili powder, and fresh cilantro.

SERVES 6

FOR THE RECIPE:

½ cup Mexican crema or sour cream

¼ cup mayonnaise

1 teaspoon guajillo chili powder, divided

¼ cup finely chopped fresh cilantro,
  plus more for garnish

½ cup finely crumbled Cotija cheese or queso
  anejo, plus more for garnish

6 ears of grilled corn (page 205)

1 lime, cut into 6 wedges

Combine the crema, mayonnaise, ½ teaspoon of the guajillo chili powder, and the cilantro in a medium bowl. Stir to combine.

While the grilled corn is still warm, use a pastry brush to "paint" the corn with the crema mixture. Garnish each cob with a layer of crumbly Cotija cheese and chopped cilantro and a light dusting of guajillo chili powder. Serve each cob with a wedge of lime.

MACQUE CHOUX WITH SMOKED TOMATO & CORN

This classic dish from south Louisiana is an excellent side to serve with seafood and poultry main dishes, particularly shrimp and grits or Smoked Turkey (page 45). It's also the kind of recipe you can fiddle with to no end: add sliced, sautéed okra to the mix, serve it alone or over rice, or add smoked, diced chicken or sausage.

SERVES 6 TO 8

FOR THE RECIPE:

2 tablespoons bacon fat or unsalted butter

1 cup diced yellow onions

½ cup chopped red or green bell pepper

1 tablespoon minced jalapeño pepper

1 teaspoon kosher salt or rub of choice

6 ears of grilled corn, kernels removed and milk extracted (page 205)

1 cup (about 4) smoked tomatoes (page 263)

½ cup heavy cream or whole milk

Melt the bacon fat or butter in a large, heavy-bottomed skillet over medium heat. Add the onions, bell pepper, jalapeño, and salt or rub to the skillet and cook for 3 minutes, stirring occasionally with a wooden spoon. Add the corn (including the milk and pulp) and tomatoes to the skillet and use the spoon to break the tomatoes into smaller pieces. Cook the mixture over medium heat for 10 minutes, stirring occasionally. Stir in the cream and cook for 2 more minutes, until warm. Taste and adjust the seasonings as necessary before serving.

POTATO SALAD WITH
SMOKY CREOLE MUSTARD

Backyard cookouts and potato salad go hand in hand. For added flavor, instead of boiling, you can smoke-roast the cut potatoes until they are fork tender, about 1 hour.

SERVES 4 TO 6

FOR THE RECIPE:

3 pounds medium red potatoes, scrubbed and cut into 1-inch pieces

1 tablespoon kosher salt

⅓ cup mayonnaise

⅓ cup sour cream

⅓ cup smoked Creole Mustard (page 262)

½ teaspoon Gary Wiviott's Beef Rub (page 232)

½ teaspoon granulated sugar

5 slices cooked bacon, 1 tablespoon of fat reserved

1½ cups diced tomatoes

2 tablespoons thinly sliced scallions

Place the potatoes and salt in a large pot and fill the pot with enough cold water to completely cover the potatoes. Bring the water to a boil over high heat, then reduce the heat to low and simmer until the potatoes are fork tender, about 20 minutes. Drain the potatoes.

While the potatoes are boiling, whisk together the mayonnaise, sour cream, mustard, rub, sugar, and bacon fat in a large mixing bowl.

Pour the drained, warm potatoes into the bowl with the dressing. Add the tomatoes, bacon, and scallions, and gently toss to coat.

Cover and refrigerate the salad for at least two hours before serving. Serve chilled. The potato salad can be stored in an airtight container in the refrigerator for up to 5 days.

HUSH PUPPIES
WITH CHARRED JALAPEÑOS

A tip of the hat to the late "Big Jim" Whitten in Florida, a true barbecue man I had the honor of knowing in the early days of my low and slow learning. He passed away in 2014, and he was one of the greats—little known by all but the most devoted barbecue men. On a table piled high with glorious meat at annual Q-Fest gatherings, his hush puppies managed to stand out. The trick, he told me, is to use fresh baking powder. I've added my own touches, but the technique and spirit of this recipe is 100 percent Big Jim. RIP, friend.

FOR THE RECIPE:

4 jalapeño peppers

2 cups cornmeal

½ cup all-purpose flour

2 teaspoons baking powder

1 tablespoon granulated sugar

¼ teaspoon kosher salt

½ teaspoon Gary Wiviott's Beef Rub (page 232), or a spicy rub your choice

1 large egg, beaten

¾ cup whole milk

4 scallions, finely chopped (white and green parts)

Vegetable oil, for frying

Char the jalapeños over a hot, direct fire until the skin is blackened and blistered. Stem, seed and roughly chop the jalapeños. Sift together the cornmeal, flour, baking powder, sugar, salt, and rub into a large bowl. Using a wooden spoon, gently fold in the egg and milk. Add the scallions and jalapeños and stir just until they are incorporated in the batter. Over mixing the batter will make the hush puppies tough. Let the batter rest at room temperature for 20 minutes to allow the cornmeal to absorb the liquid. The batter should be thick enough to drop in spoonfuls, but not too dry. If it looks dry or too thick, gently stir in more milk or water to loosen the batter.

Clip a candy or deep-fry thermometer to the inside of a heavy pot that is at least 6 inches deep (like a 6-quart Dutch oven), and heat 2 to 3 inches of oil to 375°F. If the oil is not hot enough, the hush puppies will absorb too much oil. You will need to adjust the heat throughout the cook to maintain a steady 375°F.

Drop 1 tablespoon of the batter into the hot oil using two oiled spoons or an ice-cream/cookie scoop. Repeat with the remaining batter, but only fry four or five hush puppies at a time to avoid crowding and lowering the oil temperature. When one side is fried to golden brown, use a slotted spoon or wooden chopstick to flip the hush puppies and fry the other side. When the hush puppies are cooked, transfer them to a paper towel–lined platter to drain. Serve warm.

OKRA SAUTÉ

This is one of my wife's all-time favorites—a side dish I serve with everything from brisket to smoked turkey. You can also serve this as a main course over rice or pan-fried slices of polenta.

FOR THE RECIPE:

2 tablespoons olive oil

1 medium yellow onion, diced

3 garlic cloves, minced

½ teaspoon red pepper flakes

1 pound mushrooms, sliced

1 pound small okra, stems removed, sliced in half lengthwise

3 large tomatoes or 5 smoked tomatoes (page 263), roughly chopped, juices reserved

2 teaspoons soy sauce

¼ cup water or chicken stock

1 tablespoon unsalted butter

1 tablespoon freshly squeezed lemon juice

Salt and freshly ground black pepper

Heat the oil in a medium saucepan over medium heat, and sauté the onion and garlic until the onion is translucent, about 5 minutes. Add the red pepper flakes, mushrooms, okra, tomatoes, soy sauce, and water or stock. Cover the pan and simmer until the okra are tender, about 20 minutes. If the okra are still not tender at this point, add more water, cover the pan, and simmer for another 5 minutes.

When the okra are tender, increase the heat to medium high. Stir in the butter and lemon juice, and season with salt and pepper. Serve immediately or store in an airtight container in the refrigerator for up to 2 days.

BARBECUE-BAKED POTATOES

This is a side dish that risks out-doing the main dish in effort and richness, so pair it wisely with a meat that doesn't require a lot of prep or fuss, like rib-eye steak, Smoke-Roasted Beef Tenderloin (page 127), or Smoked Turkey (page 45). If you don't have the time or yen to smoke the potatoes (which will take more than an hour), nuke the potatoes in a microwave for 10 to 15 minutes until they are tender, then finish by browning the stuffed potatoes on the cooker for a more subtle smoke flavor.

SERVES 8

FOR THE RECIPE:

4 large russet potatoes

1 tablespoon vegetable oil

1 teaspoon kosher salt or dry rub of your choice

CHEESE SAUCE:

3 tablespoons unsalted butter

¼ cup diced white onion

1 teaspoon kosher salt

1 teaspoon freshly ground black pepper

3 tablespoons all-purpose flour

2¼ cups whole milk, at room temperature

½ cup grated white Cheddar cheese, at room temperature

6 strips cooked bacon, chopped

¼ cup chopped scallions

Scrub the potatoes clean with a stiff-bristled brush under cold running water, then pat them dry with paper towels. Coat the potatoes with the oil and season with the salt or dry rub. Place the potatoes on the grate of a cooker set for low-and-slow cooking (225°F to 250°F) or hot smoke-roasting (300°F to 350°F). Refresh the fire with 1 wood chunk if the wood from the initial setup is burned through. Smoke the potatoes until fork-tender, about 2 hours at a low-and-slow temperature or 1 hour at a hot smoke–roast temperature, depending on the size of the potatoes.

While the potatoes are smoking, prepare the cheese sauce: Melt the butter in a medium saucepan over medium heat. Add the onion, salt, and pepper; cook until the onion is translucent, about 3 minutes. Sprinkle the flour over the onions and whisk the mixture to combine. Use the whisk to break up any lumps and incorporate the flour into the butter to form a paste. Cook, whisking constantly, until the roux is pale yellow and frothy, about 2 minutes. (If the paste starts to brown, reduce the heat to low.) Slowly stir in the milk, whisking steadily to prevent lumps.

Continue whisking, and increase the heat to medium high. Bring the mixture to a boil, stirring frequently to prevent scorching on the bottom. Simmer the sauce until it has thickened, 2 or 3 minutes, then remove the pan from the heat. Stir in the grated cheese until it has melted completely and the sauce is smooth. Taste and adjust the seasonings as needed.

When the potatoes are fork tender, remove them from the cooker and allow them to rest until they are cool enough to handle. Using a sharp knife, slice ¼ inch off of the long side of the potatoes. With a spoon, carefully scoop the pulp from the potatoes into a medium mixing bowl, leaving about ¼ inch of flesh and the skin intact. If you want a rustic, chunky filling, mash the pulp to your desired consistency with the back of a fork. If you want a smoother filling, use a potato ricer to mash the potatoes. (Be careful when mashing. The potato will turn thick and gluey if you mash it too much.) Add the cheese sauce, scallions, and bacon to the potato and stir to blend. Taste the mixture and adjust the seasonings as needed. Divide the cheesy potato mixture among the potato shells.

Add 1 wood chunk to the fire in the cooker and open the vents to increase the temperature in the cooker to 300°F to 350°F. After the wood engages and the billowing clouds of smoke die down, place the stuffed potatoes directly on the grate of the cooker and cook them until the tops are lightly browned and the skins are crisped, about 30 minutes. Carefully remove the potatoes from the cooker with a large spatula and serve them warm.

SOUPY RANCH BEANS

These tasty beans are a staple of Texas Hill Country BBQ joints and abuelita *kitchens south of the border. You can cheat and use 2 (15-ounce) cans of pinto beans (including the liquid), but the beans will not have nearly the same depth of flavor and, more importantly,* abuelita *would not approve.*

FOR THE BEANS:

1 pound dry pinto beans, sorted and rinsed

3 quarts water

½ yellow onion, chopped

½ teaspoon ground cumin

½ teaspoon ground coriander

1 bay leaf

½ teaspoon freshly ground black pepper

FOR THE SEASONING:

1 tablespoon olive oil

5 slices bacon, chopped

½ white onion, diced

2 jalapeños, diced

4 garlic cloves, chopped

4 medium tomatoes, roughly chopped

1 teaspoon ground cumin

½ teaspoon guajillo chili powder

½ teaspoon ground coriander

½ teaspoon kosher salt

6 ounces (¾ cup) Mexican beer

To cook the beans, combine the beans, water, onion, cumin, coriander, bay leaf, and black pepper in heavy-bottomed, 12-quart pot over high heat. Bring the water to a boil, then reduce the heat to low and simmer for 2 to 3 hours, or until the beans are tender.

To make the seasoning, heat the olive oil in a large skillet over medium-high heat, and sauté the bacon, onion, jalapeños, and garlic until the onion starts to turn translucent, but not brown, about 3 minutes. Reduce the heat to medium and add the tomatoes, cumin, chili powder, coriander, and salt. Cook the mixture until the tomato liquid starts to evaporate.

When the beans are tender, add the sautéed vegetable mixture to the pot, then return the empty skillet to the stove over medium heat. Pour the beer into the skillet and scrape up any brown bits from the bottom of the pan. Remove the skillet from the heat and pour the beer mixture into the pot with the beans and vegetables. Stir to combine and cook the beans over medium heat until the flavors meld, about 10 minutes. The beans should be soupy. Add more water or beer as needed, and season with salt, black pepper, and chili powder before serving.

Garnish the beans with fresh cilantro, queso fresco, diced raw white onion, and/or diced jalapeños.

NOT SALT LICK COLESLAW

My wife loves this coleslaw, which is a riff on the famous Texas barbecue joint's beloved recipe. The sesame seeds are unusual for a Texas barbecue side that dates back to the 50s, and many people credit Hisako Roberts, the Japanese wife of the founder Thurman Roberts, for this and other distinctive flavors at Salt Lick.

SERVES 6 TO 8

FOR THE RECIPE:

¾ cup white vinegar

¼ cup granulated sugar

½ tablespoon kosher salt

⅛ teaspoon freshly ground white pepper

1 head of cabbage, shredded

1 carrot, shredded

3 scallions, thinly sliced on the diagonal (white and green parts)

⅛ cup vegetable oil

2 tablespoons sesame oil

¼ teaspoon celery seeds

¼ cup toasted sesame seeds

In a medium nonreactive saucepan over medium-high heat, bring the vinegar to a boil, then slowly add the sugar and salt, stirring constantly, until they are completely dissolved, about 1 minute. Remove the pan from the heat.

Place the white pepper in a medium bowl. Slowly whisk the warm vinegar mixture into the pepper. Cover the bowl and refrigerate the vinegar mixture until chilled, at least 30 minutes.

In a large mixing bowl, toss together the cabbage, carrot, scallions, vegetable oil, sesame oil, celery seeds, and sesame seeds until thoroughly mixed. When you are ready to serve the slaw, pour the chilled vinegar dressing over the cabbage mixture and toss to combine. Serve immediately, while the slaw is cold and crisp.

9.

BRINES

& MARINADES

DEAR STUDENT,

BRINES AND MARINADES INFUSE MEAT WITH MOISTURE AND FLAVOR, WHICH IS important when you're cooking with charcoal because even a clean-burning, controlled fire can result in overcooked, dry meat. Brining uses a strong salt/water solution to force moisture into meat by osmosis, and it is an essential in low and slow cooking because it makes the meat juicier and less prone to drying out. If you add extra seasoning (herbs, spices) to brine, those flavors are also absorbed into the meat. Marinades use a strong acidic component (citrus, vinegar) that coats and flavors the outer layer of the meat. Although the salt solution in a marinade can also lightly brine meat by the same chemical reaction, marinades are primarily about external flavoring.

As you experiment with brines and marinades, remember: you can pair a brine or marinade with a rub that has complementary flavors, but if you plan to use an aggressive rub, there's no point getting fancy with the brine or marinade—subtle flavors will be lost and strong flavors can clash.

Enjoy!

Gary Wiviott

BASIC 24-HOUR BRINE

Think of this brine as a template—a base recipe that works perfectly on its own, but one you can also customize to create nuances of flavor. Add up to ⅓ cup of various seasonings and spices per gallon of liquid, but be judicious with aggressive or acidic ingredients like citrus or hot chile peppers. This brine recipe makes more than enough to completely immerse a whole 12- to 14-pound turkey, a couple of ducks or chickens, or several pounds of fish or seafood in a large container, with brine to spare. You can easily cut the recipe in half if you are brining smaller quantities of food.

MAKES 2 GALLONS

2 gallons water, divided	⅔ cup light brown sugar, packed
1 cup kosher salt	

In a stock pot or large sauce pan over medium-high heat, combine 2 quarts of the water with the salt and brown sugar. Bring the mixture to a low boil and stir until the salt and brown sugar are completely dissolved. Remove the pot from the heat.

In a nonreactive 4-gallon container, combine the concentrated brine with the remaining 1½ gallons of water and allow the mixture to cool. When the brine is completely cool, submerge the meat in the liquid, cover the container, and refrigerate for up to 24 hours.

LAZY BRINE

There are times when you need to slam it together and get the meat in a brine so you can focus on more important cooking tasks. No spice cabinet is complete without Old Bay seasoning, and the classic seafood boil flavor works surprisingly well with poultry, as well as with fish or seafood.

MAKES 2 GALLONS

2 gallons water, divided	⅔ cup light brown sugar, packed
1 cup kosher salt	½ cup Old Bay seasoning

In a stock pot or large sauce pan over medium-high heat, combine 2 quarts of the water with the salt, brown sugar, and Old Bay seasoning. Bring the mixture to a low boil and stir until the salt and brown sugar are completely dissolved. Remove the pot from the heat.

In a nonreactive 4-gallon container, combine the concentrated brine with the remaining 1½ gallons of water and allow the mixture to cool. When the brine is completely cool, submerge the meat in the liquid, cover the container, and refrigerate for up to 24 hours.

BASIC BUTTERMILK BRINE

I love the distinct twang buttermilk gives to poultry, and it creates a great foundation for whatever additional herbs and spices you want to add. The second list of ingredients creates my favorite go-to buttermilk brine for turkey and chicken (particularly Smoky Low & Slow Wings, page 62). The kick from the hot sauce is subtle, and the other flavors complement it perfectly.

MAKES 2 GALLONS

1 gallon water, divided

1 cup kosher salt

⅔ cup light brown sugar

1 gallon (4 quarts) buttermilk

¼ cup molasses or dark cane syrup

¼ tablespoon freshly ground black pepper

4 tablespoons Louisiana-style hot sauce, such as Tabasco or Crystal

2 tablespoons garlic powder

2 tablespoons onion powder

1 teaspoon ground coriander

2 teaspoons ground allspice

In a stock pot or large sauce pan over medium-high heat, combine 2 quarts of the water with the salt and brown sugar. Bring the mixture to a low boil and stir until the salt and brown sugar are completely dissolved. Remove the pot from the heat.

In a nonreactive 4-gallon container, combine the concentrated brine with the buttermilk and the remaining 2 quarts of water. If you are making my amped-up brine, stir in the molasses, black pepper, hot sauce, garlic powder, onion powder, coriander, and allspice. Allow the mixture to cool. When the brine is completely cool, submerge the meat in the liquid, cover the container, and refrigerate for up to 24 hours.

BUTTERMILK & HERB BRINE

Steeping fresh herbs in hot brine retains the bright, potent flavor of the herbs—a flavor that gets a boost from the zing of buttermilk. You can save it for your next Thanksgiving turkey, or try it on a batch of smoked chicken quarters or legs for a picnic.

MAKES 2 GALLONS

1 gallon water

1 cup kosher salt

⅔ cup light brown sugar, packed

5 sprigs fresh thyme

5 sprigs fresh flat-leaf parsley

5 fresh sage leaves

1 gallon (4 quarts) buttermilk

In a stock pot or large sauce pan over medium-high heat, combine 2 quarts of the water with the salt, brown sugar, thyme, parsley, and sage. Bring the mixture to a low boil and stir until the salt and brown sugar are completely dissolved. Reduce the heat to low and allow the mixture to simmer for 10 minutes, until the water turns light green. Remove the pot from the heat. Strain the liquid through a fine-mesh sieve into a nonreactive 4-gallon container and discard the herbs. Pour the buttermilk and the remaining 2 quarts of water into the container with the concentrated brine, and allow the mixture to cool. When the brine is completely cool, submerge the meat in the liquid, cover the container, and refrigerate for up to 24 hours.

BOURBON BRINE

Because everything is better with bourbon. Plus, adding a small amount of booze to a brine works with the salt to loosen up the proteins in meat, which will make your turkey, chicken, or duck even juicier.

MAKES 2 GALLONS

1½ gallons (6 quarts) water

1 cup kosher salt

⅔ cup light brown sugar, packed

6 to 8 bay leaves

1 tablespoon whole black peppercorns

Zest of 2 lemons

½ gallon (2 quarts) apple cider

1 cup bourbon

In a stock pot or large sauce pan over medium-high heat, combine 2 quarts of the water with the salt, brown sugar, bay leaves, peppercorns, and lemon zest. Bring the mixture to a low boil and stir until the salt and brown sugar are completely dissolved. Remove the pot from the heat.

In a nonreactive 4-gallon container, combine the concentrated brine with cider, bourbon, and the remaining 1 gallon of water, and allow the mixture to cool. When the brine is completely cool, submerge the turkey in the liquid, cover the container, and refrigerate for up to 24 hours.

TERIYAKI WING MARINADE

The provenance of this wing marinade is in dispute—it may belong to my wife's sister, Rita, or it may be my wife Ellen's. But I only live with one of those women, and she does a terrific job with these wings. Although the marinade works just fine on Smoky Low & Slow Wings (page 62), I prefer it on wings headed for a hot smoke roast (page 57)—just be careful to keep the cooker at 350°F or below to prevent the sugar in the marinade from burning.

MAKES 2½ CUPS

2 cups light or dark brown sugar, packed

1 cup soy sauce

1 cup chopped scallions

¼ cup minced garlic

3 tablespoons toasted sesame oil

2 tablespoons grated fresh ginger

¾ cup white sesame seeds

In a container large enough to fit all of the wings (or whatever meat you intend to marinate), combine the brown sugar, soy sauce, scallions, garlic, sesame oil, and ginger and whisk until the mixture is blended. Add the wings to the marinade and toss to coat. Cover the container and refrigerate the wings for 3 to 4 hours. Stir the wings every hour to redistribute the marinade. Before hot smoke-roasting, sprinkle the wings with the sesame seeds.

MIDDLE EASTERN YOGURT MARINADE

Ron Kaplan, aka Ronnie_Suburban in Chicago, is a friend and all-around terrific cook. This marinade is one of his signature greats, a recipe I turn to often when I'm smoking chicken and other poultry or lamb. This marinade makes enough to coat a whole butterflied turkey, but you can cut the recipe in half if you're smoking chicken halves, quarters, legs, or thighs. Use this marinade in lieu of brining.

MAKES ABOUT 5 CUPS

4 cups plain, whole-milk Greek yogurt

8 garlic cloves, crushed

Juice of 4 lemons (about ¾ cup)

3½ tablespoons kosher salt

4 teaspoons freshly ground black pepper

4 teaspoons whole coriander seeds, freshly ground

4 teaspoons ground turmeric

Combine all of the ingredients in an airtight container large enough to fit the turkey or chicken. Whisk the mixture to blend. Marinate your choice of poultry for a minimum of 6 hours or overnight for a whole turkey and 3 to 6 hours for chicken parts.

LEMON-DILL MARINADE

This is a terrific marinade for Smoke-Roasted Leg of Lamb (page 165) or Smoke-Roasted Beef Tenderloin (page 126). Pour it into a zip-top bag or container large enough to hold the meat. Refrigerate the marinating meat for 3 to 4 hours for smaller cuts or at least 5 hours or up to 24 hours if you are marinating a leg of lamb. Flip the bag or stir the marinade often to redistribute the liquid.

MAKES ABOUT 2¼ CUPS

1 cup dry red wine

½ cup freshly squeezed lemon juice

1 cup chopped fresh dill

2 tablespoons fresh oregano leaves

1 tablespoon kosher salt

2 teaspoons mustard powder

⅔ cup olive oil

In a medium bowl, whisk together the wine, lemon juice, dill, oregano, salt, and mustard powder. Slowly drizzle in the oil as you whisk the mixture to emulsify.

HONEY-SOY MARINADE

This spicy, sweet, and savory blend is a barbecue guy's riff on Jacques Pepin's classic summer lamb. Slather the mixture over a leg of lamb and let it marinate for 2 to 4 hours in the refrigerator, turning the leg every hour to redistribute the marinade.

MAKES 3¾ CUPS

1 medium onion, quartered

4 garlic cloves

1-inch piece fresh ginger, peeled and sliced

1 jalapeño pepper, stemmed, seeded and quartered

¼ cup soy sauce

1 tablespoon freshly squeezed lemon juice

1 teaspoon freshly grated lemon zest

¼ cup honey

3 cups olive oil

½ teaspoon guajillo chili powder

Combine the onion, garlic, ginger, and jalapeño in a food processor and pulse the mixture until the pieces are roughly chopped and approximately the same size. Add the soy sauce, lemon juice, lemon zest, honey, olive oil, and guajillo powder to the mixture and process until smooth. Store the marinade in an airtight container in the refrigerator for up to 1 week.

GARLIC-ROSEMARY MARINADE

The fresh garlic and citrus echo the flavors of Chimichurri Sauce (page 250), which makes this a good match for the Tri-Tip cook (page 121). But think of this as an all-purpose marinade you can use on turkey (page 45), or even in lieu of brining the pork tenderloin for the Pitmaster Porchetta (page 181).

MAKES ABOUT ¾ CUP

½ cup olive oil

8 garlic cloves, finely chopped

2 teaspoons dried rosemary

Zest and juice of 1 lemon

½ tablespoon kosher salt

½ tablespoon freshly ground black pepper

In a medium bowl, whisk together the olive oil, garlic, rosemary, lemon zest and juice, salt, and pepper. Place the meat in a 1-gallon zip-top bag and pour in the marinade. Seal the bag and turn and roll the meat to coat it in the marinade. Place the bag in the refrigerator and allow the meat to marinate for at least 2 hours, or up to 8 hours. Let the meat reach room temperature in the marinade before cooking.

FIERY HARISSA MARINADE

Harissa is a Tunisian chili pepper paste made from a variety of sweet and spicy peppers and spices like coriander and cumin. Compared to the heat of a habañero, it's not a very spicy condiment and is often used as a straight-up rub on grilled meats. Paired with lime and garlic, the flavor takes on a brighter, fruity heat in this marinade, and I like to use it on Hot Smoke–Roasted Tri-Tip (page 121) or Smoke-Roasted Beef Tenderloin (page 126).

MAKES ABOUT ¾ CUP

¼ cup harissa paste

¼ cup canola oil (or other neutral vegetable oil)

4 tablespoons cider vinegar

1 teaspoon kosher salt

½ teaspoon freshly ground black pepper

3 garlic cloves, minced

Juice of 1 lime

1 teaspoon freshly grated lime zest

In a medium bowl, whisk together all of the ingredients. Place the meat in a 1-gallon zip-top bag and pour in the marinade. Seal the bag and turn and roll the meat to coat it in the marinade. Place the bag in the refrigerator and allow the meat to marinate for at least 2 hours, or up to 8 hours. Let the meat reach room temperature in the marinade before cooking

10.
RUBS

DEAR STUDENT,

WET AND DRY RUBS ARE ANOTHER WAY TO APPLY FLAVOR AND TEXTURE TO smoked meats. The following recipes are my favorites, but feel free to use them as guidelines for building your own repertoire of signature rubs. Start playing with the Flavor and Grind (page 14), and mix coarse, medium, and fine grinds of the same spice or herb to produce different layers and textures of flavor. Dig deeper into flavor affinities to find new, interesting herb and spice pairings. (*The Flavor Bible*, by Karen Page and Andrew Dornenburg, is a great resource for inspiration.)

Enjoy!

Gary Wiviott

ALL-PURPOSE RUB

The flavor profile of my rubs will almost always skew spicy. I love the depth and complexity of combining different dried, freshly ground Mexican chiles. I have every one of these ingredients on hand at all times in my kitchen, and this rub is something I can throw together simply by scooping or pinching from a row of prep bowls within arm's reach.

MAKES ABOUT ½ CUP

¼ cup Toasted Mexican Chile Blend (page 15)

2 tablespoons kosher salt

1 tablespoon freshly ground black pepper

½ tablespoon dried thyme

½ tablespoon mustard powder

Combine all of the ingredients in a medium bowl and stir until blended. Store the rub in an airtight container at room temperature for up to 1 month.

CITRUS-HERB RUB

Smear this over and under the skin of turkey or chicken headed for the cooker—the bright, fresh citrus notes make a great counterpoint to the flavor of wood smoke.

MAKES 1 CUP

2 tablespoons chopped fresh thyme

2 tablespoons chopped fresh rosemary

2 tablespoons olive oil

2 teaspoons kosher salt

2 teaspoons freshly ground black pepper

4 garlic cloves, chopped

Zest and juice of 1 orange

Zest and juice of 1 lemon

Combine all of the ingredients in a medium bowl and whisk until blended. Use this rub immediately, or within 3 to 4 hours of blending the ingredients. The citrus juice will break down and change the flavor of the fresh herbs after several hours.

SZECHUAN FIVE-SPICE RUB

This rub is no joke. It delivers serious heat, but it's a winner on brined, hot smoke–roasted duck or turkey served with Ginger-Scallion Sauce (page 243).

MAKES ABOUT ⅔ CUP

4 tablespoons Chinese five-spice powder

4 tablespoons kosher salt

2 teaspoons freshly ground Szechuan pepper

1 teaspoon freshly ground white pepper

Combine all of the ingredients in a medium bowl and stir until blended. Store the rub in an airtight container at room temperature for up to 1 month.

HERBES DE PROVENCE RUB

Whenever I want to stray from the heat of the ground Mexican chile pepper spice blend, herbes de Provence is my default. I use this on duck and other poultry, as well as salmon fillets and other seafood. You can make your own herbes de Provence blend by combining dried tarragon, savory, sage, thyme, lavender, and marjoram, but I love the balance of flavors in Spice House's blend, which you can buy online at www.thespicehouse.com.

MAKES ABOUT ⅓ CUP

4 tablespoons herbes de Provence

1 tablespoon kosher salt

1 teaspoon freshly ground white pepper

Combine all of the ingredients in a medium bowl and stir until blended. Store the rub in an airtight container at room temperature for up to 1 month.

MAGRET-STYLE DRY CURE

I can't guarantee that Hot Smoke–Roasted Duck (page 51) cured in this blend will get you out of trouble the way it does for me, but it's worth a shot. The fresh ingredients in this cure give it a shorter shelf-life—you can cover and store it in the refrigerator for up to 1 day, but it's best used immediately.

MAKES ABOUT ¾ CUP

½ cup minced shallots

4 tablespoons chopped fresh flat-leaf parsley

1 tablespoon kosher salt

1 tablespoon freshly ground black pepper

2 teaspoons crumbled dried bay leaves

2 teaspoons crushed dried thyme

4 garlic cloves, chopped

Combine all of the ingredients in a medium bowl and stir until blended.

PASTRAMI RUB

I created this blend on Goose Breast Pastrami (page 69) or Duck Breast Pastrami (page 74). After coating the prepared breasts with Master Cure (page 68), sprinkle and press a generous, even layer of this rub onto the breasts, about 2 tablespoons per goose breast lobe or 1 tablespoon per duck breast lobe.

MAKES ABOUT ½ CUP

3 tablespoons freshly ground black pepper

1 tablespoon coriander seeds, coarsely ground

3 teaspoons garlic powder

3 teaspoons onion powder

3 scant teaspoons guajillo chili powder

4½ teaspoons brown mustard seeds, coarsely ground

Combine all of the ingredients in a medium bowl and stir until blended. Store the rub in an airtight container at room temperature for up to 1 month.

BRISKET RUB

The last thing a perfectly smoked brisket needs is a complicated rub with 17 ingredients that mask the flavor of the meat. Simple is best, particularly if you plan to make the Texas Brisket Sauce (page 248) with a hunk of the fat or lop off the point to make Burnt Ends (page 87). And nothing is simpler than this salt-and-pepper combo accented with chili powder.

MAKES ⅔ CUP

¼ cup coarsely cracked pepper
  (aka butcher pepper)

¼ cup kosher salt

2 tablespoons Toasted Mexican Chile Blend
  (page 15) or 2 teaspoons cayenne pepper

Combine all of the ingredients in a small bowl and stir to blend. Store the rub in an airtight container at room temperature for up to 2 months.

CHICKEN WING WET RUB

I developed this wing rub in the early days of my barbecue tinkering—about 20 years ago—and it perfectly captures the signature flavors I love: a good amount of heat balanced with subtle sweetness.

MAKES ABOUT 1¾ CUPS

⅓ cup kosher salt

⅓ cup dark brown sugar, packed

⅓ cup vegetable oil

⅓ cup Louisiana-style hot sauce,
  such as Tabasco or Crystal

¼ cup soy sauce

¼ cup minced white onion

7 garlic cloves, crushed

2 tablespoons minced fresh cilantro

1 tablespoon ancho or guajillo chili powder

1 teaspoon cayenne pepper

Combine all of the ingredients in a large bowl and stir until the mixture is well blended and the consistency of a very wet rub or a thick marinade. Coat chicken wings in the mixture and refrigerate in a covered container for 8 to 12 hours.

These wings are delicious straight off the cooker, but if you want to gild the lily, make a Buffalo-style sauce: Combine ½ cup melted butter with ½ cup of Louisiana-style hot sauce. Toss the wings in the butter sauce to coat. Serve with Blue Cheese Dip (page 247) and crisp carrot and celery sticks.

GHOST PEPPER VOLCANO WING RUB

Every backyard barbecue master needs at least one recipe like this spicy, hot-hot chicken wing rub. But unlike some absurd, hot-for-the-sake-of-hot rubs, the flavors here are remarkably balanced. You'll bite into a wing, the first wave of molten heat will hit you immediately, and just before you think your brain might melt, your last cogent thought will be, "Wow, this is delicious." Then the ghost pepper heat kicks in, and you'll start crying for your mama. Ghost peppers (aka Bhut Jolokia) measure at least 500,000 Scoville units hotter *than habañeros.*

Use the rub sparingly, no more than ⅓ cup to coat 5 pounds of Smoky Low & Slow Chicken Wings (page 62) or Crispy Hot Smoke–Roasted Chicken Wings (page 57). If you want even more kick, dust the wings lightly with rub after the cook.

MAKES ABOUT ¾ CUP

4 tablespoons light brown sugar, packed

3 tablespoons half-sharp paprika

2 tablespoons kosher salt

1 tablespoon freshly ground black pepper

1 tablespoon ghost pepper (Bhut Jolokia) chili powder

2 teaspoons garlic powder

1 teaspoon onion powder

1 teaspoon cayenne pepper

1 teaspoon guajillo chili powder

½ teaspoon dried oregano

½ teaspoon dried thyme

Combine all of the ingredients in a medium bowl and gently stir with a whisk to combine. Mix the rub carefully to avoid stirring up a cloud of the pepper powder—it will burn if it gets in your eyes. Store the rub in an airtight container at room temperature for up to 1 month.

PITMASTER RUB №1

The coffee in this rub makes an incredible companion to the fatty richness of Beef Short Ribs (page 91). Be sure to grind the coffee to a powder—bigger granules will give the rub a gritty, unpleasant texture on the meat. I typically don't recommend using sugar in rubs because it starts to burn at about 325°F, but this recipe is an exception and should only be used on low-and-slow (225°F to 250°F) cooks. Be particularly careful if you're using a kettle grill, which tends to run hotter than the other cookers.

MAKES ABOUT 2½ CUPS

1 cup light brown sugar, packed

½ cup half-sharp paprika

½ cup freshly ground black pepper

6 tablespoons kosher salt

2 tablespoons finely ground coffee

½ tablespoon ground cinnamon

¾ teaspoon cayenne pepper

½ teaspoon ground allspice

½ teaspoon garlic powder

½ teaspoon onion powder

½ teaspoon ground cumin

Combine all of the ingredients in a medium bowl and stir to blend. Store the rub in an airtight container at room temperature for up to 2 months.

GARY WIVIOTT'S BEEF RUB

This recipe makes far more rub than you'll use on a few racks of beef ribs, but it's a great blend to use in many beef cooks, particularly brisket. I like my beef ribs fiery-hot, but if you like a little less punch, cut the amount of cayenne to 1 tablespoon.

MAKES ABOUT 2¾ CUPS

6 tablespoons garlic powder

6 tablespoons kosher salt

5 tablespoons freshly ground black pepper

5 tablespoons hot Hungarian or half-sharp paprika

5 tablespoons sweet paprika

5 tablespoons Toasted Mexican Chile Blend
(page 15)

3 tablespoons cayenne pepper

3 tablespoons onion powder

2 tablespoons dried oregano

2 tablespoons dried thyme

1 tablespoon ground cumin

Combine all of the ingredients in a medium bowl and stir to blend. Store the rub in an airtight container at room temperature for up to 2 months.

STANDING RIB ROAST WET RUB

This simple wet rub is strong enough to stand up to the heat of a hot smoke roast, but subtle enough not to overpower the nuance of smoke. Best of all, this spicy, savory mixture is what produces the delicious, spicy, fatty bark on my favorite vegetable, the Standing Rib Roast (page 110).

MAKES ¾ CUP

½ cup olive oil

¼ cup Worcestershire sauce

3 tablespoons kosher salt

2 tablespoons freshly ground black pepper

1 tablespoon Toasted Mexican Chile Blend (page 15)

1 tablespoon garlic powder

2 teaspoons onion powder

Combine all of the ingredients in a medium bowl and stir to blend. Store the rub in an airtight container in the refrigerator for up to 1 week.

SMOKED CORNED BEEF RUB

You'll taste the brightness of coriander and black pepper—classic flavors in deli pastrami—but this "shortcut pastrami" rub is slightly amped up by the fresh chili powder blend. Note that there's no salt in this rub; it is designed for a piece of meat that has already been cured in salt. Add 2 tablespoons of kosher salt if you want to turn this into a rub to use on brisket (page 78) or a chuck roast.

MAKES ABOUT ¾ CUP

5 tablespoons coarsely ground black pepper

2 tablespoons coriander seeds, coarsely ground

1 tablespoon garlic powder

1 tablespoon onion powder

½ tablespoon Toasted Mexican Chile Blend (page 15)

¾ teaspoon brown mustard seeds, coarsely ground

Combine all of the ingredients in a medium bowl and stir to blend. Store the rub in an airtight container at room temperature for up to 2 months.

HUNTER BEEF RUB

Hunter beef is kind of like the Pakistani version of chopped corned beef: a brisket cured in spices that echo the flavors of the region. The origins of this recipe start with two friends: Nab Uddin, who introduced this childhood dish to a forum of Chicago foodies, and Mike Sula, a James Beard–award-winning Chicago writer who has made a career of pursuing the obscure, the undiscovered, and the forgotten in food and drink culture. In Sula's words, this recipe might be of interest to about thirteen people, but I think he's being modest. At least twenty-five of you will find the dish fascinating enough to attempt, and I challenge the rest of you to reach outside your comfort zone and give it a shot. Sula developed a spice blend that mimics the flavors of the traditional Hunter Beef, minus the heavy curing salts found in packaged spice mixes. (You can also substitute a smaller corned beef cut from the point of a brisket. Be sure there's a good layer of fat attached and cut the rub and cook time based on the weight of the meat. Do not use a corned beef flat, which is too lean and will dry out on a smoker.)

MAKES ABOUT 1½ CUPS

4 tablespoons cayenne pepper	4 teaspoons garlic powder
4 tablespoons freshly ground black pepper	5 teaspoons ground ginger
3 tablespoons ground cumin	3 teaspoons ground cinnamon
3 tablespoons ground coriander	3 teaspoons ground cardamom
2 tablespoons ancho chili powder	1½ teaspoons ground cloves
4 teaspoons onion powder	1½ teaspoons ground mace

Combine all of the rub ingredients in a medium bowl and stir to blend. The mixture can be stored in an airtight container at room temperature for up to 2 months.

Follow the meat preparation and cook instructions for Smoked Corned Beef (page 102) on your cooker of choice (page 103). Use a generous layer of rub on the meat, about ¾ cup for a full brisket.

After the cook, or after steaming the meat (see page 110), shred the meat with a fork while the meat is still warm. Use a cleaver to chop the strands of meat to a uniform size and incorporate the bark. Serve this shredded meat with paratha or naan bread, sautéed onion and green bell pepper, and Cucumber Raita (page 252).

BALTIMORE PIT BEEF RUB

This is a fairly straightforward rub you can use on beef cooked low and slow, but it is a powerhouse on hot Smoke–Roasted Baltimore Pit Beef (page 116). If you use this on brisket or other big cuts of beef, double or triple the recipe.

MAKES ABOUT ⅓ CUP

2 tablespoons kosher salt

1 tablespoon half-sharp paprika

2 teaspoons garlic powder

2 teaspoons dried oregano

1 teaspoon freshly ground black pepper

1 teaspoon Toasted Mexican Chile Blend (page 15)

Combine all of the ingredients in a small bowl and stir to blend. Store the rub in an airtight container at room temperature for up to 2 months.

SANTA MARIA–STYLE TRI-TIP RUB

These are the classic herbs and spices found in the California Central Coast's signature "barbecue" tri-tip (page 121), and the ingredients should be at the ready in any cook's spice cabinet.

MAKES ½ CUP

4 tablespoons garlic powder

3 tablespoons kosher salt

2 tablespoons dried parsley

2 teaspoons freshly ground black pepper

2 teaspoons half-sharp paprika

Combine all of the ingredients in a small bowl and stir to blend. Store the rub in an airtight container at room temperature for up to 2 months.

BEEF TENDERLOIN RUB

You can take the mildly flavored tenderloin in a lot of different directions based on the ingredients you choose for the rub. Start with the straightforward ingredients as listed, and customize the blend with flavors that suit your palate from the list of optional add-ins.

MAKES ¼ CUP

2 tablespoons kosher salt

1 tablespoon freshly ground black pepper

1 teaspoon half-sharp paprika

1 teaspoon onion powder

1 teaspoon garlic powder

½ teaspoon guajillo chili powder

OPTIONAL ADD-INS:

½ teaspoon fish sauce

½ teaspoon Worcestershire sauce

½ teaspoon ground cumin

½ teaspoon finely ground coffee

¼ teaspoon cayenne pepper

Combine all of the ingredients in a small bowl and stir to blend. Store the rub in an airtight container at room temperature for up to 2 months. (If you add Worcestershire or fish sauce to the rub, store it in an airtight container in the refrigerator for up to 1 week.)

LEMON OIL WET RUB

I whipped this lemon oil together a few times and discarded the strained "goop" before having the a-ha! moment to use the pulp as a wet rub on whole fish. In the immortal words of J. J. Evans Jr., "it's dy-no-MITE!" The beauty is, you use the whole lemon—seeds, skin, pith, pulp, and all. Everyone asks the same question, and I assure you, the seeds, pith, and skin do not turn the oil or rub bitter. Use the same proportions if you double or triple the recipe (½ cup olive oil per lemon, etc.). The oil is delicious as a finishing drizzle on Smoked Whole Fish (page 133), Smoke-Roasted Leg of Lamb (page 165), warm polenta or pasta, or emulsified into vinaigrette for salads.

MAKES ABOUT ⅔ CUP

1 lemon, scrubbed clean
½ cup olive oil
½ teaspoon salt

2 garlic cloves, quartered
Optional: ¼ cup chopped fresh herbs,
    such as mint, basil, or cilantro,
    or 1 teaspoon herbes de Provence

Cut the lemon into eighths and place them in the bowl of a food processor, along with the oil, salt, and garlic cloves. Purée the ingredients until smooth. Add the herbs, if using, and pulse several times to blend. Strain the oil through a fine-mesh sieve into a small bowl, and reserve the goopy solids.

To use, slather the meat with the wet rub "goop" before cooking; when the meat is finished cooking, drizzle it with a thin streak of the lemon oil. Store the oil and wet rub separately in small containers with tight-fitting lids. Both will keep for up to 2 weeks in the refrigerator or 3 months in the freezer.

SALMON DRY CURE

This quick cure for Smoked Salmon (page 140) mimics the flavors of a classic gravlax. Air-drying the cured salmon for several hours is a key step that produces a rich, decadent piece of fish.

MAKES ABOUT 1 CUP

1 tablespoon white peppercorns

1 tablespoon dried juniper berries

1 tablespoon whole allspice

4 crushed bay leaves

¾ cup kosher salt, divided

⅓ cup light brown sugar, packed

In a spice grinder, combine the peppercorns, juniper berries, allspice, and bay leaves. Pulse to grind until the mixture is medium-fine, like coarse sand. Add 2 tablespoons of the salt to the grinder and pulse 2 or 3 more times to combine. Pour the ground spice mixture into a small bowl, and whisk in the remaining salt and the sugar until blended.

Store the cure in an airtight container at room temperature for up to 2 months.

FIVE-PEPPER LAMB RUB

When you're smoke-roasting Lamb Breast (page 170), this peppery wet rub cuts through the fattiness of the meat and, over the course of a low-and-slow cook, the rub crisps and forms a delicious, spicy bark. The fish sauce is an oddball ingredient, but I use it more and more often to impart that mysterious, savory umami flavor in rubs, marinades, and sauces.

MAKES ABOUT ⅓ CUP

2 tablespoons olive oil

1 tablespoon coarsely ground white peppercorns

1 tablespoon freshly ground black pepper

1 tablespoon Szechuan peppercorns, coarsely ground

1 tablespoon red pepper flakes, coarsely ground

1 teaspoon garlic powder

½ teaspoon onion powder

1 tablespoon kosher salt

1 tablespoon fish sauce

Combine all of the ingredients in a medium bowl and stir to blend. This rub will lose some of its punch over time and is best used immediately. If you have to make it ahead of time, store the rub in the refrigerator in an airtight container for up to 3 days.

SZECHUAN WET RUB

Although cumin, garlic, and ginger are the top flavors in this rub, the subtle, numbing kick of Szechuan pepper adds a distinct but not overwhelming hit of heat. Slather this wet rub on Lamb Breast (page 170).

MAKES ABOUT ½ CUP

2 tablespoons whole cumin seeds

1 teaspoon Szechuan peppercorns

½ teaspoon whole black peppercorns

4 garlic cloves, chopped (about 2 tablespoons)

1 tablespoon chopped fresh ginger

1 tablespoon red pepper flakes

2 teaspoons kosher salt

⅓ cup vegetable oil

In a skillet preheated over medium heat, lightly toast the cumin seeds, Szechuan peppercorns, and black peppercorns until the spices are fragrant, about 2 minutes. Coarsely grind the seeds together in a spice grinder. In a medium bowl, combine the cumin, Szechuan pepper, black pepper, garlic, ginger, red pepper flakes, and salt. Drizzle in the oil and use the back of a spoon to mash the mixture together and release the oil and flavor of the aromatics.

This rub will lose some of its punch over time and is best used immediately. If you have to make it ahead of time, store the wet rub in an airtight container in the refrigerator for up to 3 days.

PITMASTER PORCHETTA SPICE RUB

This rub mirrors the flavors of a classic Italian porchetta, but gets an extra kick from the red pepper. Make a double or triple batch—you can use the leftovers for Smoke-Roasted Leg of Lamb (page 165).

MAKES ABOUT ½ CUP

¼ cup plus 2 tablespoons kosher salt

3 teaspoons chopped fresh rosemary

3 teaspoons fennel seeds, toasted and crushed

3 teaspoons red pepper flakes

3 teaspoons freshly ground black pepper

Zest of 2 lemons (about 1½ tablespoons)

In a small bowl, combine the salt, rosemary, fennel seed, red pepper flakes, and black pepper; stir to blend. If you plan to make this rub more than 1 or 2 days ahead of time, or if you plan to double the recipe and have leftovers, do not add the lemon zest until you are ready to use the rub. Store any extra rub, minus the zest, in an airtight container for up to 2 months.

LEMON-ROSEMARY WET RUB

This fresh citrus and herb pairing lends a bright, light flavor to Smoked Fresh Ham (page 187). Slather this all over the surface of the scored ham and work the rub deep into the crosshatched slits.

MAKES ABOUT ⅓ CUP

1 lemon, scrubbed clean

2 tablespoons fresh rosemary leaves

4 garlic cloves

½ tablespoon half-sharp paprika

½ teaspoon kosher salt

¼ teaspoon freshly ground black pepper

2½ tablespoons cider vinegar

¼ cup olive oil

Cut the lemon into eighths. Place the cut lemon in the bowl of a food processor, along with the rosemary, garlic, paprika, salt, and pepper. Pulse the mixture several times to roughly chop and blend the ingredients. With the food processor running, slowly drizzle in the cider vinegar, then the olive oil. Process the rub until it forms a loose paste.

Store the rub in an airtight container in the refrigerator for up to 1 week.

CHINESE FIVE-SPICE WET RUB

Chinese five-spice is a blend of spices that have a natural affinity for pork. Use this rub on Smoked Fresh Ham (page 187), working the blend deep into the slits of the scored ham before cooking.

MAKES ABOUT 1 CUP

1½ tablespoons kosher salt

½ teaspoon freshly ground black pepper

¼ teaspoon Chinese five-spice powder

¼ teaspoon mustard powder

Pinch of ground cloves

¼ cup light brown sugar, packed

⅓ cup cider vinegar

Combine all of the ingredients in a small bowl and stir to blend. The mixture will resemble a thick syrup.

If you want to make this rub ahead of time, combine the dry ingredients and store the mixture in an airtight container at room temperature for up to 1 month. When you are ready to use the rub, mix in the cider vinegar.

11.
SAUCES &
CONDIMENTS

DEAR STUDENT,

I HAVE A LOT OF OPINIONS ABOUT SAUCE IN BARBECUE AND CHARCOAL COOK-
ing, but most of them aren't printable. So I'll say it like this: always treat sauces as a condiment—a little something extra you can serve on the side, in a separate vessel, to complement flavors or add a touch of richness. Never (ever) sauce before serving the barbecue or charcoal-roasted meats that you just spent hours of your life brining, marinating, rubbing, and smoking.

Enjoy!

Gary Wiviott

GINGER-SCALLION SAUCE

This punchy, green dip is a classic Chinese accompaniment to poached chicken and fish dishes—the kind of foods that need a real wallop of flavor. Although brined, smoked turkey, duck, and chicken are anything but plain, this sauce is transcendent and adds an extra kick to duck rubbed in the Szechuan Wet Rub (page 239), or any poultry soaked in a brine made with ginger, soy, scallions, and black pepper.

MAKES ⅓ CUP

6 scallions, finely chopped (white and green parts)

4 tablespoons grated fresh ginger

¼ cup corn oil

½ teaspoon kosher salt

Preheat a small skillet or saucepan over medium-high heat.

Combine the scallion and ginger in a medium heatproof bowl and set them aside. Pour the corn oil into the hot skillet and let it heat up until the oil starts to shimmer. Do not let the oil heat to the point of smoking.

When the oil is shimmering (but not smoking) hot, carefully pour it over the scallion and ginger mixture. The mixture will sizzle a bit and release a heavenly scent. Stir in the salt. Allow the sauce to cool to room temperature before serving.

BLUEBERRY-HABAÑERO SAUCE

Duck, turkey, chicken, planks of wood—this unique sauce is good on everything. Sure, it's a little spicy, but the sugar, ginger, and citrus really balance the heat. If you need to dial it down for sensitive palates, cut back to one minced habañero.

MAKES 3 CUPS

1 (24-ounce) package frozen blueberries, ½ cup reserved

⅓ cup light brown sugar, packed

¼ cup water

¼ cup freshly squeezed orange juice

2 whole fresh habañero peppers, minced

2 tablespoons freshly squeezed lemon juice

1 tablespoon grated fresh ginger

½ teaspoon freshly grated lemon zest

½ teaspoon freshly ground black pepper

½ teaspoon kosher salt

1 tablespoon unsalted butter (optional)

In a large saucepan over medium heat, combine all of the ingredients, except the ½ cup of reserved blueberries. Simmer the mixture for 15 minutes, stirring occasionally, until the sauce thickens and develops into a thin syrup.

Remove the pan from the heat and stir in the reserved ½ cup of blueberries and the butter, if using. Taste the sauce and adjust it with more salt and sugar as needed.

BARBECUE GUY'S DUCK
À LA RASPBERRY SAUCE

This riff on duck à l'orange sauce uses raspberry preserves to give the smoked duck a different dimension. You can also substitute orange, fig, apricot, and other fruit preserves.

MAKES 2½ CUPS

1 tablespoon cornstarch

2 tablespoons sherry, port, or Madeira

2 cups raspberry preserves

Zest and juice of 3 to 4 navel oranges
  (about 2 cups juice and ¼ cup zest)

½ cup light brown sugar, packed

¼ cup red wine vinegar

In a small bowl, whisk together the cornstarch and sherry; set it aside. Combine the raspberry preserves, orange zest and juice, brown sugar, and vinegar in a medium nonreactive saucepan over medium heat. Bring the sauce to a boil and simmer for 15 to 20 minutes or until the sauce thickens to a syrupy consistency. Whisk in the cornstarch slurry and simmer the sauce for an additional 5 minutes.

To serve, pour a thin layer of the sauce onto a serving platter and arrange the sliced duck, skin-side up, on top of the sauce. (This prevents the skin from losing its crunch in the sauce.) Serve the remaining sauce on the side.

CLASSIC DUCK
À L'ORANGE SAUCE

My duck à l'Orange is an homage to Julia Childs' recipe in Mastering the Art of French Cooking, *amped up with orange zest and more vinegar and sugar. The sweetness of navel oranges varies widely depending on the season and your geography, so if the sauce has too much of a bitter edge, add brown sugar to balance it out. Too sweet? Add a teaspoon or two of orange zest or red wine vinegar.*

MAKES ABOUT 4 CUPS

2½ tablespoons cornstarch

3 tablespoons sherry, port, or Madeira

½ cup granulated sugar

½ cup red wine vinegar, plus more to taste

2 cups duck or chicken stock, divided

Zest and juice of 2 navel oranges
 (about 1 cup juice and 2 tablespoons zest)

1 scant teaspoon kosher salt

1 tablespoon brown sugar (optional)

1 tablespoon softened butter (optional)

In a small bowl, whisk together the cornstarch and sherry; set it aside.

In a nonreactive saucepan over medium-high heat, combine the granulated sugar and vinegar. When the mixture comes to a low boil, reduce the heat to low and simmer for 3 to 5 minutes until the liquid thickens into a syrup. Whisk in ½ cup of the duck or chicken stock. Simmer for 1 minute, stirring until the liquid is absorbed into the syrup.

Whisk in the remaining 1½ cups of stock, along with the cornstarch slurry, orange zest and juice, and salt. Simmer for 5 minutes or until the sauce is slightly thickened. Taste the sauce and adjust the flavor, adding ½ teaspoons of red wine vinegar or brown sugar in increments to adjust the sweetness as you like it. Remove the pan from the heat and stir in the softened butter (if using) to finish.

To serve, pour a thin layer of the sauce onto a serving platter and arrange the sliced duck, skin-side up, on top of the sauce. (This prevents the skin from losing its crunch in the sauce.) Serve the remaining sauce on the side.

BLUE CHEESE DIP

I think you'll realize you only need a cold beer and a pile of wet naps to go with your smoke-roasted or low-and-slow chicken wings, but people expect this creamy dip when you serve those wings Buffalo style.

MAKES 2 CUPS

1 cup Hellman's or Duke's mayonnaise

½ cup sour cream

¼ cup crumbled blue cheese

¼ cup finely chopped flat-leaf parsley

2 tablespoons minced white onion

1 tablespoon freshly squeezed lemon juice

1 tablespoon white vinegar

1 teaspoon minced garlic

¼ teaspoon cayenne pepper

Kosher salt and freshly ground black pepper

Combine all of the ingredients in a medium bowl and stir to blend. Season with salt and pepper before serving. Store the dip in an airtight container in the refrigerator for up to 5 days.

HORSERADISH SAUCE

The bracing heat of horseradish sauce gives Smoke-Roasted Baltimore Pit Beef (page 116) an intense, sinus-clearing whack of flavor that goes hand in hand with the rich beefiness of top round. For a unique take on this sauce, substitute Prepared Smoked Horseradish Root (page 251) for the bottled variety. This sauce is also a great match for Smoke-Roasted Beef Tenderloin (page 126) and Smoked Salmon (page 140).

MAKES ABOUT 1¼ CUPS

1 cup mayonnaise

3 tablespoons prepared horseradish

1 tablespoon freshly squeezed lemon juice

½ tablespoon olive oil

¼ teaspoon kosher salt

¼ teaspoon freshly ground black pepper

Combine all of the ingredients in a medium nonreactive bowl. Whisk to blend. Cover the bowl with plastic wrap and refrigerate for at least 1 hour before serving.

TEXAS BRISKET SAUCE

This is my clone of the sauce that underscored my barbecue epiphany at Cooper's in Llano, Texas. It's a fairly typical ketchup/vinegar-based sauce with one exception: the addition of a big hunk of trimmed, seasoned, and smoked brisket fat. You can lop off a crispy section from the point of a cooked brisket, but for aesthetics, I prefer to season and smoke the trimmed fat from a brisket separately. Start making the sauce ahead of time and, when the smoked fat is dark and crisped, stir it into the sauce. This recipe makes enough sauce for a crowd of Texans eating a 12-pound brisket, but if your guests are pro-sauce, you can easily double this recipe.

MAKES ABOUT 2½ CUPS

Large scraps of fat from trimmed brisket, about ½ cup

1 teaspoon yellow mustard

2 teaspoons brisket rub of your choice

1 cup white vinegar

1 cup ketchup

1 cup water

½ tablespoon Louisiana-style hot sauce, such as Tabasco or Crystal

½ tablespoon Worcestershire sauce

½ teaspoon garlic powder

½ teaspoon onion powder

Kosher salt and freshly ground black pepper

As you are trimming a brisket (for instructions see page 85), remove the fat in long, thick strips or chunks. Coat the pieces of fat in mustard and the same rub you are using on the brisket. Place the fat on a piece of aluminum foil and set it on the grate in the cooker next to the brisket. Smoke the fat for 1 to 2 hours, or until the fat is crisped and very dark. Flip the fat halfway through cooking to expose all sides to the smoke and heat.

While the fat is cooking, combine the vinegar, ketchup, water, hot sauce, Worcestershire sauce, garlic powder, and onion powder in a large saucepan over medium heat. Whisk to blend, and simmer the mixture for 20 minutes, stirring occasionally.

When the fat is dark and crispy, add it to the warm sauce. Cook the sauce over medium heat for 10 to 15 minutes, until the crispy pieces of bark break down and disperse into the sauce. If you want a smoother sauce, use an immersion blender to break it down further. Season the sauce with salt and pepper and serve it warm. The sauce will keep for up to 1 week stored in an airtight container in the refrigerator.

BLACK GARLIC BUTTER

Black garlic is made by slowly caramelizing the heads—for weeks at a time, the ultimate low and slow—which gives the cloves a complex savory sweetness akin to an earthy balsamic vinegar. It's a very unique flavor that pairs deliciously with the Standing Rib Roast (page 110). Add one anchovy fillet to the mix for a mind-blowing compound butter on a Smoke-Roasted Leg of Lamb (page 165).

MAKES 1 CUP

4 black garlic cloves

½ teaspoon fine sea salt

¼ teaspoon freshly ground black pepper

¼ teaspoon cayenne pepper

1 cup (2 sticks) unsalted butter, at room temperature

1 teaspoon honey

Mash the black garlic and sea salt in a mortar and pestle, or with the back of a spoon in a medium bowl, until the mixture forms a rough paste. Incorporate the black pepper and cayenne into the paste. Add the butter and honey and stir to blend. Adjust the seasonings, adding more honey, sugar, or salt as desired.

Scrape the butter mixture onto the long edge of a sheet of a parchment paper, waxed paper, or plastic wrap. Fold the paper over the mound of butter and press and roll the butter into a cylinder. Twist the ends closed. Refrigerate the butter until solid, about 1 hour. The butter will keep for up to 2 weeks in the refrigerator or up to 3 months in the freezer, tightly wrapped.

CHIMICHURRI SAUCE

This bright, fresh, green sauce from Argentina is a classic condiment served with marinated and grilled beef. It's an excellent accent drizzled over slices of Hot Smoke–Roasted Tri-Tip (page 121), and it perfectly echoes the flavors of the Garlic-Rosemary Marinade (page 223).

MAKES ABOUT 2 CUPS

1 cup fresh flat-leaf parsley leaves, packed

1 cup fresh cilantro leaves, packed

¼ cup fresh oregano leaves, packed (or 1 teaspoon dried oregano)

3 garlic cloves, smashed

2 teaspoons red pepper flakes

2 teaspoons kosher salt

1 teaspoon freshly ground black pepper

⅓ cup red wine vinegar

1 cup extra-virgin olive oil

In the bowl of a food processor, combine the parsley, cilantro, oregano, garlic, red pepper flakes, salt, black pepper, and vinegar. Pulse until the mixture is finely chopped, stopping to scrape the sides of the bowl with a rubber spatula as needed, about 1 minute total.

With the food processor running, add the oil through the feed tube in a steady stream. Scrape the sides of the bowl and pulse a few times to combine. Transfer the sauce to an airtight container, and let it sit at room temperature before serving to allow the flavors to meld. Just before serving, stir and season the sauce with more salt and pepper as needed. The chimichurri will keep in an airtight container in the refrigerator for up to 1 week.

PREPARED SMOKED HORSERADISH ROOT

Smoked fresh horseradish is an outstanding substitute for store-bought horseradish, in part because you're in control of how much punch the condiment will have. When you introduce vinegar to freshly ground horseradish root, it stabilizes the heat of the root. Add vinegar immediately after grating the horseradish if you want a mellower result, or wait up to three minutes before adding the vinegar if you like it hot-hot.

MAKES ABOUT ½ CUP

1 (8- to 10-inch) section fresh horseradish root

6 tablespoons white vinegar

2 tablespoon water

1 teaspoon kosher salt

½ teaspoon granulated sugar

Shave the woody outer skin and any blemishes off of the horseradish root with a vegetable peeler. When your cooker is burning a fresh batch of wood—either in the beginning of a cook or after you've added fresh wood chunks to the fire—smoke the horseradish root over a low-and-slow KISS fire (225°F to 250°F) for 1 to 2 hours, depending on the level of smokiness you desire.

Remove the root from the cooker. When it is cool enough to handle, cut the root into ½-inch cubes. In a food processor fitted with the metal blade, pulse the root until it is finely chopped. (If you don't have a food processor, grate the whole root on the fine holes of a box grater or microplane.)

Scrape the horseradish root into a medium bowl. To make the condiment mild, immediately combine the grated root with the remaining ingredients. For a hotter version, wait 2 to 3 minutes after chopping or grating to add the remaining ingredients. Whisk to blend. If the mixture is too dry, add 1 to 2 teaspoons of water to reach your desired consistency.

CUCUMBER RAITA

A classic condiment in Indian and Pakistani cuisine, raita lends a sharp, bright, and cooling note to high-ly-spiced meats. It's an excellent foil to the spices in the Hunter Beef Rub (page 234), but it also works with smoke-roasted lamb or even as a unique sauce for lamb spare ribs (page 170) rubbed with a curry blend. I've been known to add ¼ teaspoon of habañero powder to give it even more oomph.

MAKES 4 CUPS

1 quart plain, whole-milk Greek yogurt

1 English cucumber, grated on a microplane

3 garlic cloves, grated on a microplane

½ teaspoon ground cumin

½ teaspoon cayenne pepper

Juice of 2 lemons

Zest of 1 lemon

Kosher salt and freshly ground black pepper

Combine all of the ingredients in a medium bowl and stir to blend. Season with salt and pepper to taste. Store in an airtight container in the refrigerator for 2 to 3 days.

SEAFOOD COCKTAIL SAUCE

It doesn't get any simpler than this, the perfect cocktail sauce to serve with Smoked Shrimp (page 148). If you can find fresh horseradish, make the Prepared Smoked Horseradish Root (page 251) to give this sauce a hint of smoke.

MAKES 1½ CUPS

1 cup ketchup

¼ cup white vinegar

¼ cup prepared horseradish

Juice of 1 lemon

1 teaspoon Worcestershire sauce

1 teaspoon Louisiana-style hot sauce, such as Tabasco or Crystal

⅛ teaspoon freshly ground black pepper, or more to taste

Combine all of the ingredients in a medium bowl and whisk until the sauce is blended. Taste and adjust the seasonings as needed. Cover the bowl and refrigerate the sauce for at least 30 minutes before serving. Store in an airtight container in the refrigerator for up to 2 weeks.

PITMASTER REMOULADE SAUCE

Think of this as Creole tartar sauce. You can't go wrong pairing this with fish or seafood. Use this as a dressing for peeled Smoked Shrimp (page 148), as a side sauce for Smoked Salmon (page 140), or slathered on Hot Smoke–Roasted Soft-Shell Crabs (page 158).

MAKES ABOUT 1⅓ CUPS

1 cup mayonnaise

½ small red onion, roughly chopped

2 scallions, chopped (white and green parts)

3 sprigs fresh flat-leaf parsley

2 tablespoons pickle relish

1½ tablespoons freshly squeezed lemon juice

1 teaspoon salt

1 teaspoon Smoked Creole Mustard (page 262)

1 teaspoon prepared horseradish

½ teaspoon hot sauce

Combine all of the ingredients in a medium bowl and whisk to blend. Store the sauce in an airtight container in the refrigerator for up to 1 week.

OLD BAY TARTAR SAUCE

Please don't ever use jarred tartar sauce, especially on fresh, quality fish or seafood that you've spent an hour or so prepping and cooking. This is the sauce your Smoked Whole Fish (page 133) deserves. You can smoke the jalapenos while your fish is cooking, or use a stemmed, seeded, and chopped raw jalapeno.

MAKES ABOUT 1⅓ CUPS

1 cup mayonnaise

1 smoked jalapeno pepper

1 tablespoon drained capers

1 tablespoon chopped dill pickles

1 tablespoon freshly squeezed lemon juice

1 tablespoon chopped scallions

1 tablespoon Dijon mustard

1½ teaspoons Old Bay seasoning

Freshly ground black pepper

In a medium bowl, whisk together the mayonnaise, chipotle, capers, pickles, lemon juice, scallions, Dijon, and Old Bay. Season the sauce with black pepper. The sauce can be stored in an airtight container in the refrigerator for up to 5 days. Bring it to room temperature before serving.

OLD BAY BUTTER SAUCE

Use this sauce as a finishing drizzle on Smoked Whole Fish (page 133) or Soft-Shell Crabs (page 158), or as a decadent dip for Smoked Shrimp (page 148).

MAKES ½ CUP

½ cup (1 stick) unsalted butter, at room temperature

1 garlic clove, minced

1 small shallot, minced

1 teaspoon Old Bay seasoning

2 teaspoons freshly squeezed lemon juice

Melt the butter in a small saucepan over medium heat. Add the garlic, shallot, and Old Bay seasoning. Cook until the garlic is fragrant and the shallot turns translucent, about 3 minutes. Remove the pan from the heat and stir in the lemon juice. Store the sauce in an airtight container in the refrigerator for up to 2 weeks.

COMPOUND BUTTERS

Compound butter is ridiculously easy to make, and it's a good condiment to have on hand to light up the flavor of a simple dish. It is my go-to for finishing fish, seafood, and other smoked meats that aren't heavily rubbed or marinated. You can also toss the butter with smoke-roasted or grilled vegetables.

MAKES ½ CUP

OLD BAY BUTTER

½ cup (1 stick) unsalted butter,
    at room temperature

1 teaspoon Old Bay seasoning

1 teaspoon freshly grated lemon zest

GINGER-SOY BUTTER

½ cup (1 stick) unsalted butter, at room
    temperature

2 tablespoons soy sauce

2 tablespoons chopped scallions

1 tablespoon grated fresh ginger

CHIPOTLE-LIME BUTTER

½ cup (1 stick) unsalted butter,
    at room temperature

1 canned chipotle in adobo, chopped

2 teaspoons freshly grated lime zest

½ teaspoon kosher salt

1 teaspoon tequila (optional)

In the bowl of a stand mixer fitted with the paddle attachment, whip together the butter and seasoning ingredients until smooth. Scrape the butter mixture onto the long edge of a rectangular sheet of parchment paper, waxed paper, or plastic wrap. Fold the paper over the mound of butter and press and roll the butter into a cylinder. Twist the ends closed. Refrigerate the butter until solid, about 1 hour. The butter will keep for up to 2 weeks in the refrigerator or up to 3 months in the freezer, tightly wrapped.

TAPENADE

You'll want to eat this straight up on a cracker, but save it all for serving with Smoke-Roasted Leg of Lamb (page 165) or Rack of Lamb (page 176). The anchovies are essential—they reinforce the flavor of the anchovy-studded lamb—but if you're leery of the strong flavor, reduce the amount of anchovies to 2 or 3 fillets and taste the mixture before adding more.

¾ cup pitted dry-cured olives

5 anchovy fillets, drained

2 garlic cloves, roughly chopped

3 tablespoons drained capers

2 tablespoons sliced almonds

2 tablespoons freshly squeezed lemon juice

¼ cup olive oil

Kosher salt and freshly ground black pepper

In the bowl of a food processor or blender, combine the olives, anchovies, garlic, capers, almonds, and lemon juice. Pulse the mixture until all of the ingredients are coarsely chopped. With the food processor running on low, slowly pour the olive oil through the feed tube. Season the tapenade with salt and pepper before serving.

TZATZIKI SAUCE

Greeks know lamb like Texans know brisket. This cold yogurt sauce, is a must if you're serving Greek-style Smoke-Roasted Leg of Lamb (page 165).

MAKES ABOUT 2½ CUPS

1 large cucumber, peeled

1 teaspoon kosher salt

2 cups plain, whole-milk Greek yogurt

¼ cup chopped fresh mint

2 tablespoons chopped fresh dill

1 tablespoon chopped fresh flat-leaf parsley

4 garlic cloves, minced

2 tablespoons olive oil

Slice the cucumber in half lengthwise. Scrape the seeds out with a spoon, and roughly grate the cucumber. In a colander set over the sink, toss the grated cucumber with the salt and let it drain for 30 minutes, tossing occasionally. Rinse and drain the cucumber, then scoop it into a clean dish towel, fold the towel up around it, and squeeze out any excess water.

In a medium bowl, mix the cucumber with the remaining ingredients. Let the sauce sit at room temperature for 30 minutes before serving. Store the sauce in an airtight container in the refrigerator for up to 2 days.

SKORDALIA

This thick Greek spread is traditionally served with fried fish, but I serve it with Smoked Whole Fish (page 133) and Smoke-Roasted Leg of Lamb (page 165). You can add a kiss of smoke by throwing the whole head on the cooker with a sliver of the top cut off for 20 to 30 minutes or until the cloves are tender.

1 head of garlic cloves, peeled

½ teaspoon kosher salt

2 russet potatoes, boiled to fork tender

1 cup olive oil, divided

1 tablespoon red wine vinegar

1 teaspoon freshly squeezed lemon juice

¼ cup room temperature water, as needed

In the bowl of a food processor, combine the garlic and salt and purée until smooth. Add the potatoes, ½ cup of the olive oil, the vinegar, and the lemon juice, and pulse to blend. With the food processor running, slowly add the remaining olive oil through the feed tube. If the mixture is too thick, add up to ¼ cup of water, 1 tablespoon at a time. Store the spread in an airtight container in the refrigerator for up to 1 week.

SALSA VERDE

You'll probably find at least seventeen dishes you'll want to serve with this zesty sauce. It's a must if you're making the Pitmaster Porchetta (page 181), but the flavors also pair well with lamb recipes in Chapter 6 (page 163).

MAKES ABOUT 1½ CUPS

2 cups fresh flat-leaf parsley leaves, packed

1 cup olive oil

2 teaspoons fennel seeds, lightly toasted

2 teaspoons coriander seeds, lightly toasted

2 teaspoons red pepper flakes

½ teaspoon freshly ground black pepper

2 anchovy fillets

2 garlic cloves

Juice of 2 lemons

Zest of 1 lemon

Kosher salt

In a blender or food processor, combine all of the ingredients except the salt; purée until smooth. Scrape down the sides of the bowl and pulse to ensure that all the ingredients are uniformly puréed. Season with salt before serving. Serve at room temperature. Store in an airtight container for up to 1 week.

MINT SALSA VERDE

This sauce is an amped-up Salsa Verde I serve with Pitmaster Porchetta (page 181). If you go this route, consider adding ¼ cup each of fresh mint leaves and tarragon to the fresh herb mix that gets rolled into the roast. I also serve this with Smoke-Roasted Leg of Lamb (page 165) and adjust the lamb rub accordingly.

MAKES ABOUT 1½ CUPS

1 cup fresh mint leaves, packed

1 cup fresh flat-leaf parsley leaves, packed

1 tablespoon chopped fresh tarragon leaves

1 tablespoon chopped capers

1 teaspoon toasted fennel seeds, coarsely ground

1 teaspoon toasted coriander seeds, coarsely ground

2 teaspoons red pepper flakes

½ teaspoon freshly ground black pepper

2 garlic cloves

1 cup olive oil

Juice of 2 lemons

Zest of 1 lemon

2 anchovy fillets

Kosher salt

In a blender or food processor, combine the mint, parsley, tarragon, capers, fennel, coriander, red pepper flakes, black pepper, garlic, olive oil, lemon juice, lemon zest, and anchovies. Purée until smooth. Scrape down the sides of the bowl and pulse to ensure that all ingredients are uniformly puréed. Season with salt before serving. Serve at room temperature. Store in an airtight container for up to one week.

PICKLED MUSTARD SEEDS

I love the briny, citrus flavor of these mustard seeds, but the best part is the texture—it pops like caviar. Buy quality mustard seeds from a spice purveyor like The Spice House or Penzey's. I've noticed some varieties sold in grocery stores and ethnic markets tend to turn bitter.

I serve this condiment with any smoked meat that has an affinity for citrus and mustard, including Smoked Fresh Ham (page 187), Goose Breast Pastrami (page 69), and Smoke-Roasted Leg of Lamb (page 165). You can also stir this into mayonnaise and use it as a spread on sandwiches.

MAKES 3 CUPS

1½ cups white vinegar

1½ cups water

1 cup medium-hot mustard seeds

½ cup granulated sugar

1 tablespoon kosher salt

1 cup freshly squeezed orange juice

In a nonreactive saucepan over medium-low heat, combine the vinegar, water, mustard seeds, sugar, and salt. Bring the mixture to a very low simmer—just barely bubbling—then reduce the heat to low and cook for 30 minutes. Add the orange juice and stir to blend. Continue to cook at a low simmer until the mustard seeds are tender, about 10 minutes. Taste the mixture. The seeds should "pop" when you bite into them. You may need to simmer the mixture 15 to 20 minutes longer, but continue tasting to avoid overcooking. The seeds will lose their "pop" if you overcook them. Store in an airtight container in the refrigerator for up to 2 weeks.

SMOKED CREOLE MUSTARD

Wood smoke and a dash of apple cider give grainy Creole mustard a deeper, more concentrated flavor. Use this as a spread on sandwiches, tossed into potato salad, or whisked into vinaigrette for a smoky accent.

MAKES 1 CUP

1 cup Creole mustard   1 tablespoon apple cider

Combine the mustard and cider in a shallow, nonreactive pan. Place the pan on a cooker running a KISS method or lower-and-slower cook, after the wood is engaged and the billowing clouds of white smoke have tempered. Smoke the mixture for 30 to 45 minutes, stirring occasionally. Store in an airtight container in the refrigerator for up to 1 month.

SMOKED TOMATOES

Smoking really concentrates the savory flavor of tomatoes, and this is one of those ingredients that I never run out of creative ways to use. Smoked tomatoes can be roughly chopped to use in a fresh salsa or on bruschetta; whirred into butter (page 264), pizza sauce (page 202), or vinaigrettes (page 264); or stirred into polenta or Okra Sauté (page 210).

Fresh plum tomatoes are best in this recipe, but when tomatoes are out of season, I use canned plum tomatoes (preferably Roma or San Marzano). Simply pour two or three 28-ounce cans, juice and all, into a shallow baking dish or disposable aluminum pan cast-iron , and smoke the tomatoes low and slow for 1 hour until most of the juice has evaporated, stirring frequently.

MAKES ABOUT 5 POUNDS

5 pounds whole plum tomatoes	3 tablespoons olive oil

Cut the tomatoes in half lengthwise and place them in a large bowl. Drizzle the oil over the tomatoes and gently toss to coat.

Place the tomatoes skin-side down in a perforated pan or grill basket. Place the pan on a cooker running a low-and-slow cook (225°F to 250°F), and smoke the tomatoes for 30 to 45 minutes, until the skin around the edges of the tomatoes shrivels and shrinks away from the flesh.

Remove the pan from the cooker and allow the tomatoes to cool for 10 minutes. When the tomatoes are cool enough to handle, carefully remove the skins, reserving any juice from the tomatoes. Discard the skins and use the tomatoes and reserved juice as desired.

Store the tomatoes in an airtight container in the refrigerator for up to 1 week, or in the freezer for up to 2 months.

SMOKED TOMATO VINAIGRETTE

A drizzle of this dressing will brighten any salad, particularly one topped with Smoked Shrimp (page 148) or tossed with big pieces of Smoked Salmon (page 140) or tuna. You can also brush this vinaigrette on bruschetta or stir a little into mayonnaise to give it more zip.

MAKES ABOUT 1¼ CUPS

1 cup (about 4) smoked tomatoes (page 263)

⅓ cup red wine vinegar

¼ teaspoon cayenne pepper

1 tablespoon freshly squeezed lemon juice

2 teaspoons Smoked Creole Mustard (page 262)

Pinch of granulated sugar

¾ cup olive oil

Gently remove the skin and stem point from the smoked tomatoes, reserving any juice that spills. In the bowl of a food processor or blender, combine the skinned tomatoes, reserved juice, vinegar, cayenne, lemon juice, Smoked Creole Mustard, and sugar. Process the ingredients until smooth. While the machine is running, slowly drizzle in the olive oil through the feed tube. Store in an airtight container in the refrigerator for up to 1 week.

SMOKED TOMATO BUTTER

Drizzled on grilled steaks or seafood, stirred into polenta, smeared on bread—you'll never run out of ways to use this compound butter.

5 Smoked Tomatoes (page 263)

½ cup (1 stick) unsalted butter, at room temperature

Kosher salt and freshly ground black pepper

Gently remove the skin and stem point from the tomatoes. For a perfectly smooth butter, press the tomatoes through a fine-mesh sieve to remove the seeds. Combine the tomatoes and butter in the bowl of a stand mixer fitted with the paddle attachment. Whip the mixture on medium-low speed to combine.

Scrape the butter mixture onto the long edge of a rectangular sheet of parchment paper, waxed paper, or plastic wrap. Fold the paper over the mound of butter and press and roll the butter into a cylinder. Twist the ends closed. Refrigerate the butter until solid, about 1 hour. The butter will keep for up to 2 weeks in the refrigerator or up to 3 months in the freezer, tightly wrapped.

SMOKED TOMATO REMOULADE

I use the term "remoulade" loosely here—most of these ingredients have nothing to do with a classic remoulade. It's a great spread on smoked meat or grilled fish sandwiches, and I also serve it with Smoked Shrimp (page 148) and Hot Smoke–Roasted Soft-Shell Crabs (page 158).

1 cup mayonnaise

4 Smoked Tomatoes (page 263), chopped, juices reserved

2 tablespoons drained capers

2 tablespoons chopped fresh flat-leaf parsley

2 teaspoons half-sharp paprika

1 teaspoon cayenne pepper

1 teaspoon yellow mustard

Juice of ½ lemon

1 garlic clove

2 anchovy fillets, finely chopped

Dash of Worcestershire sauce

Kosher salt and freshly ground black pepper

In a medium bowl, whisk together the mayonnaise, tomatoes, capers, parsley, paprika, cayenne, mustard, lemon juice, garlic, anchovies, and Worcestershire sauce. Season the sauce with salt and pepper before serving. The sauce will keep in an airtight container in the refrigerator for up to 1 week.

INDEX